D1483685

King of the World

King of the World

The Life of Cyrus the Great

MATT WATERS

OXFORD
UNIVERSITY PRESS

Oxford University Press is a department of the University of Oxford. It furthers
the University's objective of excellence in research, scholarship, and education
by publishing worldwide. Oxford is a registered trade mark of Oxford University
Press in the UK and certain other countries.

Published in the United States of America by Oxford University Press
198 Madison Avenue, New York, NY 10016, United States of America.

© Oxford University Press 2022

Library of Congress Cataloging-in-Publication Data
Names: Waters, Matthew W. (Matthew William), author.
Title: King of the world : the life of Cyrus the Great / Matt Waters.
Other titles: Life of Cyrus the Great
Description: New York, NY : Oxford University Press, 2022. |
Includes bibliographical references and index.
Identifiers: LCCN 2021058974 (print) | LCCN 2021058975 (ebook) |
ISBN 9780190927172 (hb) | ISBN 9780190927196 (epub) | ISBN 9780197584316
Subjects: LCSH: Cyrus, the Great, King of Persia, -530 B.C. or 529 B.C. |
Achaemenid dynasty, 559 B.C.–330 B.C. | Iran—Kings and
rulers—Biography. | Iran—History—To 640.
Classification: LCC DS282 .W38 2022 (print) | LCC DS282 (ebook) |
DDC 935/.05092 [B]—dc23/eng/20220121
LC record available at https://lccn.loc.gov/2021058974
LC ebook record available at https://lccn.loc.gov/2021058975

DOI: 10.1093/oso/9780190927172.001.0001

1 3 5 7 9 8 6 4 2

Printed by Sheridan Books, Inc., United States of America

Contents

Preface

Cyrus the Great, the founder of the Achaemenid Persian Empire, reigned from 559 to 530 BCE. He was a transformational figure in world history, and many things to many people. To the early Persians and Elamites, Cyrus was an exceptional leader who launched them onto a world stage stretching from Central Asia to Anatolia and beyond, a visionary responsible for a dramatic rise in their fortunes, both figuratively and literally. To the ancient Babylonians, he was cast as a king in the frame of Hammurabi; although of foreign origin, he was represented as fully vested in their traditions. To the ancient Judeans, he was a foundational figure responsible for their freedom from Babylonian domination, literally termed a messiah figure, who facilitated the rebuilding of the Temple of Solomon and inaugurated what today is called the Second Temple period. To ancient Greek and Roman writers, Cyrus was a model ruler, in whom were crystallized the highest qualities of leadership and ingenuity, but who could also be a relentless and ruthless general. In modern times the same superlatives are also applied to Cyrus, who remains for many a nationalistic symbol that encapsulates the glory of the earliest periods of Iranian history.

What made him so "great"? Beyond the epithet "Great King," of course, which was a title claimed by a host of kings in antiquity, but one that did not often stick after their reigns. For that matter, the epithet "great" has been applied to a number of people throughout history, often (but certainly not always) assigned after their lifetimes: a function of being remarkable in their physical characteristics or outstanding in their abilities or accomplishments. These all applied to Cyrus, the particulars of which will be explored throughout this book. Cyrus the individual remains elusive, however, as he left no surviving testimony beyond a handful of royal inscriptions. We must sift several, often disjointed, ancient perspectives to get a sense of the man. Nonetheless, Cyrus was an object of fascination even in antiquity, among several peoples, and it is remarkable that he attained, and maintained, such positive press in almost all sources, across cultures and across centuries. Cyrus thus remains a worthy object of attention for the imprint he left on world history, anywhere the ancient Achaemenid Empire touched in antiquity, and its extensive but sometimes subtle legacy thereafter. Unless noted otherwise, references to "Cyrus" are to be understood throughout this book as referring to Cyrus II, in other words, Cyrus the Great. There were other Cyruses, notably Cyrus the Great's grandfather, who when discussed will be referred to as Cyrus I. Another prominent Cyrus dates from the late fourth century, Cyrus the Great's great-great-great-grandson, called Cyrus the Younger in modern literature. The name "Cyrus" is, of course, anglicized from the Latin spelling of the name; in Greek it was *Kuros*, in Hebrew *Koresh*, in Elamite and Babylonian *Kurash*, and in Old Persian *Kurush*.

The title of this book is taken from one of the royal epithets from Cyrus' few extant inscriptions, dedicated shortly after his conquest of what had been the Babylonian Empire in 539 BCE. The Babylonian title *šar kiššati*, the "King of the World," as it applied to Cyrus both implied and indicated just that. (The *š* is pronounced "sh" in English.) The word *kiššati* meant totality, encompassing everything, and indeed some modern translations prefer the translation "universe" to relay that sense. The translation "world" seems sufficient here to demarcate Cyrus' rule over the realm of humans as distinct from that of the gods. The title *šar kiššati* was not new, but when Cyrus became "King of the World," it was closer to a literal reality than for any ruler before him in history.

But even then Cyrus did not rule Egypt, for centuries part of the same world, the ancient Near East, the region referred to as the Middle East today. And, of course, the title did not allow for lands beyond the Indus Valley or especially beyond the Himalayas. Nonetheless, Cyrus' dominion dwarfed the largest empire that preceded him, the Assyrian Empire, and within two generations after his death his successors Cambyses (Cyrus' son), Darius I (married to Atossa, one of Cyrus' daughters), and Xerxes (Cyrus' grandson) had added additional territories, including Egypt and other parts of northeastern Africa as well as the Indus valley (this is shown in Map 1). This, the Achaemenid Persian Empire, was eclipsed only briefly by Alexander the Great upon his conquest of it, and only matched again by the height of the Roman Empire a few centuries later.

For a figure of such historical import, the record on Cyrus is unfortunately thin. This in turn is no doubt part of the reason Cyrus has not received as much airtime in modern times, especially when considered with other famous conquerors who followed in his footsteps, such as Alexander the Great, Julius Caesar, or Chinggis Khan. Cyrus may be matched with any of these, though books dedicated to him are far fewer in number than for any of the preceding. Several academic conferences and museum exhibitions have raised the profile of Cyrus and the Achaemenids in recent years. For Cyrus himself, the importance of the inscription called the Cyrus Cylinder continues to reiterate his historical importance during the last generation. The loan of the artifact, usually housed in the British Museum, to the National Museum of Iran in 2010 and, subsequently, a museum tour of the United States in 2013 served as the impetus for several publications and an international conference commemorating Cyrus himself. Important tributes and articles relevant to these events have been published in Curtis 2013, Finkel 2013, Daryaee 2013, and Shayegan 2019.

History is context and interpretation, and that certainly applies to historical reconstruction from a thin, and at times contradictory, record. This treatment of Cyrus is written for the general reader; it examines Cyrus' life from birth to emperor as it may be tracked from a variety of documentary, archaeological, and art historical evidence. I have endeavored to present a balanced view of what we know, what we do not know, and (at least as of the present writing) what we cannot know: to acknowledge uncertainties or instances where there are multiple interpretations of the varied evidence. Primary source references and allusions to the wide-ranging scholarly literature—discussing the particulars of numerous contested interpretations and the related caveats—are for the most part relegated to endnotes and the bibliography, wherein the interested reader may find references to a variety of Cyrus-related topics. For the reader new to this material, I recommend first consultation of the brief timeline and chronological table, and especially Appendix A on the ancient source material and its difficulties, to get some initial orientation into the diverse and complex world that was the ancient Near East in the mid-first millennium BCE.

This book is a distillation of scholarly work that has occupied much of my research focus for close to three decades. The ideas and syntheses from several articles and parts of two books—revisited, reconsidered, and rewritten for an introductory audience—find expression here. My own fascination with Cyrus, and the Achaemenid Empire, stems from its unrivaled place as the preeminent geopolitical power for more than two centuries in the ancient world, heirs to and innovators within several streams of tradition, and diverse cultures, in the ancient Near East. The written records of these civilizations reach back centuries before the Persian Empire's genesis. Somewhat ironically, we still rely on the Persians' contemporaries, the ancient Greeks, for narrative material describing what they knew, or thought they knew, about Cyrus. Despite the Greeks' own foundational place in the Western tradition, it is important to remember that during Cyrus' time many of them were subject peoples on the western fringe of the Achaemenid Empire.

Translations of most documentary sources herein are my own, unless otherwise noted. Translations from the Hebrew Bible are adapted from *The New Oxford Annotated Bible with the Apocrypha*.

Where used in the endnotes, abbreviations follow those in *The Oxford Classical Dictionary* and in *The Assyrian Dictionary* of the University of Chicago, a multivolume work more commonly called the Chicago Assyrian Dictionary or, just simply, *CAD*. The English spelling of the names of various ancient authors and actors (and, for that matter, places and other names) is not always consistent. This is an unavoidable issue in normalizing words from different languages and scripts, and there is thus significant variety of spelling in modern works. Herein, more recognizable names from ancient Near Eastern history are generally spelled in their Latinized form, for example, Cyrus (rather than Kurush, or Kurash) or Darius (rather than Dareios or Darayavaush). Other names approximate standard usage in modern works, for example, Ashurbanipal.

Several individuals deserve acknowledgment and deep thanks for their help along the way. I thank Stefan Vranka for first proposing this project to me in spring 2017, and his sage guidance during its progression along a meandering path, often subjected to other responsibilities that intruded. I thank also Timothy DeWerff, Leslie Anglin, and OUP staff for their copy-editing acumen, James Perales for the cover design, as well as Suganya Elango and the team at Newgen for guiding this work through the various production stages. Anonymous reviewers—of both the book proposal and the manuscript itself—gave me much food for thought and saved me from a few howlers. For images, maps, permissions, advice, and consistent support on all matters Achaemenid, I deeply thank Rémy Boucharlat, Beth Dusinberre, Mark Garrison, Dan Potts, Karen Radner, Chessie Rochberg, and Margaret Root. In particular I wish to acknowledge David Stronach, to whose memory and influence this work is dedicated. David's work will be cited frequently throughout the volume for his seminal contributions as excavator at Cyrus' capital, Pasargadae, for his fundamental publications on Cyrus' career, and not least for his interest and support of my own work. He is missed. Finally, and the last shall be first, my thanks and appreciation to my wife Michelle, the embodiment of patience.

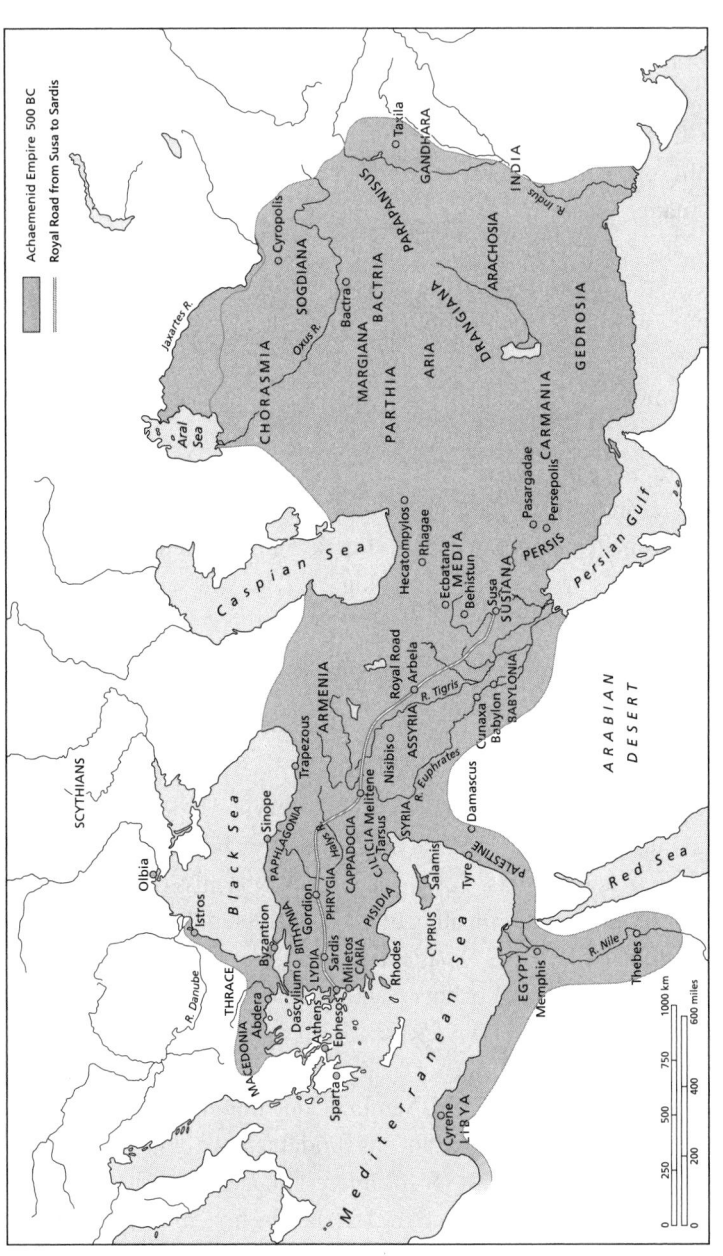

Map 1 The Achaemenid Empire, c. 500 BCE (reign of Darius I), after *The Oxford Handbook of the State in the Ancient Near East and Mediterranean*, ed. P. Bang and W. Scheidel, 2013.

Chronological Table

	Iran		Anatolia	Greater Mesopotamia			Egypt
	Susa (Khuzistan)	Anshan/Parsumash (Fars)		Levant	Assyria	Babylonia	
1000 BCE	Middle Elamite period (c. 1500–1000)		Collapse of Hittite Empire, c. 1200				
	Neo-Elamite period I			Kingdoms of Israel and Judah	Neo-Assyrian period (until 609)	Neo-Babylonian period (until 539)	Third Intermediate period Dynasties XXI–XXV
	Persian/Iranian migrations	Persian/Iranian migrations Semi-sedentary pastoralism			Shalmaneser III	Frequent friction with Assyria	
	Neo-Elamite period II			(subject to Assyria)			
750 BCE	Shutruk-Nahhunte II	(subject to Elamite king in Susa)	Kingdoms of Urartu, Phrygia, Lydia		Sargon II	(subject to Assyria)	
					Sennacherib		
650 BCE	Te'umman	Teispes			Esarhaddon		
	Huban-haltash III	Medes dominant in northern Iran / Cyrus I			Ashurbanipal		Dynasty XXVI
	Neo-Elamite period III	Cyaxeres / Cambyses I		Sack of Jerusalem	Fall of Assyria	Nabopolassar Nebuchadnezzar II	
550 BCE		Astyages	Croesus of Lydia			Nabonidus	Amasis
500 BCE		Cyrus the Great					Psammetichus III
	ACHAEMENID PERSIAN EMPIRE						

Timeline

Major chronological markers and kings referenced in this book (all dates BCE):

1000–609	Assyrian Empire
721–705	Reign of Sargon II, King of Assyria
717–699	Reign of Shutruk-Nahhunte II, King of Elam
705–681	Reign of Sennacherib, King of Assyria
681–669	Reign of Esarhaddon, King of Assyria
c. 680–540s	Mermnad Dynasty of Lydia (last king was Croesus)
669–630	Reign of Ashurbanipal, King of Assyria
664?–653	Reign of Te'umman, King of Elam
c. 650	First evidence of Persian military activity in Elam
646	Assyrian sack of Elamite Susa
c. 640	Cyrus I, King of Parsumash (Anshan) pays homage to Ashurbanipal; Cyrus' son Arukku sent to Assyrian court at Nineveh
626–539	Babylonian Empire
c. 620–550	Height of Median power
612	Sack of Nineveh by Medes and Babylonians
587/586	Sack of Jerusalem by Babylonians (Nebuchadnezzar II)
559–530	Reign of Cyrus (II) the Great
556–539	Reign of Nabonidus, King of Babylon
550	Cyrus defeats Astyages, King of the Medes
540s	Cyrus conquers Anatolia and defeats Croesus, King of Lydia
539	Cyrus conquers Babylonia; Cyrus Cylinder dedicated shortly thereafter

538	Cyrus and Cambyses II take part in the New Year Festival rites at the Marduk temple in Babylon
538	Death of Cyrus' primary wife, Queen Cassandane
530s–510s	Main construction at Pasargadae
530	Death of Cyrus the Great
530–522	Reign of Cambyses II
525–522	Cambyses conquers Egypt
522	Death of Cambyses II in April. Reign of Bardiya (6 months) and usurpation of Darius I
522–486	Reign of Darius I
520–519	Bisotun Inscription of Darius I
510s	Darius I's campaigns into Europe (Balkans) and Indus Valley
499–493	Persians quell Ionian revolt
490	Persian expedition to Eretria and Attica; Battle of Marathon
486–465	Reign of Xerxes
484	Revolts in Babylonia
480–479	Xerxes' invasion of Greece

1

Introduction

The Kings of Anshan

I am Cyrus, King of the World, Great King, Strong King,
King of Babylon, King of the Four Quarters, the son of
Cambyses, Great King, King of Anshan, grandson of Cyrus,
Great King, King of Anshan, great-grandson of Teispes,
Great King, King of Anshan, of an eternal line of kingship.

—Cyrus Cylinder, lines 20–21, 539 BCE

Scope and Scale: The Cusp of the First World Empire

Two million square miles. That is the estimated expanse of the
Achaemenid Empire at its height c. 500 BCE. It included terrain
of all types and climes: mountains, plateaus, flood plains, wide
rivers and seas, forbidding deserts, vast steppes, and thick forests.
From its core in Parsa, the modern Iranian province of Fars, the
Empire encompassed the known world from the western spurs of
the Himalayas and modern Kazakhstan to the Sahara Desert and
modern Libya and Sudan, from the Indus Valley to the Balkans
(Map 1). Most of this territory was conquered by Cyrus the Great,
the founder of the Empire, who reigned from 559 to 530 BCE, the
fourth king in his dynastic line as relayed in the opening quote
from the Cyrus Cylinder, a foundational text for the study of Cyrus
shown in Figure 1.1 and that will be referenced many times in

Figure 1.1 The Cyrus Cylinder from Babylon, BM 90920, 539 BCE.
© Trustees of The British Museum.

this book. His conquests included the three major powers of his time: the Medes in northern Iran, the kingdom of Lydia in Anatolia, and the Babylonian Empire that encompassed Mesopotamia as well as much of the Levant. Cyrus' military and organizational accomplishments were without rival in world history to that point, and one seldom surpassed since. The Achaemenid Persian Empire as a geopolitical unit lasted from c. 550 to 330 BCE, from the reign of Cyrus the Great to Darius III, whose death in 330 marked for all intents and purposes the formal passing of the throne to Alexander III ("the Great") of Macedon. The word "Achaemenid" is both a dynastic and a periodizing label. It stems from the name Achaemenes (Old Persian *Haxāmaniš*), the eponymous ancestor from whom Darius I (r. 522–486) traced his lineage and to whom he also linked the lineage of the Empire's founder, Cyrus.

Cyrus the Great is one of the most pivotal, yet underappreciated, figures in history. He nonetheless remains an enigma in many ways, viewed through multiple traditions in which he still looms large. But before we consider Cyrus himself, attention is due to the milieu in which he lived, the influences upon him, those nations and peoples beyond his own with whom his forefathers interacted. This involves assessment of a broad range of documentary, archaeological, and art historical evidence, as well as their manifold problems of interpretation (see Appendix A). In other words, this book is more than a simple narrative of what Cyrus did while on military campaign. Cyrus' empire may be considered the culmination of 2,000 years of ancient history. His military and diplomatic acumen resulted in a unification of all the major kingdoms that encompassed the ancient Near East: broadly defined, the widely diverse populations of Iran (ancient Elam and various Iranian kingdoms, including the Medes), of Anatolia (ancient Urartu, Phrygia, and Lydia), and of Greater Mesopotamia and the Levant. The only exceptions to these sprawling conquests were northeastern Africa—the kingdom of Egypt and territories stretching into Libya, the Sudan, and Ethiopia—and the Indus Valley; these were conquered by his son Cambyses and by his son-in-law Darius I in the two decades after Cyrus' death in 530.

Cyrus' conquests in Anatolia in the 540s included several Greek city-states, those Ionian and Dorian Greeks who had colonized several important cities in the western part of what is now Turkey. Cyrus' extension of Persian power in these municipalities, separated by the Aegean Sea but still closely linked to their mother-cities in Greece, laid the foundations for the so-called Persian wars fought by Darius I and Xerxes in the early fifth century BCE. To the Persians, of course, these were Greek wars, campaigns unto the far western fringes of their empire, the impetus for which was both retribution and imperialism, which brought Cyrus' grandson Xerxes into Europe and the Greek peninsula. The infamous battles

of Thermopylae and Salamis are touchstones of the Western tradition, the tipping points of traditional, historical narratives that
symbolize the epitome of a free people fighting to remain so.
These battles remain such powerful symbols that they overshadow
Xerxes' successful campaign in the sacking (twice!) of Athens and
the receipt of tribute from many city-states of Greece, itself symbolic of their inclusion in the Empire. That perspective frames the
narrative from the Achaemenid point of view.

The extent of Cyrus' conquests, and the staying power of the
Achaemenid Empire, can be difficult to grasp, especially considered
in light of the previous era. For the periods before 500 BCE, detailed
chronological tables organized by regions such as Mesopotamia,
Egypt, Anatolia, and Iran usually indicate a distinct dynasty or
kingdom for each region, occasionally one that overlaps its immediate geographic neighbors. Less frequently, a single power will
fill multiple sections of the table, for example, Egypt in the fourteenth century or Assyria in the eighth and seventh centuries.
In the time of Cyrus and his successors, almost all the timeline's
sections are subsumed under one power, Achaemenid Persia. The
rapid pace and efficiency with which Cyrus spread Persian rule
laid the foundations for an empire that endured for more than two
centuries, one that left an indelible, if not always traceable, impact
on its successors (see Chronological Table).

To study Cyrus is also to study the Persian imperial impetus,
the seminal, if often overlooked, impact of the Empire on many
subject and peripheral peoples, not just Greeks. To take yet another example, within the biblical tradition, Cyrus was, literally,
the anointed one, a messiah figure—termed as such in the Book of
Isaiah.[1] He was Yahweh's chosen one to unite the lands and to lay the
foundations for the so-called Second Temple period of Judean history. Jerusalem had been sacked, the Temple of Solomon destroyed,
and many of its people (including the royal house) removed to
Babylon by the Babylonian king Nebuchadnezzar II in 587–586.
After Cyrus' conquest of Babylonia in 539, these Judean exiles were

allowed to return home. This resulted in the reconstruction of the Temple and inaugurated its renewal under Persian aegis. These returning exiles arrived bearing Cyrus' message of liberation and incorporated it into their own traditions (see Chapters 4 and 6).

To frame Cyrus' life, conquests, and empire, it is fitting to start with a series of questions that have spurred modern historians for generations. Pierre Briant in the prologue to his monumental work on Achaemenid history, *From Cyrus to Alexander*, framed them as appropriate to the entire Achaemenid dynasty but particularly apropos to Cyrus' rise in the mid-sixth century BCE:

> How can we explain this sudden outburst into history by a people and a state hitherto practically unknown? How can we explain not only that this people could forge military forces sufficient to achieve conquests as impressive as they were rapid, but also that, as early as the reign of Cyrus, it had available the technological and intellectual equipment that made the planning and building of Pasargadae possible?[2]

This book aims to broach these same questions, as it frames Cyrus the Great's place in history. He was more than a successful general and charismatic leader. He deserves a place in the reckoning of other famous leaders and conquerors in world history who came after him: from Alexander the Great, for whom Cyrus served in many ways as a model (Chapter 6), to Julius Caesar and beyond. In fact, it is not until the time of Chinggis Khan that a comparable case may be fielded, one who, like Cyrus, built his empire from modest beginnings and, so it may seem to the present-day observer, exploded onto the world stage with little warning.[3] That Cyrus was able to conquer so much territory, and yet receive almost universally positive press as an individual and as a ruler in both contemporary and later sources—Babylonian, Hebrew, Greek, Roman, and Persian—is a stunning testimony to the man and to the king.

Cyrus' legacy in modern times can be conflicted, especially within Iran itself and among the Iranian diaspora after the 1979 revolution and the foundation of the Islamic Republic of Iran. In no small part, this conflicted legacy stems from his near absence in the indigenous, ancient Iranian documentary tradition after the Achaemenid period; this phenomenon poses several problems in studying such a major historical figure, problems that will be discussed in more detail in Chapter 6. In the twentieth century, Cyrus the Great became a nationalistic symbol of the Pahlavi dynasty, which privileged Iran's pre-Islamic (especially the Achaemenid) heritage over the Islamic. Indeed, this pre-Islamic history—to the exclusion of a millennium and a half of Iran's more recent Islamic heritage—was the centerpiece of the Pahlavi view of Iranian national identity. This adaptation culminated in 1971 with an over-the-top celebration of the 2,500th anniversary of Iranian monarchy, held at Persepolis and sponsored by Mohammad Reza Shah, complete with a full-scale parade and a lavish recreation of Achaemenid court spectacles. The criticisms of this event, prominent among them by the exiled Ayatollah Khomenei who had accused the Shah of indifference to Islam, were quite fierce.[4]

An Achaemenid Renaissance

In consideration of the scale of his achievements and the dearth of surviving information about him, Cyrus the Great remains a larger-than-life legend. With the rediscovery of several ancient Near Eastern languages over the last roughly 150 years, we have a better, but still evolving, sense of the whole of ancient Near Eastern history. The languages recorded by various cuneiform scripts, including the main ones of the Achaemenid Empire's royal inscriptions and administration, were lost to memory: Old Persian, Elamite, and Akkadian were only deciphered in the later nineteenth century. Study of these sources, their translation, and interpretation of those already in museum collections worldwide, let alone those awaiting discovery, remains a work-in-progress. Extant sources in the other main language of the Empire, Aramaic, though the language itself was never lost, are minimal. Most of these documents were parchment, and as such, with few exceptions, they rarely stood the test of time. It is only within the last few decades of modern scholarship that the traditional picture of Achaemenid history—one almost entirely reliant on ancient Greek sources like Herodotus and Ctesias, with the occasional spicing from material in the Hebrew Bible—was modified in any substantial way through incorporation of indigenous evidence.

Greek sources preserved fantastic stories, still necessary to write any narrative history of the Achaemenid period, but their accuracy and reliability must be considered at every point. The Greeks were not writing history as we define it today, though Herodotus especially is considered a founding father of what became, centuries later, an academic discipline. Rather, Herodotus and other Greek authors were seeking information to allow them to understand the world, and the Greeks' place within it, in terms that went beyond the traditional renderings of what we call myth or legend. Many of the Greek accounts straddle that line too effectively, as is the case, for example, of Herodotus' narrative account of Cyrus the Great. Differentiating fact from fiction can be a daunting task. For a longer treatment of the various sources and their difficulties, the reader is directed to Appendix A.

During the 1980s, a series of academic conferences gave impetus to a fundamental reworking of our understanding of the first Persian Empire.[5] The perspective introduced by this sea change in Achaemenid studies is often termed the "New Achaemenid History" in academic circles. Its purpose was to loosen the so-called tyranny of Greece over early Persian history. This colorful phrasing has been used to describe the principal reliance on, and often uncritical acceptance of, Greek sources in reconstructing Achaemenid history. As alluded to above, the increasing availability, accessibility, and approachability of indigenous sources—textual, art historical, and archaeological—have afforded new vistas and allowed a Near Eastern (more specifically here: a Persian) perspective to be applied to this history. Such an approach seems nothing more than common sense. But it is easier acknowledged than applied, again, a function of source availability and the weight of scholarly tradition through the later twentieth century. It is difficult to understate the impact that this change in perspective, stemming from a primary reliance on indigenous sources, has had on our views of early Persian history. That noted, the pendulum at times can swing too far the other way, dismissing or minimizing what ancient Greek and other sources from the Empire's peripheries are able to tell us. In many cases, of course, reading these external sources tells us more about Greeks' (or others') views about the Persians than about the Persian themselves. But there is still much to be learned from, as just one example, early Persian royal ideology refracted through the lens of Herodotus' narrative.

This is not the place for an extended discourse on Achaemenid historiography, or Greek historiography of the Achaemenids, but it is an important phenomenon about which the reader of this period should at the least be aware. With regard to Cyrus the Great, it is necessary to emphasize that modern assessment of him is in many ways a construct of Western historical traditions, with echoes of colonialism. Such assessments stem not only from the continued, albeit necessary, reliance on Greek sources to write a narrative of early Persian history but also from the actuality that *ancient* Middle Eastern studies remains a discipline with firm roots in Western academia. The foundational archaeological work and interest of Western explorers and excavators in the nineteenth and early twentieth centuries has resulted in major collections of artifacts (including tens of thousands of cuneiform tablets) housed in Western museums, with all the cultural baggage that that implies. This is also a critical epiphenomenon with implications far beyond what may be discussed in a short introduction.

Setting the Historical Stage

Summarizing ancient Near Eastern history for the roughly two millennia before Cyrus is an impossible task, at least in a few pages. A bewildering number of ethnicities, tribes, languages, and peoples left their mark on Greater Mesopotamia and the Levant, the modern countries of Iraq, Syria, Jordan, Lebanon, and Israel, as well as Egypt and Iran. All nonetheless were in frequent contact with one another, immediate neighbors or not, even though for much of ancient history the nature of the surviving evidence does not permit us to track the economic or social interchange, or in many cases even the geopolitical situation, as well as we would like. When it comes to empire, there were several predecessors to Cyrus—the dynasty of Akkad and the Ur III kings of early Sumer, Babylonians, Hittites, Egyptians, and especially the Assyrians the most famous among them—but none approached even near the same scale as the foundations that Cyrus laid for the Achaemenid Persian Empire.[6]

With the decline and fall of the Assyrian Empire during the late seventh century, we enter a new era termed by modern scholarship the Long Sixth Century. The Long Sixth Century is called thus because it encompasses not only the sixth century BCE itself but also the latter part of the seventh and first part of the fifth. Ancient Near Eastern specialists typically define the Long Sixth Century more precisely as beginning with the reign of the Babylonian king Nabopolassar, who threw off the Assyrian Empire's yoke in 626 and established the empire that succeeded it after Assyria's final fall, until Cyrus conquered the Babylonians in 539. The end point of the Long Sixth Century is often taken to be the unsuccessful Babylonian revolts against Xerxes in 484. As considered within Mesopotamia itself, those parameters are fairly straightforward. They are less suitable when considering the Achaemenid Empire as a whole, a far vaster area. From a wider perspective, the Long Sixth Century may be considered to encompass the last decade or two (at least) of the Assyrian Empire through its last gasp in 609

BCE; the span of the Babylonian Empire (ca. 626–539 BCE) and its contemporary powers the Medes, Lydians, and Egyptians; Cyrus' conquests of all of the preceding; and the early Achaemenid period into the reign of Xerxes. From a wider Mediterranean perspective, the Long Sixth Century coincides roughly with the early Archaic period in Greece (i.e., the age of the tyrants), the nascent formulation of the first democracies in some city-states such as Athens, to the eve of Xerxes' invasion of Greece in 480–479. The Romans to the west, and likewise the kingdoms in India to the east, had yet to achieve wider historical relevance beyond their own, immediate regions.

In the study of ancient civilizations, the Achaemenid Empire as a historical period has often been an outlier, another reason Cyrus the Great has been often given short shrift in many modern treatments. In college courses on the ancient Near East, the tidal wave of Cyrus overwhelms the wider ancient Near East at the very end of the term, a phenomenon shoehorned into the last day or two of class and overshadowed by the previous several weeks of sorting two millennias' worth of several other interesting and important civilizations (for which consult the Timeline). In courses focused on Greek history, Cyrus and the Achaemenid Empire share time with, but are entirely overshadowed by, the so-called late Archaic and Classical periods of Greece. That is understandable, based on course focus, if ironic: in geopolitical terms, the Greeks were generally minor players in the ancient eastern Mediterranean dominated by the Persian Empire. In other courses, the Persian Empire sets the stage, as a foil, for the arrival of Alexander of Macedon and his singular, but ephemeral, achievement.

Persians and Iranians

The terms "Persian" and "Iranian" will appear many times in this book, at times applied fluidly. For the period in question, they are not quite synonymous. For all intents and purposes, the terms ultimately become so, although that phenomenon postdates Cyrus the Great. His successors Darius I and Xerxes frequently emphasized their Persian *and* Iranian ethnicity (in Old Persian terms *Pārsa* and *Ariya*), with heavy emphasis on the former. More than 700 years later, the Sasanians anchored the concept of "Iran" as a nation: *Ērānšahr*, "the Empire of Iranians." With vicissitudes over time, after Sassanid rule the region was more often called "Persia" until formally replaced by "Iran" in 1934 of our own era.

The precise meaning of the word "Aryan"—*Ariya* in the Achaemenid inscriptions—is yet debated, but it is taken by most to mean, literally, "Iranian." The term is used technically now as a linguistic term denoting Indo-Iranian, an eastern branch of the Indo-European language family.[7] In this book, "Iran" and "Iranian" will be used as a geographic term and a linguistic or ethnic term, respectively. There were many distinct Iranian groups in antiquity, before and after the Achaemenid Empire, often independent of one another. The Medes, about whom there is much more to say in Chapter 3, were just one example. The Persians were, of course, another subset of this group, who became the dominant ethnonym over their fellow Iranians during the Achaemenid ascendancy. Thus, the term "Persia" or "Persian" will be applied herein primarily to the ruling dynasty and its people—but also by extension as a label for the Empire as a whole—encompassing not only the Persians themselves but also applied in that more general sense, as in "Persian Empire," including those whom they ruled as well. Occasionally, as a geographic term, "Persia" may refer to the core area of the Empire, but in such instances the original term *Parsa*, roughly equivalent to the modern province of Fars, is typically used to avoid confusion.

In the mid-first millennium BCE, "Iran," as a geographic term, encompassed not only ethnic Iranians. Elamites and Semitic-speaking peoples dwelt throughout. The Elamites were the earliest inhabitants of the land now called Iran. The Elamite language does not clearly belong to any language grouping, so it is considered a linguistic isolate.[8] The anglicized geographic term "Elam" comes ultimately through Hebrew from Akkadian *Elamtu*, to describe the land that the Elamites themselves called *Haltamti*. We know much less about Elamite history and culture than we do about Mesopotamian, a function of accessible material and focus, a consequence of modern excavations and scholarly interest. This lack of knowledge does not mean, of course, that the Elamites were removed from the constant contact and interchange among their neighbors and various other peoples; the situation was quite the opposite. Elamite civilization may be traced to the fourth millennium, roughly contemporary with the earliest Sumerians in Mesopotamia, and the Elamites remained the dominant power in Iran until the Medes and Persians, along with other Iranian groups, established themselves in the Zagros Mountains during the first half of the first millennium.

Persian-Elamite, or Iranian-Elamite, acculturation—also sometimes termed "ethnogenesis"—was a formative phenomenon in the blending of populations and cultures that underlay the evolution of the Achaemenid Persian Empire. The Persian-Elamite distinction became erased over time, with the Elamites absorbed and, especially from the perspective of external sources, effectively disappearing. One manifestation of this ethnogenesis was the different names applied in antiquity to the heartland of Cyrus' kingdom, modern Fars. It was labeled Parsa in Old Persian, Anshan (Anzan) by the Elamites, Parsumash by the Assyrians, and Persis by the Greeks.

Herodotus demarcated two groups of Persian tribes. Those who worked the land included the Pasargadae, Maraphians, Maspians, Panthialaei, Derusiaei, and Germanii. The Pasargadae tribe included the Achaemenid clan, so Herodotus relayed his understanding of the origins of the Empire's ruling dynastic family, based in turn on his understanding of the genealogy propagated by Darius I. The tribes who were nomadic included the Daï, Mardians,

Dropici, and Sagartians. Xenophon relayed that there were twelve tribes, though he did not name them, and Strabo's later list contains some differences still.[9] It is evident that the Greek authors were not always consistent in labeling clans or tribes, which makes historical reconstruction difficult. Further, while the approximate locations where some of these groups dwelt is known, it is pure guesswork on others.

Scholars believe that Iranian migrations into western Iran began in the second millennium BCE, but migration movements of specific ethnicities are notoriously hard to track without complementary data from textual sources. Some connect the migrations' origins to a Bronze Age society called in modern literature the Bactria-Margiana Archaeological Complex (BMAC) that flourished circa 2000 BCE. It is also termed the Oxus Civilization, named after the Oxus River (the modern Amu Darya) that runs through the region: modern northeastern Iran, northern Afghanistan, and parts of Turkmenistan and Uzbekistan. Whether or not Indo-Iranian groups were some of the original inhabitants of the BMAC is yet debated. Thus, we can only generalize about the earliest stages of the migrations of Iranians into the land that would ultimately bear their name.

The two main Iranian groups of the first millennium BCE, Medes and Persians, first appeared in the written record of the ninth century BCE. The Assyrian king Shalmaneser III (r. 858–824) described several campaigns into the central western Zagros Mountains, northwest of the modern Mahidasht, during which he encountered several clusters of Medes and Persians. The famous royal inscription called the Black Obelisk, a roughly 6-foot-tall stela, noted that Shalmaneser "received tribute from twenty-seven kings of Parsua" and from there he also campaigned in the lands of the Medes and other peoples in that vicinity (Figure 1.2). Shalmaneser III's inscriptions give the impression of dozens of discrete Iranian groups, or tribes, in that region. This is roughly akin to Herodotus' description, 400 years later, of the multiple Persian

Figure 1.2 The Black Obelisk of Shalmaneser III from Nimrud, c. 825 BCE, BM 118885.
© Trustees of The British Museum.

tribes. It was certainly not Shalmaneser III's intent to differentiate the political relationships or kinship ties, if any, between these Persian groups, so those elements remain opaque. Roughly a century after Shalmaneser III's reign, as a consequence of consistent campaigning and territorial acquisition, the Assyrians created a formal province of Parsua in the central Zagros.

During the last half of the seventh century and into the sixth, Cyrus the Great's predecessors ruled in Anshan (Fars), the region that the Assyrians called Parsumash, spelled similarly but distinct from the Parsua of the central Zagros. It remains an open question whether these Assyrian toponyms, Parsua and Parsumash, indicated that the inhabitants of those regions were primarily people of Persian ethnicity. It is generally assumed so, though such assumptions can be fraught and, if accepted, engender questions about the links, if any, between Persians dwelling in the central Zagros and Persians dwelling in Fars. Archaeological evidence has also tendered more questions than answers—for example, what may be gleaned from the disbursement of various types of pottery, always problematic (if not impossible) to equate with ethnic groups. In other words, tracking the movements of discrete Iranian tribes or groups, such as the Persians, through Iran in the first half of the first millennium continues to prove a frustratingly elusive task.[10] There remain questions that modern scholarship is simply not able to answer definitively.

The Kingdom of Anshan/Parsumash among the Great Powers

In the lines of the Cyrus Cylinder quoted at the beginning of this chapter, Cyrus the Great assumed the standard royal titles that generations of Babylonian and Assyrian kings did before him. These lines of text also provide the only genealogical list preserved from Cyrus himself, which lists three generations of his forefathers to his great-grandfather Teispes (Chart 1). It is there that one must begin in order to explore the geopolitical world in which Cyrus' forebears were located. While we do not have exact regnal dates for these early kings, the story as it can be traced goes back to the later eighth

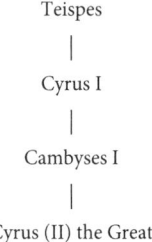

Teispes
|
Cyrus I
|
Cambyses I
|
Cyrus (II) the Great

Chart 1   Linear descent of Cyrus the Great as relayed in the Cyrus Cylinder, line 21.

and early seventh centuries, when the Assyrian Empire was the premier power in the ancient Near East. Extensive Assyrian records allow significant insights into how they organized their empire and their relations with its peripheries. The Assyrians were the imperial model par excellence, until the Persian Empire co-opted its legacy and superseded it.

Anzan—or as more commonly spelled in the literature, Anshan—was the name the indigenous Elamites used for the region roughly coterminous with the modern Iranian province of Fars, called *Parsa* in Old Persian and *Parsumash* by the Assyrians. In the early seventh century, Elamite Anshan was a region of only peripheral concern to the Assyrians. A more vital geopolitical consideration than who ruled distant Fars was control of the Babylonian-Elamite border zone, meaning the foothills of the central Zagros Mountains that gave access to lucrative trade routes. Assyrian dominion was frequently tempered by the dynamic rivalries they had with Babylonia and Elam, their neighbors to the south and southeast, respectively. Babylonia and that part of Elam around the important city of Susa (the wider region often called Susiana, roughly equivalent to modern Khuzistan) were more than 200 miles apart on the Babylonian alluvium. Southern Babylonia was home to Aramaean and Chaldean tribes, many of which had strong ties with—and were often beholden to—Elamite political authority.

The interplay between these three powers—Assyria, Babylonia, and Elam—is conspicuous throughout the extant source material c. 900–625. Despite the vicissitudes in the tripolar relationship, in general Assyria was much more effective at projecting its power. Until the decline of the Assyrian Empire in the 610s, fighting occurred outside of their core territory, that is, along the Elamite-Babylonian frontier or within Babylonia or Elam itself. The necessity of frequent military activity against Elam and Babylonia reveals, though, that even at its height Assyria never fully quieted those regions. This is a striking contrast to the ability of Cyrus and his successors to keep all these regions, with few and short-lived exceptions, firmly under their control for more than two centuries.

The Assyrian-Elamite dynamic in particular is of great import as backdrop for the rise of Cyrus the Great's dynasty. Elamite territory had included Anshan for centuries, and by the seventh century (and likely earlier) Elamites and Persians were sharing, and occasionally sparring over, the same ground. Shutruk-Nahhunte II (r. 717–699) was one of the most preeminent Neo-Elamite kings on record.[11] He used the traditional Elamite title "king of Anshan and Susa" in his royal inscriptions, and he meant it, mobilizing troops from throughout Khuzistan and Fars. Shutruk-Nahhunte II proved to be one of the Assyrians most vexing and powerful opponents at the height of their empire, a consistent thorn in their side through his military activities in the Elamite-Babylonian border regions. At the Battle of Der—near modern Badra, Iraq—in 720 an Elamite-Babylonian coalition was able to forestall, at least for a few years, Assyrian ambitions in the south. The battle appears to have been a draw, perhaps even an Elamite victory on the field. Later sources indicate that the Elamites did most of the fighting.

As is almost always the case, our evidence for these events is not what we would like it to be. And, even when we have it, the record is often fragmentary. That last bit may be considered a weak pun intended, meant as a necessary reminder: the actual tablets are worn or broken in key spots. During his struggles with the Assyrians in the Zagros Mountains north of Khuzistan, Shutruk-Nahhunte II recruited troops from a new place (new to us, at least, in the extant record), one of the first recorded references to Parsumash in Fars.[12] Roughly two decades later, the Assyrian king Sennacherib (r. 705–681) recounted in several of his inscriptions a great victory at the Battle of Halule (near modern Samarra, Iraq) in 691 over a wide-ranging coalition of peoples led by the Elamite king Huban-nimena. Among them were contingents from Parsumash and Anshan, which suggests the Elamite king's continued rule, or influence, over the area of Fars. Subsequent references in Assyrian sources did not differentiate Anshan and Parsumash, and the terms became essentially synonymous, the former fading from Assyrian usage.[13] The toponym "Anshan" did not, however, fade entirely, as we have seen from the opening quotation of this chapter. The title "King of Anshan" was used by Cyrus the Great, and was attributed to his forebears, to describe his rule as king of the entire region called Anshan. After Cyrus the Great's reign, with few exceptions, the toponym Anshan essentially disappeared from the corpus.[14]

Assyrian references to Parsumash suggest that what was once entirely Elamite territory was giving way, over the course of the later eighth and early seventh centuries, to a significant change. Persians—to the Assyrians, "Parsumashians"—were becoming more visible, and aggressive (see below), and a new nation was crystallizing from an Elamite-Persian ethnogenesis alluded to previously. Teispes, Cyrus the Great's grandfather, was certainly involved in this milieu, although pinpointing his activities is an impossible task—he is named in no contemporary sources of the mid-seventh century. At that time, the slow burn of Assyrian-Babylonian-Elamite tension was flaring up into major confrontations. Our main sources for the period, still Assyrian, remain focused on the intractable problems posed by recalcitrant Elamites and Babylonians, often working together to thwart Assyrian domination. Elam had some success in doing so, Babylonia not so much. The late 650s and 640s marked a breaking point, when a significant upsurge in Elamite aggression, followed by a major revolt in Babylonia supported by the Elamites, turned the full might of Assyria upon them. These confrontations overshadowed most other geopolitical concerns in the extant sources. If Teispes was on the move in Fars at about the same time, a foreshadowing of later Persian expansionism, it was as yet barely on the Assyrian radar of concerns. The Elamites would have had a different take on the matter, an alarmed one perhaps, but it must be noted again that we do not have Elamite or Persian documentary sources extant from the period that shed light on this matter. It is a pity that so much critical data is missing. Assyrian-Babylonian-Elamite interchanges directly informed the rise of the Persian Empire.

Frequent Babylonian-Elamite cooperation may have been based on ties of intermarriage between members of royal and elite families, a phenomenon that modern scholars are still tracking in the sources. Common efforts against Assyrian included not only active, military alliance on the battlefield but also clandestine assistance with refugees or fugitives. These last, in Assyrian eyes, were rebels or criminals on the run from Assyrian justice, or, better put, vengeance. The Assyrian annals often justify accounts of the kings' campaigns against Babylonia or Elam, or both, for the reasons just noted: to punish oath-breaking or the cossetting of refugees, among a variety of other offenses to Assyria, its gods, and its king. These narrative renderings were highly stylized, cast in an ideological framework that also heavily influenced Cyrus and his successors. The Assyrian annals rarely indicated weakness or defeat. They vividly portrayed their enemies as impious, accursed, treasonous, inane, or insane—or some combination of the preceding—and, as an added touch, occasionally as possessed by demons.

One example was Assyria's Elamite arch-enemy of the mid-seventh century, the Elamite king whom the Assyrians called "Te'umman," an abbreviated form of his Elamite name Tepti-Huban-Inshushinak. It was Te'umman who gave impetus to the decade or more of intensive Assyrian involvement in Elamite affairs, a reaction to the Elamites' transgression and aggression. Ashurbanipal, the Assyrian king at the time, was not a fan. In his annals, Ashurbanipal frequently described Te'umman as "the image of a malevolent demon," as one who frequently "sought out evil" and "sent insults" or "provocative speech"—he offended in a variety of colorful and compelling ways. Such outrages did not go without consequences of divine and royal retribution, as indeed happened to Te'umman: a mishap befell him, his lip was paralyzed, his eye afflicted, he suffered a seizure. Te'umman was a resourceful and resilient enemy, but in the year 653 at the Battle of Til Tuba along the Ulai River, he was defeated, humiliated, and killed: not necessarily in that order.

A celebrated relief sequence from Ashurbanipal's palace at Nineveh portrays vignettes from the battle—including the pursuit, capture, and execution of Te'umman—and the grisly aftermath. Te'umman's humiliation persisted even after his death: his head a macabre necklace for other offenders and a grotesque backdrop for the famous palace relief scene of Ashurbanipal's banquet (see Figure 1.3).[15] A persistent motif in the annals finds Assyrian

Figure 1.3 Relief with banquet scene from the North Palace of Nineveh, reign of Ashurbanipal c. 640 BCE, BM 124920. The head of Te'umman hangs from a tree on the left side of the relief.
© Trustees of The British Museum.

enemies in flight, as various Elamite kings targeted by Assyrian campaigns were compelled to scramble to safety in the "distant mountains." That the highland peripheries of eastern Khuzistan, particularly along the southern route toward Fars, served as important centers is demonstrable from both contemporary and later evidence. Assyrian involvement in Elam increased in the late 650s and 640s, bringing them and their geopolitical concerns closer to Fars. There, at the same time Elam was collapsing, a nascent kingdom under Teispes and Cyrus I was rising.

After Te'umman's defeat, multiple and mostly short-lived (or, at least, short-reigned) kings are attested in Elam through the 640s, some ruling concurrently. The Elamite kings' relationships with each other are rarely clear, and the geopolitical situation remained fluid and chaotic. Kings and counter-kings swiftly entered and departed the scene, as Ashurbanipal launched no fewer than a half-dozen campaigns against Elam from 653 into the mid-640s. At the same time, Ashurbanipal was battling a major Babylonian revolt (abetted by the Elamites) begun by his brother, the regent of Babylon, Shamash-shum-ukin. This rebellion was finally quashed in 648, and then it was the Elamites' turn. After one or two initial forays against Elamite territory, in the year 646 Ashurbanipal condensed decades of frustration with the Elamites' meddling, their intransigence, and their consistent ability to flout Assyrian power. Ashurbanipal's account of the sack of Susa contained one of the most detailed, and dramatic, despoliations of enemy territory extant from Assyrian annals. More than two dozen Elamite cities were listed before the following account of a campaign against the last Elamite king of any note, named Huban-haltash III:

[T]he cities I swept away, I demolished them, I burned them with fire . . . the guardians of the temples, the fierce bulls, the fitting ornaments of the gates, I defiled until they did not exist. His (the Elamite king's) gods and goddesses I counted as ghosts. . . . (In Susa) their secret groves into which no foreigner had penetrated,

my seasoned troops entered into their midst, they saw their
secrets, and they burned them with fire. The graves of their previous kings, those who did not reverence Ashur and Ishtar, my
gods, those who made trouble for the kings, my fathers, I swept
them away, I demolished, I exposed them to the sun. Their bones
I took away to Assyria. Their spirits were not at rest. . . . For
1 month and 25 days the districts of Elam I laid waste. Salt and
thorns I sprinkled upon the fields. . . . I deprived them the voices
of men, the tracks of oxen and of sheep, the sounds of the joyous
harvest song. Upon those fields I made wild onagers and gazelles
lie in their midst.

The preceding is only a sampling. Within the full dramatic rendering, not quoted here, Ashurbanipal also listed dozens of gods and
kings (i.e., divine and royal statues) by name, described mounds
of treasures plundered, and hundreds of prisoners sent back to
Assyria. The casual reader may be forgiven for assuming that Susa
was, as Ashurbanipal clearly meant to imply, utterly destroyed.[16]
While any semblance of a centralized Elamite political authority
was undone, it is clear that Susa was not annihilated. At the least,
it proved resilient. Within a generation Susa was reoccupied, likely
never completely abandoned entirely, though its history for the
century after 646 is opaque. Reconstructed on a grander scale by
Darius I more than a century later, Susa became one of several enduring symbols of the Elamite legacy that profoundly shaped the
Achaemenid Empire.

Our data for this transitional period in Elam, leading to Cyrus
the Great's rise, is quite thin even by the usual standards, and the
historian's task in reconstructing the geopolitical situation unen-
viable. There is little more to go on than names in sporadic and
fragmentary royal inscriptions, a few corpora of administrative
documents, and scant archaeological evidence. One spectacular
find, however, from Arjan (near Behbahan in southwestern Iran)
testifies to a diversity of styles mixing in this region in roughly the

century before Cyrus the Great's rise. A bathtub-like coffin found there contains the burial of one Kidin-Hutran, son of Kurlush. Kidin-Hutran was entombed with several precious objects, some of which inscribed with his name, including an ornately incised ring, scabbard, stand, and bowl, among other high-value artifacts. The bowl in particular is notable here (Figures 1.4a and 1.4b). Its intricate artwork, in several registers, includes a recasting of a royal court scene that was eclectic in its influences but shows remarkable similarity to an eighth-century Assyrian example from Til Barsip in northern Syria, along with stylistic elements that anticipated portrayals at the Achaemenid capital of Persepolis. We do not know the story behind this Kidin-Hutran, a man with an obviously Elamite name buried in an Elamite region, but with grave goods revealing a heterogeneous backdrop. Debate continues whether the objects interred with him were of local manufacture or gained elsewhere, for example, as trophies or souvenirs. Whether made there

Figure 1.4a The interior of the Arjan bowl.
Photo courtesy of J. Álvarez-Mon and used by permission.

Figure 1.4b Drawing of the interior of the Arjan bowl.
Courtesy of David Stronach.

or brought there, the finds from the tomb of Arjan attest to a diverse milieu, hardly confined to this one example, testimony to the variety of inputs impactful within a process of Elamite-Iranian acculturation.[17] The tomb's date is also debated; most situate it within the formative period, c. 650–550, the time when Cyrus the Great's forebears ruled.

How do we proceed from a centralized Elamite polity c. 700, through the geopolitical chaos of the mid-to-late seventh century, to Cyrus the Great conquering much of the known world in the mid-sixth? There are scattered hints in the sources. While Assyrian engagement in Elam was at its height, in the decade after the defeat of Te'umman in 653 discussed previously, we find a handful of tantalizing references to Persians, the inhabitants of Parsa (see Map 2), called "Parsumashians" in the Assyrian royal correspondence. These letters as a corpus contain information on military and other matters relayed among Assyrian officials, foreign dignitaries or messengers, and the king. There are two letters in particular, broken in many places, but with clear reference to armed conflict between Elamites and Persians in the Zagros foothill regions. They included warnings about Persians raiding the area around the city of Hidalu, transport of prisoners, and skirmishes between Elamite and Persian forces. In one letter addressed to Ashurbanipal, the author urged the king to dispatch two commanders with troops to thwart the Persians' raiding activities, so that Assyrian control of the region was not compromised. There is urgency in the letter's call for assistance, which suggests the seriousness of Persian

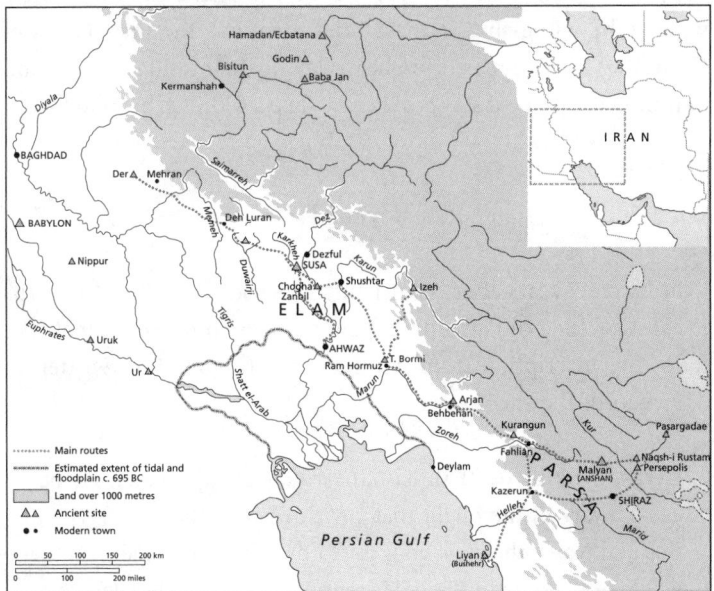

Map 2 Map of Mesopotamia and Western Iran (after Waters 2014a, 135).

incursions. The action described in another letter is closely related. An Assyrian general named Bel-ibni reported to Ashurbanipal that Persians had been plundering the Elamite areas of the Shallukeans and Hidalu.[18] These Persian military activities may be suggestive of wider tensions, as it seems unlikely that the situation referred to in these two letters was an anomalous situation.

For Assyrian military officials, the primary concern was the Persians' potential disruption of Assyrian attempts to stabilize Elam. The situation described in these letters may be considered as a backdrop for Ashurbanipal's later encounter with Kurash of Parsumash, that is, Cyrus I, Cyrus the Great's grandfather. Based on the time frame, and comparing Cyrus' own genealogy as relayed in line 21 of the Cyrus Cylinder, it is tempting to attribute this Persian military activity not only as a contributing factor in the disintegration of Elam as a political unit but also as heralding the appearance of Teispes himself, or his son Cyrus I, on the scene. In other words, we may be witnessing in these brief mentions the first phases of Cyrus the Great's dynastic forebears flexing their military might and outlining the nascent stages of Persian expansionism beyond Fars.

Cyrus I

Within a few years after Ashurbanipal's sack of Susa in 646, Cyrus I (*Kurash*), king of Parsumash, paid homage to Ashurbanipal. The following inscription from Ashurbanipal (Figure 1.5), written in 639, records the encounter:

> Cyrus, the king of Parsumash, heard about my victory. He became aware of the might that I wielded with the aid of Ashur, Bel, and Nabu, the great gods my lords, with which I leveled the whole of Elam like a flood. He sent Arukku, his eldest son, with his tribute to Nineveh, the city of my lordship, to pay homage to me. He implored my lordship.

Figure 1.5 Hand-drawing from Weidner 1931–32: 3 of the Assyrian prism inscription mentioning Cyrus, King of Parsumash. The cuneiform signs representing his name are outlined by the rectangle with bolded line.

Another inscription, surviving in multiple copies, from the Ishtar Temple in Nineveh also recorded this incident, but with slight variation. That text does not mention Arukku specifically but noted further that, along with Cyrus of Parsumash, another ruler named Pislumê, king of an otherwise unknown place called Hudimiri, also paid obeisance to Ashurbanipal. Cyrus and Pislumê's stereotyped response—their fear of Assyrian might as manifested by the gods—was applied similarly to many other rulers who brought tribute to the Assyrian king in Nineveh. "They (Cyrus and Pislumê) sent their representatives of friendship and peace, with their substantial tribute before me, and they kissed my feet." The delivery of tribute, along with the message of friendship and peace, and for that matter the delivery of hostage(s) as relayed in the prism inscription quoted above, are all part of an Assyrian formula that implied vassalage. It is unclear whether Cyrus and Pislumê viewed the exchange, and their formal relationship to the Assyrian king, in that way. But such formalized acts of submission generally carried weighty ramifications.[19]

If this Cyrus of Parsumash is correctly identified as Cyrus I of the Cyrus Cylinder, we are thus introduced to Cyrus the Great's grandfather. That in turn makes Cyrus I's son Arukku the uncle of Cyrus the Great.[20] Royal hostages—or, more politely put, the exchange of royal children—are a well-attested phenomenon in the ancient Near East. Although nothing else certain is known of Arukku, his presence at the Assyrian court, accompanied by an entourage that facilitated frequent contact between Parsumash and the Assyrian court, had momentous implications. We may gauge in broad terms the impact of this experience on Arukku and, by extension, his family and his homeland. Arukku and other hostages (no doubt considered guests from the Assyrian view) had a front-row view of a developed, sophisticated royal ideology. Cyrus and his successors were clearly inspired by Assyria for modes of imperial organization and ideological expression, and this episode points to one way (if not the main way) that this transmission occurred.

A Royal Heirloom

A striking piece of evidence for Cyrus I is the Persepolis Fortification Seal (PFS) 93*. This seal is preserved in multiple impressions from at least nineteen tablets from the Persepolis Fortification Archive of the late sixth and early fifth centuries, an archive of administrative documents dating to the reign of Darius I. We do not know the identity of the person(s) who used the seal c. 500 BCE, but it seems more likely to have been an office seal than a personal possession. The seal was inscribed in Elamite cuneiform, as shown in Figure 1.6: "Cyrus, the Anshanite, son of Teispes," a ready match for the Cyrus son of Teispes, Cyrus I, whom Cyrus the Great mentioned in his genealogy as recorded in the Cyrus Cylinder.

The seal is invariably found on a group of texts categorized by their content: primarily, the distribution of livestock before the king himself. Notwithstanding its applications during the reign of Darius I, based on close stylistic and compositional parallels with Assyrian reliefs and seals, PFS 93* must be considered an heirloom from that earlier period, meaning that it was manufactured sometime in the later seventh century.[21] In other words, PFS 93* was a seal made for Cyrus, son of Teispes, that was handed down and reused in Persepolis Fortification Archive more than a century after its original manufacture. There are many other seals in the archive that exhibit archaizing (i.e., Assyrian) imagery and style, in effect an "Assyrianizing" phenomenon. Many seal users of the highest social stratum at Persepolis preferred either antique seals themselves,

1 cm

Figure 1.6 Line drawing of seal of Cyrus (I) of Anshan, PFS 93*, scale 2–1.

Courtesy of the Persepolis Fortification Archive Project and the Persepolis Seal Project.

such as like PFS 93*, or the archaizing imagery. These include one of Cyrus the Great's own daughters, Irtashduna (called Artystone in the Greek tradition), who used PFS 38, and the royal woman, Irdabama, who used PFS 51, a close, stylistic analog to PFS 93*. Both of these women and their seals will be discussed further in the next chapter. These seals were clearly prestige items, heirlooms from the founding decades of the dynasty.

The figures engraved on PFS 93* give no certain clues to ethnicity, and it cannot be discerned from stylistic context. The sealing's image portrays a rider running through an enemy who holds a broken bow, a common symbol of defeat and humiliation in the ancient Near East. Closely contemporary to this seal's dating, and no doubt informed by them, Assyrian texts and iconography were replete with the broken-bow motif as applied to their Elamite enemies. But the motif was certainly not exclusive to those contexts; for example, Jeremiah prophesied the breaking of the bow of Elam.[22] The fleeing figure in PFS 93* also shows remarkable similarities to some of the figures in the Assyrian relief depicting the victory over Te'umman. Such symbolism would have resonated with Cyrus the Anshanite's contemporaries beyond a superficial level. The rider is presumed to be the Cyrus of the Elamite inscription, itself a vivid reminder of the Elamite milieu in which Cyrus' family established their kingdom. It is, however, curious why the epithet "king" or even "crown prince" did not accompany this Cyrus' name on the seal. There may be any number of explanations; for example, the seal was inscribed before Cyrus I held either one of those titles. That such an heirloom persisted in use under Darius I is striking in light of the circumstances surrounding Darius' rise at the expense of Cyrus the Great's sons.

What's in a (Throne-)Name?

As may be seen, tracing Cyrus the Great's predecessors in the historical record is a tricky business, or at least a convoluted one. The identification of Cyrus the Great's grandfather with Cyrus the Anshanite of PFS 93*, as well as the identification with Cyrus of Parsumash introduced above, remain contested issues. To identify Cyrus the Great's grandfather with Cyrus of Parsumash requires an average reign of forty years for both Cambyses I and Cyrus I; such lengthy reigns are not the norm in antiquity, but they are hardly unattested. There are many examples from Near Eastern history of kings who ruled for more than forty years; the Achaemenid period alone provided two examples in Artaxerxes I (r. 465–424) and Artaxerxes II (r. 405–359). Regardless, several scholars favor lower dates for Cyrus' predecessors to ease any chronological discomfort of long-reigned kings.[23] Postulated regnal dates for Cyrus the Great's forefathers are mostly based on a generational counting and conjecture; the ranges may be shifted up or down ten, even twenty, years to prove or disprove that Cyrus of Parsumash was, or was not, identical to Cyrus I listed in the genealogy of the Cyrus Cylinder. Dating based on guesswork proves or disproves nothing, however, so, while the question may remain open, the identification of Cyrus I with Cyrus of Parsumash is so followed here.

The identification of Cyrus the Great's forebears in the historical record is also compounded by uncertainties regarding the early Persian kings' use of throne-names. In many instances it is not certain whether kings' names recorded in the sources are birth-names, throne-names, or abbreviations of a longer name (the last being what linguists term a hypocoristicon), and whether that longer name be the birth-name or a throne-name. Even a brief description of the problem reveals the potentially circular nature of the arguments. Throne-names were common in the ancient Near East, even if they were not always used upon accession or were used only in a shortened form. Throne-names are demonstrable for many of Cyrus the Great's successors, but the extant evidence does not allow us to confirm the use of one until Darius II took the throne in 424, when he adapted that throne-name Darius (Old Persian *Darayavaush*) instead of his given name Vahuka, which the Greeks rendered as Ochus.[24]

That "Cyrus" was a throne-name is suggested by an unverifiable reference by the Greek geographer Strabo from the late first century BCE or very early first century CE: "There is also a river called 'Cyrus,' flowing through so-called 'hollow' Persis near Pasargadae, from which the king took his name, taking the name Cyrus in place of Agradates." Closer to Cyrus' own time but still over a century removed, Herodotus noted that Cyrus was called something else before his true identity was learned, while he was raised by the herdsman Mitradates and his wife Spaco.[25] It is unclear whether that remark refers to a name his adoptive parents called Cyrus or, reading further into it, if Cyrus' given birth-name was otherwise before he took the name Cyrus. In other words, that story may also suggest that the name Cyrus was a throne-name, or alternate name, but Herodotus never explicitly said so. It would not be surprising for Cyrus to have taken a throne-name, as doing so would have fit centuries' worth of Near Eastern practice. But even if he did— and again it must be reiterated that we have no clear indication of this—he may not have used it.[26] A definitive discovery of Cyrus' birth-name as something different than "Cyrus"—awkward as that phrasing reads—would be big news. But Strabo's report finds no confirmation whatsoever in any of the contemporary, or even near-contemporary, sources for Cyrus the Great. It is thus unclear on what Strabo's information is based; he and other ancient authors did not provide footnotes.

To add to the mix, it is not even clear what Cyrus' name means. Or, rather, there is no agreement as to what it means. Varying explanations reveal mainly that, while etymology can be a useful tool, it is often a blunt instrument. Everything about Cyrus' name, and likewise the name of his father and of one of his sons, Cambyses, remains in dispute. This includes the orthography (spelling) of the original forms, whether or not they are hypocoristica (shortened versions of longer names), and whether either was ultimately of Elamite or Indo-Iranian etymology. All names have meaning in their original language, and for Old Persian *Kuruš* has been proposed "young" or "sun" or even "humiliator of the enemy in a verbal contest." For translation of Elamite *Kuraš* there have been proposed variations on "divinely protected" or "he who bestows care."[27] The pendulum swings among academics as it does among any other discipline, though as of this writing an Elamite etymology is generally accepted, though certainly not by all.

2

An Irresistible Force

There were a great many incentives that urged Cyrus on. . . . The first was his origin as seemingly something more than human, and the second was the good fortune manifesting in his campaigns. For in whatever direction Cyrus campaigned, it was impossible for anyone to escape him.

—Herodotus 1.204

Extant ancient Near Eastern sources tell us nothing about Cyrus' youth or life before he became king. Cyrus' father, Cambyses I, is attested in the Cyrus Cylinder and referenced likewise in a royal inscription from the city of Ur in southern Babylonia. Except for his grandfather, Cyrus I, details about Cyrus' predecessors are not much known beyond names on the clay. It seems reasonable to assume, however, that Cyrus the Great did not arise from a vacuum, and his rapid expansion should find some impetus in the activities of his predecessors, as has been discussed in the last chapter. The irresistible force that was Cyrus did not meet an immovable object for a very long time.

On the other hand, there is quite a lot of information about Cyrus the Great's birth and upbringing preserved in later Greek accounts, the focus of this chapter. These Greek accounts were in the main based on multiple oral traditions circulating in antiquity, legendary (if not fantastic) tales that are essential to consider in their own right. These stories are a rich trove of important, but embellished, material, as entertaining as they are contradictory. It remains a work in progress among modern scholars to tease out plausible historicity and, even more so, to contextualize and to interpret the significance of the legendary elements. Many interpret these stories broadly as echoes of original propaganda propagated in conjunction with Cyrus' real conquest of the Medes and the efforts to legitimize himself in the Median dynastic tradition. Although the details of this legitimization varied among Greek writers, it is also one reason why Cyrus and the early Persians were for so long in modern scholarship considered subject to the Medes. That issue will be picked up again in Chapter 3, which treats Cyrus' conquest of the Medes in more detail.

For a narrative of Cyrus' upbringing, we are primarily dependent on Herodotus, Ctesias, or Xenophon. In Herodotus and Xenophon, Cyrus was grandson of the last Median king, Astyages. In Herodotus, Cyrus was ultimately raised in Persis (Parsa) and took the throne by force; in Xenophon, he was raised at the Median court and took the throne peacefully upon marriage to a Median princess. In Ctesias, Cyrus had no royal blood at all but rose through the Median ranks by skill and hard work, and, after rebelling and defeating Astyages in battle, Cyrus arrogated the Median dynastic line by way of marriage with Astyages' daughter. These stories will be summarized and compared in the following.

A New Son Rising

Herodotus' version of Cyrus' birth and upbringing is the oldest on record, written in the mid-fifth century BCE, roughly a century after Cyrus' death. Herodotus prefaced his story by noting that he was aware of three other versions of Cyrus' life. This comment serves mainly to confirm what we would already suspect of an individual of such historical import. Cyrus had an effective publicity machine that worked hard, and was successful, at legitimizing Cyrus within multiple long-standing traditions. Herodotus dedicated much of his Book 1 to Cyrus the Great, set in the early and mid-sixth century BCE of our calendar. A favorite motif in Herodotus was the omen, and it played to great effect. As the story goes, the Median king Astyages had a dream sequence in which his daughter Mandane first flooded Asia with her urine and, in a subsequent dream, sprung from her privates a vine that overshadowed the continent. Both dreams signified the might and the destiny of her offspring.[1] The yet-to-be-born Cyrus' exceptionalism, his very existence, would pose a threat to his grandfather. Astyages' dream interpreters, who were Iranian priests and scholars called Magi, deduced these omens to mean that Mandane's child, Cyrus, would supplant Astyages on the throne.

To forestall the unease of the first dream, Mandane was married outside the Median nobility to a Persian named Cambyses. That particular detail matched Cyrus' father's name as given in Babylonian inscriptions, so Herodotus (and Xenophon likewise) got that much right. In the version Herodotus related, the Persians were described as inferior to the mighty Medes: so, by marrying his daughter to an "inferior" Persian, Astyages assumed there could be no threat. But after the second dream described above, and having learned that Mandane was pregnant, Astyages gave instructions that the child must be exposed to die in the wilderness. Heroes like Cyrus were not so easily dispatched, however; the gods watched over them.

Herodotus' story is replete with folktale motifs, including the age-old legend of the hero exposed, or hero of humble upbringing, to which we will return below. Astyages instructed one of his lieutenants, Harpagus, also a member of the extended royal family, to dispose of the child. Harpagus was deeply ambivalent about these instructions—not least because in this version Astyages had no male offspring—so he in turn delegated the job to one of his underlings, a shepherd named Mitradates. This Mitradates had, quite conveniently for the infant Cyrus' sake, a wife who had just given birth to a stillborn son. She prevailed upon Mitradates to switch the infants, and they kept Cyrus as their own. Thus, at least initially, Cyrus was raised in obscurity among the common people. Mitradates' wife's name was Spaco, a Median name that Herodotus explained meant a female dog.[2] By analogy, Cyrus was raised in the wild by a wolf, in the same vein as later Roman tradition portrayed Romulus and Remus.

Cyrus' true identity was revealed when he was ten years old. While playing a game with other boys, he was chosen to be their king. Here again, Fate foreshadowed the inevitable hero. Acting the part of king, Cyrus took the game to heart and commanded that one of the other boys, who had refused to follow Cyrus' orders, be whipped. This boy happened to be the son of a Median notable named Artembares. Artembares was enraged when he heard this, and he took his complaint to Astyages, who summoned Cyrus. Under Astyages' harsh questioning, Cyrus coolly admitted to having punished his young compatriot and added, in effect, that he had it coming. In other words, the young Cyrus, as the king in this game, had every right to punish one of his subjects who had refused to follow his commands.

As a folktale motif, the reader knows where this goes. Astyages, noting Cyrus' bearing and nobility even in these stressful circumstances, felt both a familiarity and a growing unease. Astyages suspected that he was speaking to his true-born grandson. With Cyrus led out of the room, under further questioning both Mitradates and Harpagus filled in the gaps to confirm Astyages' suspicion and thus explained how his grandson yet lived. Astyages was conflicted: wrathful because his orders to have the boy exposed had been ignored, yet pleased that Cyrus was alive. Astyages directed his ire not against Cyrus' adoptive father Mitradates but against Harpagus, to whom Astyages had given the initial order and by whom it was responsible to see fulfilled. As punishment, Astyages arranged to serve Harpagus his own children at a banquet. The unwitting diner of a cannibalistic feast is a theme that recurs elsewhere in Greek literature, such as the story of the Mycenaeans Atreus and Thyestes. Made aware of what (or, rather, whom) he had consumed after the fact, Harpagus swallowed as well his own anger and, ostensibly, accepted the macabre punishment. This act would come back to haunt Astyages, as things often did in Greek literature, when several years later Harpagus betrayed Astyages during Cyrus' rebellion. In the short term, the Magi declared the worrisome omen that Mandane's son would become a king, already fulfilled through Cyrus' play-acting the part of king with the other boys. And Asytages heard what he wished to hear, since he had quickly taken to his newfound grandson. Upon Cyrus' later rebellion, these same Magi dream-interpreters were punished with death, scapegoated because their interpretation had been wrong. The consequences of their miscalculation were enormous, Astyages was overthrown by Mandane's son, just as the dream omens had foretold. Herodotus' legendary account, despite its overall improbability on several levels, succeeded in its main narrative task to situate Cyrus firmly in the Median dynastic line.

Ctesias of Cnidus wrote his work entitled *Persica* ("Persian Matters") in the 390s, and his account represents a considerable departure from Herodotus. Though Ctesias also tied Cyrus closely to the Median royal house, Cyrus was not born into it, and his route to join it was by no means direct. In Ctesias' version, Cyrus was not of royal lineage. Only after lengthy and illustrious service as a young man, often in difficult circumstances—the mettle also needed to be forged, after all—did Cyrus become one of the Median king Astyages' high officials. Ctesias attributed Cyrus' initial humble upbringing to a very different origin story from that of Herodotus. Cyrus was born of ignoble stock, a son of Atradates the bandit and Argoste the goat-herder of the Mardian tribe.[3] Allusions to Cyrus' Mardian origins and his "wretched goat-herder" upbringing occur periodically throughout Ctesias' account, mainly via the mouth of a scornful Astyages.

Per Ctesias, the Medes had a custom where an individual of poor means could enter the service of another in exchange for upkeep and, if inclined, change masters when better circumstances presented themselves. Through this Median version of a *cursus honorum* for the poor, attested nowhere else in the sources for Cyrus before Ctesias, Cyrus undertook a variety of jobs in the palace administration. Cyrus' life from his youth was thus set within the Median palace system. One might juxtapose the version from Xenophon's *Cyropaedia* here, where Cyrus was raised in the same system but in entirely different circumstances, that is, as a royal prince. For Ctesias, Cyrus began his life as little more than a slave, before he rose to a position of high prominence in the royal court of Asytages; the story reductively cast Cyrus' increasing prominence as a function of his grace and elegance as wine-pourer, among other positive attributes. Cyrus' rise therein is better cast, in general terms, as a function of his own talent, skill, drive, and persistence, the hero of humble upbringing gradually realizing his own destiny.

There are several overlaps with Herodotus' story, but the details diverge in significant ways. Portents also played a large role, including a flood of urine as in Herodotus, but in Ctesias' rendition it was his mother herself who had the dream. Several personal names from Ctesias' version intersected Herodotus' account, but in Ctesias the individuals had entirely different roles. A certain Artembares appeared in both writers' accounts. We met briefly Herodotus' nobleman Artembares previously. In Ctesias' version, Artembares was a eunuch who became, in essence, a foster-father to Cyrus. Oibaras, a trickster figure, was quite prominent in Ctesias' version; he became Cyrus' right-hand man and, aside from Cyrus himself, was primarily responsible for his taking the throne. In Herodotus, an Oibaras made a brief appearance as a groomsman who helped Darius I secure the throne through his cleverness. The same character thus appeared in completely different circumstances, a phenomenon that likely reflects a popular oral tradition(s) about Oibaras himself. Much later Roman accounts, such as Justin's epitome of a Roman author named Pompeius Trogus (who lived during the time of Augustus Caesar), blended Herodotus' and Ctesias' versions, as though unsure of, or indifferent to, which should be given greater credibility.

Historians remain fascinated by these conjunctions, many of which appear to stem from variations in oral traditions among the ancient Persians themselves and their dissemination to the western fringes of the Empire. Less charitably in some modern interpretations, what the Persians actually thought or told had nothing to do with it: Greek writers' active imaginations, working within Greek literary paradigms, were the only source. Ctesias in particular still suffers from this judgment. While what we may more generously term creative embellishment can hardly be rejected outright, Herodotus, Ctesias, and other ancient writers viewed the writing of history as much a literary exercise as anything else. It was also another manifestation of the Greek competitive ethos, where success was in part gained by casting your rivals as bald liars, gullible doofuses, or ignorant idiots. It is well established that Ctesias intentionally relayed different traditions to "correct" his illustrious predecessor Herodotus, but there were other factors in play as well.

Although the particulars of Cyrus' birth and upbringing as relayed by Herodotus and Ctesias differ significantly, both stories are manifestations of the folktale motif of the hero exposed, or the hero of humble upbringing. In modern scholarship of the ancient Mediterranean, this motif (in its subtle variations) is often called the Sargon Legend—after the original once and future king, Sargon of Akkad, who ruled Mesopotamia c. 2350. According to the legend, Sargon was conceived in mysterious circumstances, born in secret, and exposed: literally, set afloat in a basket down a river. A canal worker, a humble man, saved him and raised him. Sargon became beloved by the goddess Ishtar and soon thereafter became ruler of the city of Akkad, located somewhere near Babylon, and from there all of Mesopotamia and beyond, thus destiny realized. The motif is also found, in varying manifestations, in the stories of Moses, Oedipus, Romulus and Remus, and several other notable figures from antiquity. In the case of Cyrus, Herodotus' version reflected a right to rule through his noble lineage: Cyrus was descended directly from the Median king. Ctesias' version was a moralizing tale, it emphasized rather a "rags-to-riches" story of a commoner who became king through his own ability and hard work—aided in no small part by destiny—despite the circumstances of his ignoble birth.[4] The inclusion of other elements, such as Ctesias' emphasis on a secondary hero, his right-hand man Oibaras (also spelled "Soebaris" in other traditions, such as Justin), indicates other inputs into the tradition—or, rather, traditions in the plural—as well.

Another version of Cyrus' upbringing was relayed by the Athenian Xenophon, but the Cyrus of his *Cyropaedia* is even more inventive than that of either of the others. The point of Xenophon's work, however, was not history even as his contemporaries understood it, but a treatise on ideal leadership. He chose Cyrus the Great as his paradigm not only because of his interests in Persian history and culture but also because of his close acquaintance with, and admiration for, the Empire's founder's great-great-great-grandson: Cyrus the Younger. In fact, the Cyrus the Great of the *Cyropaedia* was, in essence, the Cyrus the Younger that Xenophon knew, projected as a philosopher-king figure backward onto a "historical" (rather, legendary) context roughly 150 years earlier.

The Greek accounts of Cyrus' birth and upbringing are both instructive and entertaining. When it comes to reconstructing the early Persian Empire's history and Cyrus' premier place therein, they are primarily the latter. In one passage, Herodotus included the serious(?) declaration that the ancient Persians would consider any matter of great import while drunk, then reconsider it when sober—or vice versa; apparently the order was optional. They would take further action on the matter only if the same accord was reached in both states of mind. While acknowledging that this approach may have a lot to recommend it, Herodotus' anecdote is hard to gauge. In the same passage, Herodotus also informed his audience that Persian youth (the boys, at least) were educated in only three things: horsemanship, archery, and telling the truth, good bases for good Persian men, and rulers. Those three elements recurred time and again in sources, so it is no stretch to emphasize their import in Persian culture—they are no doubt accurate.

To depart from the legendary Greek accounts briefly, we can combine these Persian educational priorities with a sketch of the prince Cyrus' formal education through a close parallel. While details of the upbringing of the historical kings of Anshan are not available to us, recall that the Assyrians were their models. The Assyrian king Ashurbanipal claimed an extensive education: wisdom and insight received from the gods, as well as knowledge and skills gained through instruction and practice. As a royal prince, he no doubt received this education from experts in their respective disciplines. It is quite likely that for the prince Cyrus a similar education applied. This instruction included the arts of war (horsemanship, chariot-driving, archery, and skill with weapons) as well as reading and writing (the scribal arts) and music. Ashurbanipal also received instruction in how to run a kingdom and palace, that is, good governance, along with craftsmanship (especially of weapons and armor) and the formal science of how to read omens and other divine signs. In other words, like Ashurbanipal, Cyrus received an encompassing education to provide the future king the capability to rule effectively and wisely. For that matter, the seal of Cyrus I, PFS 93* discussed in Chapter 1, highlighted skill-at-arms on horseback.[5]

Even within the varying accounts preserved in Greek sources, there is no clear picture on the geopolitical situation in southwestern Iran that confronted Cyrus upon his accession as king. We know from Near Eastern and Greek sources that the Medes had been the dominant power in northern Iran for at least fifty years prior, the context for which will be discussed in Chapter 3.

We recall from last chapter the phenomenon of Elamite-Iranian ethnogenesis, the first instances of Persians battling Elamites in mid-seventh-century Khuzestan and, roughly a decade later, the homage of Cyrus, the king of Parsumash, to Ashurbanipal. How do we get from the important, first steps of Persian expansionism to Cyrus the Great possessing enough power to challenge the Medes? In other words, what forces was Cyrus able to command upon his ascendancy as king of Anshan in 559? The components of his burgeoning power in Iran must have been found, at least in part, in his relationships with other Persian and Iranian tribes. Indeed, the evidence indicates that Cyrus' marriage to an Achaemenid noblewoman named Cassandane served as a linchpin for his rise to power among the Persian and other Iranian clans based not only in Parsa, but throughout Iran.⁶

Cyrus and Cassandane

The marriage of Cyrus and Cassandane provides a key to understanding the relationship between Cyrus and the Achaemenids. Cassandane was the mother of Cambyses and Bardiya (called Smerdis by Herodotus and Tanyoxarkes by Ctesias), and she is assumed likewise of Atossa and Artystone. Herodotus recounted two short anecdotes about Cambyses' mother. One involves an entertaining but severely conflated story that Cambyses was the son of an Egyptian princess, ostensibly the daughter of Amasis. As Herodotus told the story, this princess—whose name is never revealed—was in fact a daughter of Amasis' predecessor, Apries. Amasis, knowing that Cyrus' request for one of his daughters would result in her being no more than a concubine, had sent a daughter of Apries to Cyrus instead of his own daughter. Herodotus also alluded to another alternate version that has the Egyptian princess requested by Cambyses himself. In any event, Herodotus strongly rejected both those versions and asserted without qualification that

"Cambyses was the son of Cassandane, the daughter of Pharnaspes, an Achaemenid, and definitely not of any Egyptian woman."

We do not know how old Cassandane was when she married Cyrus, or when she bore Cambyses. Whether or not Cassandane was Cyrus' first wife, we may assume she became his primary one, certainly by the time her son Cambyses was designated as successor. A generation later Atossa became Darius' primary wife, and not just because she was the daughter of Cyrus, although that was no doubt a key element. Atossa's prominence increased as the mother of the heir, Xerxes, regardless of the fact that she was not Darius' first wife. Cassandane did not play a large role in Herodotus' work or other sources, but it would be unwise to underestimate her importance— not just for her own qualities and not just as the mother of the heir but also what marriage to her may have gained for Cyrus.

In the Herodotus passage just discussed, Cassandane was portrayed as justifiably prideful, conscious of her own place among Cyrus' wives, and especially so as regards her son, the future king Cambyses. Cassandane, complimented on her tall and strikingly attractive children, lamented the fact that Cyrus nonetheless preferred an Egyptian concubine. Cambyses, a boy of ten at the time, then told his mother that it is for that reason that he would conquer Egypt. It was that very impetus that Herodotus attributed as the cause of Cambyses' later invasion of Egypt after he had become king. It is a fantastic anecdote. Whether or not it provides real insight into Cassandane's character, an echo preserved through oral traditions, is at best debatable. In any event, it is hardly a stretch to visualize Cassandane as a dynamic and forceful personality, a key figure in the nascent Persian Empire, and we may assume this not only by implication of her place in the story of Cyrus' rise but also on parallel with the later prominence of the princesses Atossa and Artystone, about whom more will be said below.

A series of political marriages, emphasis on the plural, in the early years of Cyrus' reign may have significantly amplified his military power. Cyrus' marriage to Cassandane looms large as a primary example, perhaps the most important one. Allusions to Egyptian concubines and indications of Cyrus' marriage into the Median royal family suggest additional possibilities of dynastic marriages, but details are unfortunately lacking. Alliances formed therefrom would go a long way to explaining the rapid conquests that will be examined in subsequent chapters. History offers many parallels. Philip II of Macedon, the father of Alexander the Great, provides one prominent example, two centuries later, of a king who greatly augmented his power through a series of dynastic marriages.[7] Further, it need not be assumed that Cyrus the Great was the first in his line to have done this; it would not be surprising to discover evidence of his predecessors having done the same during the preceding century of intensive Elamite-Persian ethnogenesis. However, something, or rather some things, momentous happened in the mid-sixth century that helped propel an impactful moment in world history. Cassandane's marriage to Cyrus should be considered of enormous consequence in this sequence. Cassandane represented an important link, perhaps "the" important link, a linchpin between Cyrus' line and that of the Achaemenids that delivered powerful clans and families—and their respective followers and resources—to Cyrus.

Based on later events, it is clear that prominent among these Achaemenids was Hystaspes, who held an important position before Darius became king. In Herodotus he was the *hyparch* of Parsa itself, though it is unclear what Herodotus meant that title to encompass; the term *hyparch* is a generic Greek title for high-level Persian officials. A passage in Darius' Bisotun Inscription indicated that Hystaspes held an important military command and may have been a satrap, though Darius did not use that term for him (Old Persian *xšaçapāvā*). Hystaspes also had a brother named Parnaka, who later became the overseer of his nephew Darius' administration at Persepolis. A man by the same name is attested as a high-ranking Babylonian judge during Cyrus' reign, but whether or not this is the same Parnaka is uncertain.[8] Cassandane's marriage to

Cyrus may have either facilitated, or reinforced, these and other ties among the Persian elite. It is a true pity that we do not know more about this remarkable woman.

The marriage may have been more than just political. Herodotus noted that Cyrus greatly lamented Cassandane's death and that he declared public mourning for her: "Cassandane had died before Cyrus himself. Cyrus had mourned greatly for her and instructed all his subjects to do likewise." Herodotus' brief report directly echoes a Babylonian source, the Nabonidus Chronicle, of an official mourning period on behalf of Cyrus' queen. Cassandane's name was not explicitly mentioned in the passage, but the Babylonian chronicles did not generally provide women's names. The passage refers to her death within a few months after Cyrus' conquest of Babylon in October 539. "In the month [Adar (i.e., early March)] the wife of the king died. From the twenty-seventh of the month Adar to the third of the month Nisan [there was] mourning in Akkad. All the people bared their heads."[9]

There are different traditions in Greek historiography about Cyrus' wives; see Chart 2 for Cyrus' marriages as recorded by

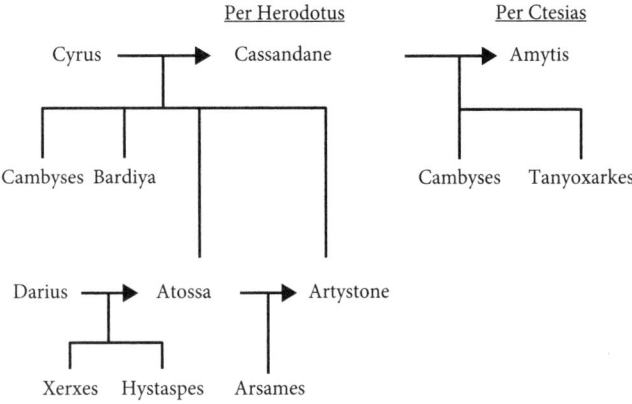

Chart 2 Cyrus' marriages and descendants as recorded by Herodotus and Ctesias.

Herodotus and Ctesias. Excerpts from Ctesias' *Persica* relay that Cyrus married the daughter of Astyages, instead of being born of Astyages' daughter (Mandane). In Ctesias' account the daughter's name was Amytis. This is another departure from Herodotus' account, but, as has been discussed previously, Ctesias represented Cyrus' entire life quite differently. And the differences did not end there. Amytis had been married to another Mede, Spitamas by name, who through their marriage was effectively Astyages' heir. In Ctesias' version of the story, after Cyrus' defeat of Astyages in the field, Cyrus slew Spitamas and married Amytis. Cyrus had two sons with her, Cambyses and Tanyoxarkes, the latter considered an alternate name of Bardiya.

The surviving text of Ctesias for this sequence is extremely telescoped. Not enough of Ctesias' original account is extant that would allow proper contextualization of the vicissitudes in Cyrus' attitude toward his once master, then threat, then vanquished enemy, then father-in-law. Regardless, once he was wedded to Astyages' daughter, Cyrus was thus legitimized as the king of the Medes. Thus, in Ctesias' version of the Cyrus story, Cyrus had no dynastic claim whatsoever to Media, but rule was gained solely through conquest (and, by implication of dreams and portents, divine favor) and then buttressed by marriage to the Median princess. The Median heroine—the female link to the throne—thus varied in the Greek tradition: Cyrus' wife (Amytis) in Ctesias and his mother (Mandane) in Herodotus. Xenophon's *Cyropaedia* in effect split the difference. Cyrus was the son of Mandane, Astyages' daughter, but Cyrus also married his cousin, the daughter of Cyaxeres, who was the son of Astyages, and with his marriage to the princess Cyrus received all of Media as a dowry. Xenophon did not bother to give the princess a name.

The conflicting traditions may be confusing but need not be mutually exclusive. In fact, it would be more surprising if Cyrus did not marry, or at least take into his household as secondary wives or concubines, any daughter(s) of Astyages. Such an act would have served the same purposes it did a generation later for Darius I, when Darius married all the women of Cyrus' family that he could find. These included not only Atossa and Artystone but also one of Cyrus' granddaughters: a daughter of Bardiya named Parmys. The practice of polygamy among Persian kings is well-attested. As noted, but bears repeating, the traditions wherein Cyrus was linked to the Median royal house by marriage may reflect Cyrus' own efforts to link himself to the Median dynasty, in fact or in appearance, one way by which Cyrus could have portrayed himself—and his successors—as legitimate Median kings.[10]

The Daughters of Cyrus: Atossa and Artystone

Before we return the focus to Cyrus himself, a few more words are due to his family, and here particularly his daughters, Atossa and Artystone. Artystone was not a major focus of Greek writers, though Herodotus noted that she was Darius' favorite wife and the mother of a son, Arsames, named after his great-grandfather on the father's side. Atossa appeared much more frequently in the Greek sources. Her name is etymologized from Avestan *Hutaosā* ("bestowing very richly"), a telling name chosen by Cyrus and Cassandane that highlighted Mazdaean traditions and that reinforced Achaemenid connections with eastern Iran, considered the homeland of Zoroaster and the religion that bears his name.[11]

Atossa loomed large in the Greek tradition, of course, as queen in her own right and as daughter (of Cyrus), wife (of Cambyses, then of Bardiya, then of Darius I), and mother (of Xerxes and several others). Enormous political influence was attributed to Atossa in several anecdotes. In one notable story preserved in Herodotus, and in a setting no less than the bedroom she shared with Darius, she convinced him to attack Greece. To Herodotus, she was purportedly (if exaggerated) the real power behind Darius' throne and it was due to her influence that her son Xerxes became the crown prince.[12] The force of personality aside, that she was Cyrus' daughter would have played no small part in Xerxes' accession. The queen mother was also a major character in Aeschylus' tragedy called *Persae* (simply "The Persians"), although Atossa was not identified by name in the play. Aeschylus assigned her a compelling role in Xerxes' tragic return—in defeat and disgrace (as per Aeschylus' version)—to Persia after his invasion of Greece in 480–479. Whether Aeschylus had much reliable information about Atossa is an open question seems unlikely; in the play her performance was mainly drawn to suit how an Athenian Greek believed a Persian queen should behave and react.

Another Greek writer, Hellanicus of Lesbos, roughly contemporary to Aeschylus, portrayed Atossa as a masculinized, tiara-and-trousers-wearing woman surrounded by eunuchs, who acted like a king and issued written judgments in her own name. This portrayal finds parallels with the legendary Semiramis, the masculinized warrior queen. Semiramis was a favorite Greek literary trope who highlighted the strangeness and effeminacy of eastern rulers, represented in Greek texts as an antithesis of what in their culture was considered proper behavior.[13] While we cannot comment in much detail about Atossa's sartorial choices, her involvement in Persian administration was not a stretch, as will be seen in the following when she and her sister Artystone are considered in their Persian context.

The influence and power of royal women is manifested through more reliable means than Greek anecdotes, however. The Persepolis Fortification Archive (PFA) provides a window into the activities of various royal women, Artystone prominent among them, and thus this material is introduced at greater length here. The PFA is named for the find spot, not the contents, of the tablets. The corpus serves as an analogous example of the rich documentation of administrative and economic documents also available from Babylonia for the Achaemenid period. Analyzing these materials remains a work in progress, and there is much more to discover. The vast majority of the PFA tablets were written in Elamite, some tablets and tags written in Aramaic (ink and incised), and a small handful in other languages (including Old Persian and Greek). The texts themselves deal mainly with the collection, storage, and redistribution of both foodstuffs and livestock. These tablets thus provide important data on the organization of labor; economy and fiscal management; the demography and cartography of the Empire's core; operations of state institutions at a basic level; religious practices and cultic personnel; travel on state business; and a host of other social and cultural aspects of Achaemenid history. Even as the tablets' continued study reveals many surprises, none of the incredible detail and sophistication manifested in these documents is the least bit surprising. Such advanced organizational control, if not at the same scale, is demonstrable for several centuries in both Mesopotamian and Elamite traditions, traceable as far back as 2100 BCE and the Ur III period.

Another important component of the Fortification archive is the variety of seals applied to the tablets, the seals authenticating the transactions described on each tablet. There were more than 1,100 distinct seals impressed upon the published Elamite tablets. These seals portray a range of activity, and their rich iconography is an invaluable resource. Some examples will be discussed in the following, including several important heirloom pieces—in addition to PFS 93* that was initially made for Cyrus' grandfather—belonging to or linked to Cyrus' daughters and other notables. The Persepolis texts and seals thus offer insights into the stratification of Persian society, but of course the emphasis is on a bureaucratic hierarchy and the people who worked within it or for it.

The royal women whose Elamite names were Irdabama, Udusa (Greek Atossa), and Irtashduna (Greek Artystone) are among those prominent in the PFA corpus. They had large retinues of staff and servants, controlled significant land holdings, managed their own private business, and went on long journeys. In other words,

Figure 2.1 Line drawing of seal of Irdabama, PFS 51, scale 2–1.
Courtesy of the Persepolis Fortification Archive Project and the Persepolis Seal Project.

they were major stakeholders, powerful movers and shakers, and were in a position to influence both politics and culture. Irdabama is the most prominent royal woman in the Fortification archive, presumably a wife or the mother of Darius, but she has not yet been identified in other sources. Her relationship with Cyrus and his family, if any, is unclear. Irdabama owned many estates, which commissioned hundreds of workers, throughout Parsa. Numerous tablets indicate the enormous amounts of food and drink dispersed before Irdabama's table, the records implying that she had a court of her own—one that, like the kings, was itinerant and was held in multiple cities, as she traveled frequently. Irdabama had her own personal seal, PFS 51, that was used on several texts from the archive (Figure 2.1). PFS 51 is a close compositional analog to PFS 93*, the seal of Cyrus I son of Teispes (Figure 1.6), and it shares several stylistic elements. PFS 51 also shows a mounted horseman, but the prey are animals, not humans as portrayed in PFS 93*.

Another seal frequently associated with disbursements is PFS 77*, an intriguing seal to consider in this context (Figure 2.2). The seal appears to have been used by Rashda, a high-level royal administrator, in Elamite called a *šaramanna*, an "apportioner." Among his other responsibilities, Rashda oversaw Irdabama's work forces. The seal portrays a compelling audience scene of a queen, a representation that recalls the vast foodstuffs recorded disbursed to

Figure 2.2 Line drawing of seal of Sherash, PFS 77*, scale 2–1.
Courtesy of the Persepolis Fortification Archive Project and the Persepolis Seal Project.

Irdabama, and just as important, another reminder that not only the king might hold audiences. PFS 77* is inscribed with the name of one Sherash, the daughter of Huban-ahpi.[14] PFS 77* is clearly part of the group of heirloom seals used by members of the royal family, including Cyrus' daughters, and members of their bureaus. Both daughter and father named in the inscription on PFS 77* are ciphers to us otherwise, but we may fairly wonder if Sherash, and her father, held prominent positions in, or were perhaps even prominent members of, the households of Cyrus the Great's forebears. To reiterate the previous discussion of PFS 93*, the seals discussed here are antiques. It has been convincingly proposed that PFS 93*, its direct companion piece PFS 51, and two known Assyrian stamp seals came from the same late seventh-century workshop, if not the same hand. This has wide-ranging ramifications for the connections between Cyrus the Great's forefathers and the Assyrian court, which have also already been discussed; if the assessment of these seals is accurate, it provides more evidence to support these connections.

Within the PFA, the royal woman Irtashduna is a much more compelling individual than her Herodotean namesake Artystone. The Elamite form Irtashduna has been etymologized as from an Iranian name, *Ṛtastūnā. Irtashduna, like Irdabama, received and dispensed sometimes large quantities of foodstuffs, for example, for feasts. Her seal, PFS 38, is one of the most elaborate in the archive (Figure 2.3). It preserves a scene of heroic encounter: a central figure in an Assyrianizing garment in a master of animals pose: holding subdued two winged-bull or griffon-like creatures with horns and human faces. To the left of the scene is an intricate, Assyrianizing floral element, above which is a similarly intricate nimbus of circles and rays, culminating in stars, within which a figure seemingly floats, presumably a deity. A number of other symbols, including a poorly preserved figure between the hero and the creature to his right, add to the complexity of this design. Whether Assyrian (i.e., manufactured in Assyria or under Assyrian influence before the fall of Nineveh in 612) or Assyrianizing (i.e., in the mode of Assyrian art but manufactured after 612), PFS 38 is yet another manifestation of the preference for archaic or archaizing imagery associated with Cyrus' royal family, as discussed above.[15]

To round out this section is a reminder as to how much remains to be discovered about Cyrus' daughters. To the consternation of several modern scholars, references to Atossa in the Fortification

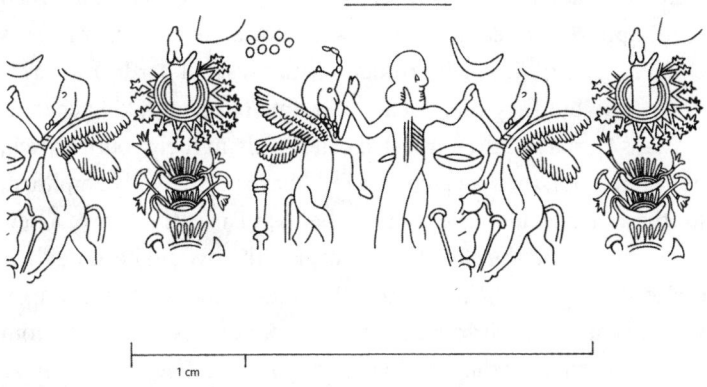

1 cm

Figure 2.3 Line drawing of seal of Irtashduna (Artystone), PFS 38, scale 2–1.
Courtesy of the Persepolis Fortification Archive Project and the Persepolis Seal Project.

archive have proven elusive. Since Atossa was the dominant queen in Greek representations of the era, it is natural to look for her among the women prominent attested in the PFA tablets. But there is no guarantee she would be there. For example, Atossa may have dwelled primarily elsewhere and was, therefore, not consistently active in the Persepolis region and thus not often mentioned in the PFA. Only recently (as of this writing) has Atossa been attested in more than a handful of texts. But the references to Udusa (the Elamite form of her name) testify to her status and influence as well, although in the PFA corpus not to the quantitative extent of texts referencing Irdabama and Irtashduna. Nonetheless, one recently published document records 11,368(!) quarts of wine expended before Atossa, meaning in her presence. If it was all consumed at one sitting, that was some banquet. We ourselves are thirsty for more. New information and insights continue to stream from the ongoing study of the Fortification archive. It is hoped that future archaeological excavations at Persepolis, and other important Achaemenid centers, will reveal new archives that complement what we are learning from the PFA.

The fascinating windows into the lives and activities of Atossa and Artystone give glimpses into the situation when these women were queens, after Cyrus' death, and at a time (c. 500 BCE) when the Empire was already close to its territorial height. Their lives as children, along with their brothers Cambyses and Bardiya, are a cipher to us, but they came of age at a time of breathtaking change. Perhaps Cyrus' children traveled extensively in their youth as well, but even if not, their awareness would have been greatly amplified, for the world would have come to them, in Parsa, the core of a new hyperpower and the site of a new capital that would become their home, Pasargadae. Within their lifetimes, Parsa went from a regional center to a world center, a nexus of peoples and goods from the four corners of the world and everything in between. To make this happen, their father Cyrus was on campaign if not constantly, then with great frequency and for long stretches, and it is to these conquests that we turn in the next chapters.

3

On the March

Leave off your dancing for me now, for when I played my
flute before you would not come out.
—Cyrus to the Ionian Greeks, offering their submission to
him way too late, from Herodotus 1.141

Cyrus' first major conquest on record was of the Medes, one of the
premier powers of the early sixth century. We rarely get glimpses
into the minutiae of ancient battles, let alone the devasting impacts
on both participants and bystanders. Inevitably the superficial accounts gloss the human cost, and the entire enterprise may seem
sanitized. This is particularly the case with Cyrus' rapid and wide-
spread conquests, for which it is again important to remind ourselves of the limited source material: in a nutshell, nothing from the
Medes or Persian themselves, hence we rely on external and later
sources to reconstruct the events. In Greek sources, the Medes were
portrayed as a powerful, centralized empire—in an entirely circular
manner—on the only model of empire available to the Greeks at the
time, the Achaemenid Empire. But the Median Empire, if it may
even be called that, was not the same as its Achaemenid successor.
It is thus important to contextualize the Medes as we understand
their history in order to set the stage for Cyrus' conquest of them.

Median Problems

Considered as a western Iranian geopolitical phenomenon, the Medes appear analogous to the Persians in the early and mid-first millennium BCE. We know they were there, but their sudden (to us) appearance in the sources as major players, in what we might call the Great Power politics of the later seventh century, is unexpected. The lack of contemporary sources for the Medes' rise, especially the impetus for their prominent involvement in the military overthrow of the Assyrian Empire, is difficult to explain. The Medes remained a force with which to be reckoned into the sixth century, until conquered in turn by Cyrus the Great in 550. But the Medes are hard to find on the ground, as it were. Archaeological remains are often not easily linked with the Medes, or any discrete ethnic group for that matter, especially minus corroborating documentary evidence. That reveals the core of the problem: there is no documentary evidence at all extant from the Medes themselves.[1] Iranian archaeological sites identified as Median—such as Nush-i Jan (roughly 37 miles south of Hamadan), Godin (Kangavar valley in Kermanshah), and Baba Jan (eastern Luristan)—indicate a decline in the first half of the sixth century: the exact time that we would expect to find evidence for a Median Empire.

The traditional picture of a Median Empire in modern scholarship, at least in most overviews from the twentieth century, is beholden mainly to Herodotus. His tale of the first Median kings thematically matches accounts of the rise of tyrants (i.e., individual rulers who seized power by force) in Greek city-states; in other words, Herodotus' version of the Median kings was, at its core, a Greek story with a veneer of the Achaemenid court of his day superimposed.[2] According to Herodotus, a Mede named Deioces arrogated power to himself, manipulated his election as king, assembled a bodyguard of spear-bearers, and implemented construction of an elaborate, fortified capital called Ecbatana. Deioces then removed himself and implemented behavioral protocols for his subjects, to whom Deioces became mostly inaccessible anyway. Herodotus then treated the reader to a survey of Deoices' descendants—for well over a century from c. 700 onward—with emphasis on military matters, such as the Medes' battles with both Scythians and Assyrians, anecdotes that in general seem plausible enough but the particulars of which modern scholars are hardpressed to corroborate.

Contemporaneous Assyrian evidence painted an entirely different picture of the Medes, one that did not involve a supraregional entity with extensive territorial dominion.[3] The Medes whom the Assyrians encountered lived in fortified settlements, apparently independent from one another, throughout the central and northern Zagros Mountains, but especially along what is called the Khorasan Road (another name for the Silk Road). Modern commentators have mixed views when it comes to labeling the extent of Median territory, at times including areas to the north of Lake Urmia and to the south into Luristan, the eastern and western extent of influence more difficult to discern.

During the Assyrian Empire's heyday from the later ninth through mid-seventh centuries, the Medes appeared frequently in their sources: as targets of Assyrian campaigning in the Zagros Mountains for horses, plunder, or manpower. By the end of the eighth century, many areas that the Assyrians identified as Median (normalized from Akkadian as *Madâ* or *Madaya*) had been incorporated into the Assyrian Empire. The rulers of these settlements are called in the Assyrian documentation "city lords" (singular *bēl āli*), a term that suggests a limited scope of their power. Many of these Median city-lords had entered formal treaty relationships, called *adê*-agreements, with Assyria. Assyria was always the dominant partner. Through the mid-seventh century, there is no indication of a centralized, Median authority, that is, a sole king, one who could be equated, for example, with Herodotus' Deioces.[4] Assyrian omen queries lead us to believe that local rulers in that region spent most of their time fighting each other, while the Assyrians attempted to keep the Khorasan Road open and safe for their own interests. The upshot of these testimonies is that there is no easy way to forge the sharply divergent Assyrian and Greek perspectives into agreement. Faced with a choice, the Assyrian evidence is given more credibility in recent assessments of the Medes, not least because the available archaeological evidence better fits the picture reconstructed from Assyrian sources.

The last references to Medes in Assyrian royal inscriptions are from the mid-650s.[5] The Medes next appear in documentary sources in records of the Babylonian chronicle series describing events of the 610s. By that time, a new Babylonian dynasty founded by Nabopolassar was in the process of asserting its independence from Assyria, already having been at war for ten years. The Medes appear in the chronicle suddenly, from our perspective, on the march with an attack on Assyrian Arrapha (modern Kirkuk, roughly sixty miles east of Ashur) in 615. In 614, attacks against Assyrian cities continued, and the Median king Umakishtar, the Cyaxeres of the Greek tradition, made a pact of alliance with Nabopolassar, the terms of which are not preserved. In 612, the Medes and Babylonians sacked Nineveh, a seminal moment in ancient Near Eastern history. There is no context given in any of these sources how Cyaxeres marshaled an army to such devastatingly effective use. The consequences of the sack of Nineveh reverberated widely. The following excerpt from the Book of Nahum is just one example:

Horsemen charging, flashing sword and glittering spear,
hosts of slain, heaps of corpses. . . . Wasted is Nineveh,
who will bemoan her?[6]

By 609, the Assyrian Empire had ceased to be an effective entity. The fall of the Assyrians, Lord Byron's "the wolf on the fold," signaled the end of the one great power that had dominated the ancient Near East for the better part of the preceding two centuries.

Recent approaches have postulated that the Medes were the leaders of a large coalition of mostly Iranian peoples from across northern Iran, a coalition unified by the forceful personality of Cyaxeres and maintained only for the purpose of defeating Assyria. This coalition, in conjunction with the Babylonians, was successful at that task, but afterward, the Median coalition splintered. If this reconstruction is accurate, it remains to be reconciled with accounts of the Medes as a major power through the first half of the sixth century, an impression given not only by Greek sources but one alluded to in Babylonian and biblical traditions. For example, in the Book of Jeremiah, the plural "kings" is used when describing the Medes in various prophetic contexts.

An inscription of the Babylonian king Nabonidus, not coincidentally the first recorded reference to Cyrus the Great (to be discussed in more detail in the following section), also referred to the king of the Medes being accompanied by additional "kings who go at his side." This seemingly incidental detail provides additional support for the Medes as a destructive force with a loose, unifying leadership: a confederation, if that is a correct term for it. Another passage in Herodotus—outside his rendition of the Medes' rise under Deioces and his successors discussed previously—parallels this perspective: "The Medes ruled all together and (directly) those living nearest; and these, further, ruled their neighbors, and so again in turn, they theirs."

Visualizing Median power as a system of loose rule of their neighbors, what some anthropologists call a "Big Man confederacy," offers a compelling model. The plurality of kings mentioned by Nabonidus and in the Book of Jeremiah fits such a reconstruction: Median domination over multiple, neighboring peoples, each of whom owed allegiance, directly or indirectly, to a Median overlord without the formal structure of an organizational empire.[7] This is the situation that confronted Cyrus from the north in the late 550s. Cyrus' victory over the Medes is the least well documented of his major conquests, but in terms of what it meant for the resources, wealth, and manpower at his disposal, it was likely the most momentous.

(More) Dreaming of Cyrus

Cyrus' rise was foretold in dreams other than those recorded by Herodotus and Ctesias about his birth, discussed previously. To consider further this phenomenon, we must turn briefly to King Nabonidus (r. 556–539) and the Babylonians, who are later in line to fall to the Cyrus juggernaut, a sequence that will be discussed in more detail in Chapter 4. For reasons unclear to us, early in his reign Nabonidus was keen to blame the Medes for preventing his desired restoration work on a temple of the moon god (the deity named Sin in Akkadian and Nanna-Suen in Sumerian). This temple was in the city of Harran (see Map 3), which had been destroyed during the last stage of the overthrow of Assyria. Whatever understanding Medes and Babylonians shared during the overthrow of Assyrian power in 610s, it was apparently no longer in effect by Nabonidus' time. In one of his royal inscriptions, the so-called Sippar Cylinder (Figure 3.1), the Medes were cast as both the cause of the temple's destruction and an impediment to its restoration.

Nabonidus' decision to blame outsiders was hardly a novel choice. The Medes were typecast as the stereotypical enemy in Mesopotamian tradition, the so-called (in Akkadian) *umman-manda*, bogeymen created by the gods as an instrument to punish wrongdoers. These *umman-manda* were periodically dragged out as the nefarious enemy by many Mesopotamian kings over the course of sixteen centuries prior to Nabonidus' day. They had great staying power as the prototypical Other. The Sippar Cylinder recorded a dream prophecy *post eventum* of Cyrus' conflict with the Median king Astyages. Concerned about the Medes, Nabonidus was assured by the god Marduk that Cyrus, the king of Anshan, would remove the threat.

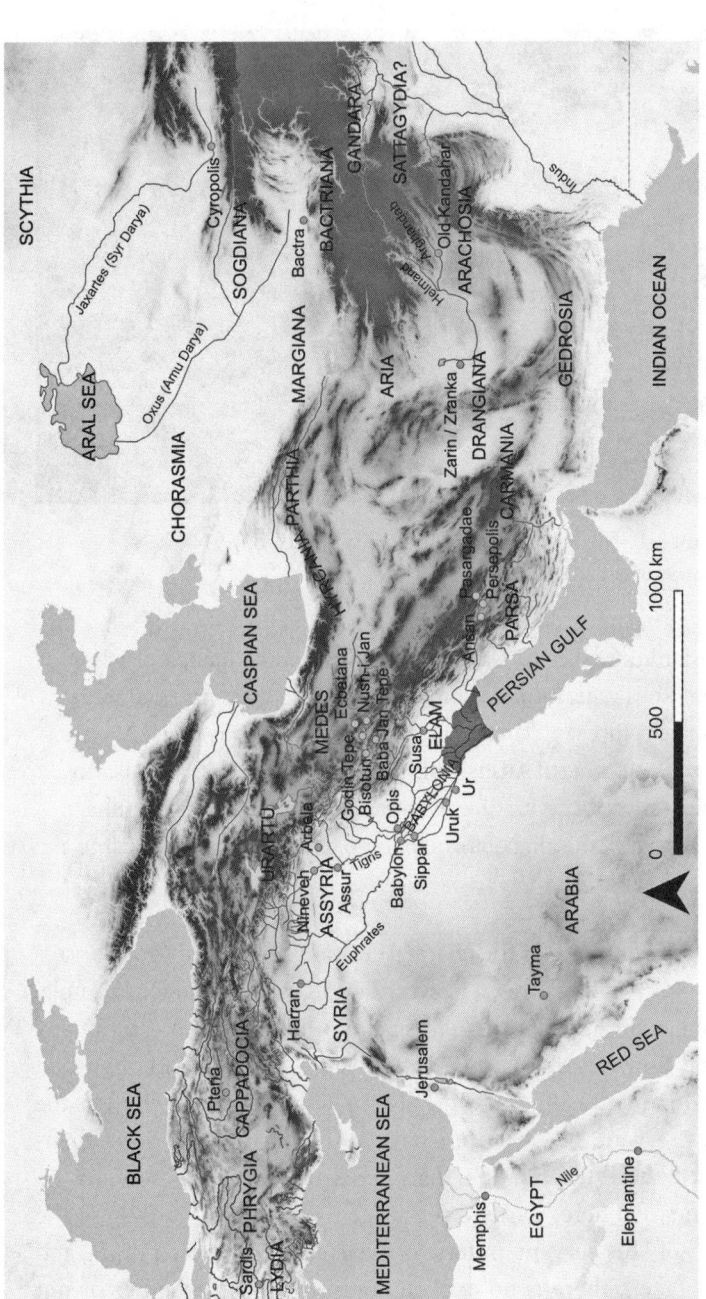

Map 3 Map of Cyrus the Great's empire, courtesy of Andrea Squitieri (LMU Munich). After Moeller, Potts, and Radner 2022, used by permission.

Figure 3.1 The Sippar Cylinder of Nabonidus, BM 91109.
© Trustees of The British Museum.

(Marduk replies to Nabonidus) "The *umman-manda* of whom you speak, he, his land, and the kings who go at his side, are no longer a threat. . . ." In the third year, they (the gods) caused to rise Cyrus, the king of Anshan, his young servant, with his small army he scattered the vast *umman-manda*. Cyrus seized Ishtumegu (Astyages), the king of the *umman-manda*, and took him captive to his land.[8]

Understanding of the characterization of Cyrus in this passage depends significantly on word choice in translation, for example, whether the "his" of the phrase "his young servant" was understood to mean that Cyrus was Astyages' servant. Although that Akkadian phrasing was typically applied to an agent who was the god's servant, by no means have all modern translations abandoned the interpretation that Cyrus was Astyages' servant. As understood here, Cyrus was the agent of the god Marduk, so the "his" of "his servant" refers to Cyrus as Marduk's servant—and thus taken, there is no explicit commentary on whether or not

Cyrus was subject to Astyages. Whether we understand Cyrus as subject to Astyages, or not, of course has enormous impact on historical reconstruction. The translation of Cyrus as "young" also carries significance, though the Akkadian word *ṣiḫru* had a variety of nuances. Did it mean in this context, as often translated, "young," and thus a commentary on Cyrus' relative age? Or is another nuance to be applied, that of "small" or "insignificant"?[9] Nabonidus' characterization of Cyrus as "insignificant"—if that is indeed what he meant—may signify little outside the literary context of this passage, a manifestation of Babylonians' ethnocentrism relegating other peoples to inferior status. But for historians attempting to piece together this period, translating Cyrus as "young" has ramifications for understanding his and his forebears' chronology.

Cyrus' War with Astyages

Before Cyrus' defeat of Astyages in 550, the political relationship between Medes and Persians is thus obscure. The difficulties in understanding the Near Eastern evidence are further confounded by contradictory Greek accounts. While the particulars vary, Greek authors generally considered the Persians subject to the Medes before Cyrus, but this arrangement finds no direct corroboration in the Near Eastern sources, barring the ambiguity in the Sipper Cylinder passage described above. One other, extant Near Eastern account tersely recorded Cyrus' victory over Astyages. The so-called Nabonidus Chronicle, a partially preserved tablet found in Babylon, indicated that in the year 550/549 Cyrus defeated Ishtumegu, the Astyages of classical sources, and plundered Ecbatana (Figure 3.2).

Like many other surviving clay tablets, the cuneiform signs of the Nabonidus Chronicle are frequently broken or difficult to read in several key places. This is reflected in the following translation with

Figure 3.2 The Nabonidus Chronicle, BM 35382.
© Trustees of The British Museum.

brackets and ellipses to indicate uncertainty of how many signs (and thus words) are missing. The relevant lines run as follows:

> Astyages mobilized his army and campaigned against Cyrus, king of Anshan, in order to conquer him. The army of Astyages rebelled, and he was taken prisoner. They delivered him to Cyrus [. . .] Cyrus marched to Ecbatana, the royal city. The silver, gold, goods, property [. . .] which he carried off as booty from Ecbatana he took to Anshan. The goods and property of the army of [. . .].[10]

Neither the Nabonidus Chronicle nor the Sippar Cylinder discussed previously offered particulars of Cyrus' progression from king of Anshan to the conqueror of the Medes. No additional information was given in the chronicle passage as to why the Median army handed Astyages over to Cyrus. That report anticipated Herodotus' embellished account of Median treachery (see below), but it offers no details to elucidate that account. Internal troubles in Media may have contributed to Astyages' downfall, as suggested by his troops' revolt, but it is unclear why disaffected Median elements would have linked their fortunes with Cyrus.

Herodotus preserved a much more colorful account of Cyrus' war with the Medes.[11] Nonetheless, as relayed, the war itself is a rather anticlimactic end to what was clearly, in Herodotus' view, the much more interesting backstory of Cyrus' rise that was discussed in Chapter 2. It is time to resume that narrative thread here, with some recap. After the discovery of the boy Cyrus' true identity, his grandfather Astyages sent him to Persia to live with his biological parents: Cambyses and Mandane, the daughter of Astyages. Meanwhile, the Median high official Harpagus, the very individual charged with exposing the infant Cyrus, paid a horrific price—despite Astyages' admitted happiness that Cyrus yet lived. For his failure to follow his lord's instructions, Harpagus unknowingly was served his own son at a banquet. Upon revelation of the macabre meal, Harpagus was stoic, but he patiently waited for the opportunity to avenge himself on Astyages. The wheel turned, and this opportunity came in the person of Cyrus. When Cyrus was old enough, Harpagus cultivated an alliance. Harpagus reminded Cyrus that Astyages had wanted Cyrus dead at birth, and that it was Harpagus himself who was responsible for Cyrus' having avoided that fate. Further, Harpagus added assurances that other Median lords also stood ready to make Cyrus their king, if Astyages could be overthrown. This was all quite convenient, and it gets better. Harpagus used a clever ruse to smuggle this message to Cyrus: a servant disguised as a hunter with the message secreted in the belly of a rabbit that he had killed.

Cyrus did not require much convincing. He persuaded his fellow Persians through a different sort of exercise. Cyrus assigned them hard labor for one day, then feasted them the next, and thereafter asked which they preferred. An easy choice, and as Cyrus presented it, one achievable to the Persians if they put away their servitude toward the Medes and joined him in rebellion. When news of this development reached Astyages, he ordered Cyrus to return before him to stand judgment, to which Cyrus responded that he would arrive sooner than Astyages wanted. Enraged, Astyages assigned none other than Harpagus to lead the Median army to crush the Persian rebellion. Astyages' choice of Harpagus to lead the Median armies against Cyrus seems inexplicable, but it worked within Herodotus' thematic approach. Herodotus used a word (*theoblabēs*) that implied Astyages' divinely inspired delusion, or recklessness, with the further implication that Cyrus was destined to be victorious. Historically accurate details take a back seat in such representations. Herodotus skated over descriptions of the battle itself. As Harpagus had already turned many of the Medes against Astyages, it was apparently not much of a fight. Cyrus won another victory and claimed the Median rule for his own, both through right of conquest and as blood heir to Astyages, via Mandane. Astyages was allowed to live, but as a prisoner at Cyrus' court—which, if true, would have made an interesting dynamic. It does fit a pattern of Cyrus' clemency toward defeated rulers, though other sources indicated that Astyages did not long survive life as a private citizen.

Ctesias' version of Cyrus' war against the Medes was clearly extensive, even in transmitted form as relayed by Nicolaus of Damascus. This counter-narrative is worth relaying at some length, not only for the different perspective that it offers but also because it is Herodotus' version that, justifiably or not, gets the most airtime in modern treatments. First, we recall that Ctesias' version had removed Cyrus' ancestry completely outside of the royal line, which is certainly not accurate. In Ctesias' rendering, Cyrus' achievements were no less impressive, perhaps more so, in that the application to Cyrus of the humble-origin motif is situated in non-royal, even ignoble, origins as discussed in Chapter 2. This alternate version is also intriguing for what it may tell us about the stories circulating about Cyrus in the century or so after this death.[12] In Ctesias' version, Cyrus became prominent among the Medes by rising through an improbable *cursus honorum* from a menial to chief wine steward. Ctesias' "chief wine steward" was probably akin to the Assyrian and Babylonian official called a *rab šāqê*, literally "chief cupbearer," an official position of immense power and authority (an illustration from the Persepolis Fortification Archive is shown in Figure 3.3). Such a connection probably underlay Ctesias' use of the title, but Ctesias often interpreted Assyrian and Babylonian titles literally, even when that literally translated title was meant as an honorific.

Cyrus brought his parents to the Median palace court to share in his success. There his mother Argoste told him of the dream she had while pregnant with him. In the dream, Argoste urinated so much that a flood swept over all Asia, akin to the dream of Asytages in Herodotus discussed in Chapter 2. A Babylonian seer interpreted

Figure 3.3 Line drawing of PFS 535*, seal of the chief cupbearer in audience before a seated female, presumably a queen, c. 500 BCE.
Courtesy of the Persepolis Fortification Archive Project and the Persepolis Seal Project.

the dream as a sign that Cyrus' destiny was to be master of Asia. But he counseled Cyrus not to reveal this portent, since it would put both their lives in jeopardy should Astyages learn of it. The seer became Cyrus' close confidant and helper. In the meanwhile, Cyrus' prestige secured prominent upgrades for his parents, including the appointment of his father Atradates as satrap of Persia. The reader may be forgiven for raising an eyebrow at this impressive promotion from bandit; a generous assessment would be that Ctesias' transmitters severely telescoped a much more extensive version from original *Persica* here, which if were available might do a lot to help contextualize this plot development.

As part of Cyrus' responsibilities as a Median official, Astyages dispatched him to negotiate terms with a certain Onaphernes, king of the Cadusians: a people whose land was in the Elburz Mountains near the Caspian Sea, north of the Medes. Rather than neutralize the Cadusian rebellion, as per Astyages' orders, Cyrus instead exchanged oaths with Onaphernes to rebel against Astyages. At this point in the narrative, an important character is introduced: Oibaras, another Persian of humble origins. Oibaras became Cyrus' right-hand man, but one who saw a rival in the Babylonian seer. And it would not be a Greek tale of the eastern kingdoms without some intrigue included. To wit, Oibaras effectively dispatched his rival, through the simple expedient of getting him drunk and burying him into a deep hole. Oibaras then took on the integral role in helping Cyrus to overthrow the Medes: encouraging, strategizing, engaging in the necessary dirty work, and displaying remarkable leadership qualities. Upon his return to Media, Cyrus granted Oibaras the requisite markers of his new stature as a Persian grandee: a horse, Persian raiment, and a retinue. These gifts mark high status in Persian culture, and more important to note, they were typically only bestowed by kings.[13] Cyrus was thus already playing the part of king, even though still Astyages' subject. Word of the imminent rebellion was sent secretly to Cyrus' father Atradates, the once-bandit, now-satrap of Persia, to prepare an army.

Shortly after Cyrus and Oibaras' departure from Media, Asytages learned of Argoste's dream-omen foretelling Cyrus' rise to power. As if that were not sufficient sign of trouble on the horizon, one of Astyages' concubines coincidentally sang him a song about a lion that had a boar in its power, and how the latter turned the tables on the former.[14] Astyages dispatched horsemen to recall Cyrus. After an initial attempt to escape—by getting the messengers drunk to the point of passing out—failed, Cyrus killed most of them in heroic combat. Cyrus' exploits here fit the expectation of a (soon-to-be) king demonstrating the necessary martial qualities, a motif that followed long-standing paradigms in Near Eastern kingship.

The situation in plain view now, Astyages cursed his own benevolence toward Cyrus, "a wretched goatherd."[15] Astyages castigated Cyrus and the Persians as beggars, and the Median king threatened all sorts of horrible punishments if they did not submit to him. The reader of Ctesias was reminded frequently of Cyrus' humble origins, which Cyrus himself embraced but also juxtaposed with his belief in the power of the gods. It is that sentiment, in fact, that is the most important element in these stories and, for that matter, in official royal ideology: divine favor. Astyages assembled an enormous army over one million strong. Ctesias, or his transmitters, took even greater liberties with numbers than many other authors. The Persians were outnumbered more than three-to-one, but those odds were not so bad considering the literary circumstances. Battles were fought at a place called Hyrba and, importantly, around Pasargadae, the latter stylized in the account as a high mountain.

As the Medes and Persians battled throughout the mountains, an exhausted Cyrus made a short detour to his parental home. There Cyrus made an offering in fire, a nod toward the Mazdaean traditions of the Achaemenid kings, though the case of the historical Cyrus' belief system is more complicated (see Chapter 5). At the same moment lightning struck, and thunder rolled. To top it off literally, propitious birds alighted upon Cyrus' house, further indicators that he would persevere. When associated with the king, such omens were replete with meaning. In his other major work, the *Indica*, Ctesias referred to swords made from special iron with which the Persian king was able to forestall storms, a phenomenon that intimated the king's powers over the forces of nature via his special relationship with the divine.[16]

Armies of hundreds of thousands battled near and around Pasargadae. Despite the Persians' innate superiority (Ctesias was telling a story about Cyrus' rise, after all), the sheer number of Median troops threatened to overwhelm them. Both Cyrus and Oibaras exhorted the Persians, who numerous times were exhausted and despairing against the Median forces. Astyages compelled his own troops to fight with threats, similar to the vignettes in Herodotus where a despotic Xerxes needed to compel his own troops forward under the whip. Whether Ctesias in the original *Persica* relayed the climactic battle is unknown; if so, it was not transmitted by later authors. The Persians eventually defeated the Medes, and Cyrus thus became king of the Medes as well.

Cyrus promptly married Astyages' daughter, named Amytis in this tradition, to legitimize his conquest. As discussed in Chapter 2, we do not know much more about this Amytis, though the name was a common one among later Achaemenid princesses. This dynastic marriage brought Cyrus the allegiance of the Hyrcanians, Parthians, Scythians, and Bactrians, effectively most of northern and northeastern Iran. If this is true, it would have gone a long way to explaining the seemingly sudden rise in Cyrus' military capabilities. The episode recalls the phrasing in the Sippar Cylinder of the Median king and the "kings who go at his side" discussed previously, an image of the Median king able to summon forces from several neighboring kings. Under Cyrus, such an arrangement became more formalized, and lasting, as an empire.

The Medes clearly maintained a special place in the Persian imperial hierarchy. As will be seen in the next section, the Medians Harpagus and Mazares were prominent generals in Cyrus' Anatolian campaigns. The Medes must have been a critical factor in the formation and organization of the Empire under Cyrus after his victory over Astyages, and this persisted with Cyrus' successors; they were foremost (if not unique) among the conquered peoples who consistently held high-ranking positions.[17] The rationale for this relationship is elusive, but it must have its origins from Cyrus and his connections—real or embellished—to the Median royal house.

Go West, Young Man

By the sixth century, the dominant power in Anatolia was the kingdom of Lydia, with its capital at Sardis (see Map 3). The wealth of the kingdom of Lydia was legendary, as was that of its last king, such that the expression "rich as Croesus" is still heard even today. Lydia's famed wealth stemmed from the gold to be found in the river Pactolus that flowed through Sardis. According to the Greek myth, the king Midas could only remove the gift (that became a curse) of the Golden Touch by washing in the river Pactolus. As will be seen below, Croesus put this wealth to good use, but in the end it did not save his kingdom, and that wealth became Cyrus'.

The Lydian king ruled most of western Anatolia, including many Greek cities on the western coast, the region that the Greeks called Ionia. Lydian control eastward is much harder to define. Until recently, the Halys River was considered the boundary between the Lydian kingdom and Median-controlled territory. But the Medes' reach is now viewed as much reduced, and the once mighty Median Empire demoted, as discussed earlier in this chapter. The kingdom of Urartu had been the dominant power in eastern Anatolia, its core territory encompassing much of modern Armenia, but the full extent of its influence is also unclear. Urartu was a powerful rival of the Assyrians through much of the eighth century, but by Sargon II's reign at the end of the eighth century its southern reach was limited.[18] A broken reference in the Nabonidus Chronicle tracking one of Cyrus' campaigns in 547/546 may refer to Urartu, as will be discussed subsequently; however, even if that is the correct reading, it is uncertain as to what that may have signified for a continuing Urartian polity until Cyrus' time.

Thus, Cyrus' Lydian conquest will be the focus of this section. There is a rich narrative tradition in Greek sources about the last Lydian king, Croesus. There is no documentary evidence from Lydia itself, however, to supplement this narrative. More than a half century of archaeological excavations at Sardis, the capital of Lydia, has demonstrated how much there is yet to learn about the periods during which the city was the capital of the Lydian kingdom and then the capital of a Persian satrapy. Ongoing work has reassessed the settlement patterns. Excavators are still coming to grips with the realization that the older model of the city's layout and environs, based on initial excavations there, was wrong.[19] Lydia's history, or rather that of its ruling Mermnad dynasty, is known to us mainly through Herodotus. Herodotus in fact began his opus with Lydia, because of its rule of the Ionian Greeks, before both Lydia and Ionia were subsumed by the rising Persian Empire under Cyrus. Herodotus' history of Lydia, like that of the Medes, contains much of interest to the historian, but even more so to the literary specialist: the account reads as more legendary than factual. That does not mean, however, that it is entirely fabricated. It is an impossible task at present to discern the factual core within Herodotus' engaging stories of Gyges and Candaules' wife, of the Athenian Solon's visit to Croesus, and of Croesus testing various Greek oracles, among other stories.

There is some external corroboration for the founding of the Lydian royal house as Herodotus relayed it. A courtier by the name of Gyges deposed the king Candaules and married Candaules' wife, thus founding a new dynasty. This Gyges appeared in Ashurbanipal's inscriptions as a ruler named Gugu, the king of Luddi (i.e., Lydia), as termed by the Assyrians.[20] A messenger from Gugu (Gyges) was dispatched to Nineveh to seek assistance from Ashurbanipal against the nomadic Cimmerians, who were wreaking havoc across Anatolia. The messenger's arrival at the court in Nineveh caused quite a stir. Ashurbanipal emphasized the Assyrians' bewilderment: the distance from which he came and the fact that no one at the Assyrian court could understand a word he said. Though Lydia was outside the Assyrian geopolitical horizon, Nineveh was a cosmopolitan place. It would not have taken long to find someone who could translate for the messenger. Gyges' request for military aid necessitated that he first make obeisance to Ashurbanipal, in effect becoming his vassal. The oaths involved were a powerful commitment, one that anticipated later Persian means of binding subjects. Although this obeisance was done, Gyges ultimately reneged on his commitments. He paid the price. Gyges died during a subsequent Cimmerian invasion, a fate that Ashurbanipal attributed to Gyges having broken his oath and suffering divine retribution.

The marvel of the message underlined the great distances and diversity between various regions and peoples that were, within roughly a century later, unified under Cyrus. A century after Ashurbanipal, the world was a smaller place. Lydia, the Greek city-states of Ionia, and other Anatolian territories that were beyond the Assyrian experience were administered by Persian satraps. Archaeological finds at Ephesus and elsewhere in western Turkey confirm the intensive mingling of Greek and Lydian styles, conjoined with an imperial (Persian) flavor that remained typical throughout the Achaemenid period. The satrapal capital Sardis was along the western edge of what the Greeks called the Royal Road; in truth it was one of many roads that served a network throughout the Empire from its core in Parsa.

Herodotus preserved a story about a war in the early sixth century between Lydians and Medes, a war that has not yet been corroborated in any contemporary source.[21] The so-called Battle of the Solar Eclipse was named after an eclipse so momentous that occurred during it—and one considered of such ill omen—that the combatants ceased the war and negotiated a peace. Although

Herodotus confused the names and geography, the kings of Cilicia and Babylonia purportedly served as witnesses for the agreed treaty, one sealed by a dynastic marriage: the Lydian king Alyattes' daughter Aryenis was married to Cyaxeres' son Astyages. If accurate, Cyrus' early conquests were thus enmeshed within an extended family affair, the implication being that Aryenis, as wife of Astyages, was the mother of Mandane and thus a grandmother of Cyrus. And this made the last Lydian king, Croesus, the brother of Cyrus' maternal grandmother as well as a brother-in-law to Astyages. It must be emphasized that these dynastic connections have not been corroborated.

Cyrus' activities in the early 540s, after his conquest of the Medes, are unknown. Presumably, they involved consolidating his hold over much of Iran. It is not until April 547 that we can again track his movements. A fragmentary passage in the Nabonidus Chronicle records that Cyrus' army marched across northern Mesopotamia, crossing the Tigris somewhere south of the Assyrian city of Arbela.

> In the month of Nisan (= March/April), Cyrus, King of Persia, mobilized his army and crossed the Tigris River downstream from Arbela.
> In the month of Ayaru (= April/May) [he marched] to [*reading of toponym uncertain*].
> Cyrus defeated its king, took its possessions, and stationed a garrison there [...]
> Later the king and his garrison were there [...]

The trajectory of this march, pinned only by the references to the Tigris and "below Arbela," raises many questions, since that route took Cyrus through what was presumably Babylonian-controlled territory. Arbela was situated on an important route, a node on the later Persian royal road mentioned previously that connected Sardis and Susa.[22]

For our present purposes, the victory is of greater concern than the route. The name of the defeated king is not preserved, and the reading of the targeted region is disputed. Most modern commentators restore "Lydia" at that spot in the tablet, others "Urartu"; a crack in the clay tablet makes the reading debatable.[23] That Cyrus conquered eastern Anatolia (wherein lay Urartu, or what was left of it) before Lydia in western Anatolia seems reasonable enough. But when it comes to Cyrus' campaigns, the modern historian is faced with the actuality of more battles than data that recount them. Even scholars who prefer to read "Urartu" in that line of the chronicle, so followed here, still date the Lydian conquest by the mid-540s.

For a narrative of the conquest, we rely primarily on Herodotus. During his preparations to confront Cyrus, Croesus sought the advice of the Oracle of Delphi, the oracle that Croesus had determined—through a variety of clever tests and application of his proverbial wealth—to be the most accurate. Concerned by the reports from the east of this new rising power, Croesus asked the oracle whether he should attack Cyrus. The response came that if he did so, he would destroy a mighty empire. Croesus took the oracle to mean that he would be victorious. But it was Cyrus who defeated him, and the mighty empire Croesus destroyed was his own. After his defeat, a further exchange highlighted Croesus' bitter disappointment in the oracle, to which the oracle blithely responded that perhaps Croesus should have sought for additional clarity.[24] Herodotus and our other main Greek sources by their nature are much more verbose—than, for example, terse Babylonian chronicles—about Cyrus' conquest of Croesus' Lydia. This is also the case, not least, because most of the earliest Greek historians were Ionians. And, a useful reminder, this region of western Anatolia was subject to Lydia before it was subject to Persia.

Herodotus cast Croesus' gambit against Cyrus as hubris: the misinterpretation of an omen along with the desire to augment his own territory. Croesus marched out to engage Cyrus and en route conquered the city of Pteria, the location of which is uncertain but presumed somewhere in north central Anatolia, where Cyrus' army met him (see Map 3). The subsequent pitched battle was inconclusive, and Croesus withdrew to Sardis to gather reinforcements. These were to include contingents from otherwise-unattested alliances with Egyptians, Babylonians, and Spartans, the last made as the result of another Delphic oracle recommending that Croesus ally himself with the most powerful of the Greek city-states.

These Spartans later provided some comic relief to what otherwise would have been a bitter and painful story for many Greeks, namely, the Ionians' forcible incorporation into the Persian Empire. The Spartans sent an ambassador to Cyrus warning him not to harm any Greek settlements. Whether the audience found it incongruous that a Spartan from mainland Greece should warn Cyrus in Anatolia, about anything, may remain open. Cyrus, when told the Spartans wished to see him, made a typical response: "Who on earth are these people?" Informed of the answer, and not terribly impressed, Cyrus announced that he had never before feared groups of people who gathered in central markets to cheat and mislead one another.[25] Herodotus was working on multiple levels here, applying both irony and multivalent meanings. Such a comment as voiced by Cyrus could have been aimed at almost any group of Herodotus' Greek contemporaries, but it was probably least appropriate to describe the Spartans, who generally disdained and shunned commercial enterprises.

To resume the narrative, winter was fast approaching. Croesus disbanded his own army, with the intention of resuming hostilities in the Spring. Cyrus, however, did the unexpected and pursued Croesus to Sardis. He took Croesus at unawares—as Herodotus put it, "Cyrus came as his own messenger to Croesus"—and defeated him in a pitched battle. The forces met on the plain outside the city before any reinforcements arrived, and Cyrus nullified Croesus' cavalry through a ploy that involved positioning pack-camels at the front of his formation, from which the Lydian horses fled. After another fierce fight, the Lydians withdrew into the city, there besieged. Outnumbered and outmaneuvered, Croesus sent renewed, desperate pleas to his allies. The siege lasted two weeks before a Persian contingent assayed a supposedly unassailable cliff to access the city, and this led to the Persian victory. Croesus was spared, according to Herodotus' version at least. Sardis was sacked, and in this case the archaeological record, including radiocarbon analysis, corroborates the textual sources. The city was looted, and its fortification wall at least partially destroyed. While the conjunction of documentary and archaeological material may not seem surprising, because of the sporadic nature of the evidence they rarely complement each other so nicely.[26] Cyrus thus took possession of the Lydian kingdom, its wealth and resources, and its territories.

Herodotus also relayed an engaging anecdote about Cyrus' relationship with the Ionian Greek cities. After Cyrus' victory, representatives from these cities visited Cyrus with the request that they be given favorable terms. Since they had not responded to Cyrus' previous offer to join him against Croesus, he was disinclined to look upon the request favorably. He instead offered them a parable of a musician upon the sea, who played his instrument in hopes that the fish he saw would come to him. When they did not, he cast a net and captured them, flopping wildly before his feet. This is the fuller backdrop for the opening quote of this chapter, as Cyrus said to the Ionians in effect: "Leave off your dancing for me now, for when I played my flute before you would not come out." The harbors of the Ionian cities would become quite useful later for the Persians kings, after they developed a fleet during the reign of Cambyses. Cyrus delegated mop-up operations in Anatolia to his Median lieutenants, while he himself returned to Ecbatana.[27]

In short order, though, some of the Lydians rebelled. One Pactyes, a Lydian to whom Cyrus had assigned the collection of tribute, instead hired mercenaries and marched on Sardis. Entrusting local elites such as Pactyes with important roles in the Empire's administration was common later, and this episode suggests the practice began under Cyrus. In this case, though, the appointment backfired. When Cyrus learned of Pactyes' revolt, he dispatched a Median named Mazares to deal with the situation. Pactyes fled to Cyme, a Greek city on the central western (i.e., Ionian) coast, from where he was passed on to various other Greek cities. The islanders of Chios were eventually induced with a payment to surrender him.

The Mede Mazares fell ill and died shortly after Pactyes was captured, but not before he began the process of systematically punishing those cities that had helped Pactyes in his revolt. After Mazares, the Mede Harpagus was sent to finish the job, a campaign that probably took several months, if not a few years. One by one, Greek cities in Ionia were subjugated. This rather dark chapter in Greek history is not preserved in much detail, especially when contrasted with the resistance of the mainland Greeks against Xerxes' invasion two generations later. This is understandably so, in light of the result of Cyrus' and his lieutenants' campaigns: a complete Persian victory. If things had gone otherwise, instead of Marathon, Thermopylae, or Salamis, the Western tradition would have perhaps celebrated the battles in the western parts of Anatolia, such as Priene, Magnesia, and Phocaea. But these cities were subjugated or destroyed by Persian and Median forces, and their territories incorporated into the Empire.

The fate of Croesus varied depending on the source. Herodotus relayed that Cyrus intended to execute him, but that the god Apollo's intervention saved Croesus. Croesus then became a stock literary character, the wise advisor, in Herodotus' narrative, a counselor to both Cyrus and his son Cambyses. This type of portrayal fits the traditions of Cyrus' magnanimity. A slightly earlier tradition from the Greek poet Bacchylides (died c. 450) suggested that Croesus was killed during the sack of Sardis. Bacchylides provided a dramatic rendering of Croesus' intended suicide on a pyre; the scene was also the subject of an early fifth-century BCE Attic amphora (Figure 3.4). The intervention of Zeus and Apollo removed

Figure 3.4 Croesus on the pyre. Attic red figure amphora, attributed to Myson, early fifth century BCE.

Photo: Tony Querrec, Musée du Louvre, Paris, France, © RMN–Grand Palais / Art Resource, NY.

Croesus to the land of the Hyperboreans, a mythical people who dwelled far in the north. The story of Croesus on the pyre occurred in multiple traditions, but Bacchylides' version implied Croesus' death, couched in divine removal to a magical place.[28] Many scholars are inclined to accept Bacchylides' version, but the truth of the matter is uncertain.

Ctesias' version of Cyrus' conquest of Lydia was preserved only in summary form by the ninth-century CE Byzantine patriarch Photius.[29] In Photius' epitome of the *Persica* it was expressly noted that Cyrus had the aid of the Saka (Scythians), whose king Amorges Cyrus defeated after the Medes. During that campaign, with Amorges captive, Cyrus himself was defeated by Amorges' wife, Sparethra. This was not one of the high points of Cyrus' campaigns, though admittedly one of the more curious. Its historicity is impossible to gauge. Ctesias was enamored of the eastern warrior-queen motif, and Sparethra was just so, cast on the more developed and better-known model of Semiramis. After a prisoner exchange, some sort of accommodation must have been made—the details of which Photius did not relay in his epitome of Ctesias' *Persica*—because Amorges became a close ally.

Augmented by these Scythian and other troops, the upshot was that the force marching against Lydia, as per Ctesias' rendition, must have been quite intimidating. Cyrus had received Croesus' son as hostage previously, when Croesus was deceived by an unspecified (i.e., the details were not preserved) divine dream. When Cyrus suspected treachery, Croesus' son was slain, and so Croesus' wife threw herself from the walls. It is difficult to know what to make of this truncated account, as it reads more like a half-baked mishmash of several Greek myths. The campaign detail most frequently mentioned by later ancient authors, who themselves consulted Ctesias, was that of a stratagem used to trick the Lydians. There were apparently variations of the ruse, whether implemented by Cyrus himself or one of his lieutenants such as Oibaras. Wooden mannequins were dressed as Persian soldiers and cleverly stationed around the city walls. Upon the Lydians' discovery of this (straw) army, they assumed they faced overwhelming numbers and fell into disarray. Thus, the Persians won the victory. While we have plenty of material that reiterates the cleverness of Cyrus and

Oibaras, this story—at least as it survived the passage of time—cannot be corroborated. In Ctesias' version, Croesus sought refuge in the temple of Apollo but was captured. As he had in Herodotus' version, Croesus escaped the bonds put upon him, to the evident consternation of both Cyrus and Oibaras, who ultimately bowed to the divine intervention on Croesus' behalf. A later tradition recorded by Justin, also based on Ctesias' version, related that after Croesus' release, Cyrus granted him territory in a city called Barene near Ecbatana.

At present, it is not possible to reconcile fully these various versions about Croesus' fate or the sequence of Cyrus' conquest of Anatolia. Regardless, by the mid-540s Cyrus had conquered the Medes and the Lydians, two of the major powers of the day. Cyrus thus controlled territory from Iran across the Anatolian plateau and was able to access the resources and manpower from an already large swath of territory encompassing diverse populations. Cyrus soon set his sights on the Babylonian Empire.

4

The Chosen One

Marduk surveyed and considered all the lands, he
searched thoroughly for a just ruler, one favored in his
heart. Marduk took him by the hand, Cyrus, the King
of Anshan, he summoned his chosen one, he named his
name to rule over all.

—Cyrus Cylinder, lines 11–12

After Cyrus the Great's conquests of the Medes and of Anatolia, he
ruled extensive territory, a fledgling empire already the largest to
that point in history. It was about to get bigger. When Cyrus turned
his full attention to Babylonia, he confronted a close neighbor but a
power more organized, and with a much longer history, than any of
his previous conquests. We have already met briefly the Babylonian
king Nabonidus (r. 556–539), who was to be the last of the dynasty
that was begun by Nabopolassar in the 620s with the overthrow of
Assyria. This dynasty, of whom the most famous of its kings was
Nebuchadnezzar II (r. 605–562), ruled what in modern scholarship
is termed the (Neo-)Babylonian Empire—its territory stretching
from the eastern littoral of the Mediterranean through what is now
Iraq.

The city of Babylon had risen to prominence under Hammurabi
in the eighteenth century BCE. Twelve hundred years later, it was the
foremost power of its time until Cyrus entered the scene and entered
Babylon as its conqueror in 539. Relative to our information for
the Medes and the Lydians, the quantity of documentary evidence

from the Neo-Babylonian period is overwhelming, though much of this documentation is better suited to the study of the economic and social history of the Babylonians themselves. Babylonian royal inscriptions were focused more on the kings' building and cultic activities than on their military deeds, so with some irony it must be noted that knowledge of their political history, especially vis-à-vis Cyrus and the Persians, remains opaque. On the other hand, temple and private archives are in such abundance—tens of thousands of clay tablets have survived, now scattered in museums through the world—that the minutiae of some temple organizations, and the social networks that linked them, may be tracked at an amazingly detailed level. Careful combing through these sources reveals that Babylon's increasing prosperity, traceable through the sixth century, began to be redirected elsewhere under the Persians. This is not surprising: new leaders meant new priorities. A fine example of this is a transfer of wealth from Babylonia applied to the massive expenditures involved in Darius I's building works at Susa, but the phenomenon may also be traced in Cyrus' and Cambyses' reigns for construction projects in or near Fars.[1] Under those two kings, it seems likely that there was a conscious design to reduce the distinctions between Babylonia and Elam. These discrete regions, even as they maintained their own cultural traditions and remained distinct satrapies, would be under one rule.

The Conquest of Babylonia

The last Babylonian king's royal inscriptions followed the age-old Mesopotamian pattern of the pious king, one concerned for and active in the building and maintenance of divine sanctuaries. More so than his immediate predecessors, however, Nabonidus also tapped the model of Assyrian royal title and epithet formulae. For this reason, it has been reasonably conjectured that Nabonidus was eager to claim the Assyrian imperial legacy. Why Nabonidus may have wanted to do so is a bit of a mystery. On the other hand, Cyrus the Great too was clearly keen to tap the Assyrian model, which may perhaps explain some of the vindictive polemic against Nabonidus after Cyrus' victory. And the reality on the ground, as it pertained to the respective kings' rule, was also different. When Nabonidus claimed the title "King of the World," the limits of his power were easily referenced. It was much harder to argue Cyrus' adoption of the title.

From a variety of Babylonian evidence, including his own inscriptions, it appears that Nabonidus had been away from Babylon for the better part of ten years (c. 553–543) at the oasis of Teima in northern Arabia. In the meanwhile Babylon was governed by Nabonidus' son Bel-shar-uṣur, the Belshazzar from the Book of Daniel 5. Nabonidus' surprisingly lengthy absence has been interpreted in a number of ways. Some associate it with his pa-tronage of the moon god, prominent at Teima, as his devotion to the deity was also evident in Harran. On that interpretation, Nabonidus has been portrayed in a negative light, even as a crazed lunatic: be-sotted by his own devotion to the moon god and seeking to prose-lytize his faith. That portrayal was probably augmented (initiated?) by the resentment of the priesthoods of other Babylonian deities, especially if they viewed their sanctuaries as receiving short shrift. Cyrus' propaganda, abetted by these Babylonian priesthoods (es-pecially, it seems, the priests of Marduk), enhanced this negative image of Nabonidus.[2] We will return to this phenomenon and some examples when discussing Cyrus' Babylonian inscriptions subsequently.

The preliminaries of the Persian-Babylonian conflict are not understood. The Babylonians, of course, would have been well in-formed of Cyrus' activities, with regular reports coming to Babylon from various officials and informers. Their intelligence network presaged that of the Persians, and both were modeled upon the Assyrian system. Of course, the free flow of people and information from Babylonian through Elam and to Parsa worked both ways.

Persian agents and merchants frequented Babylonia as well. It is unclear what spurred Nabonidus' return to Babylon in c. 543, past time in any case after a lengthy absence. Nabonidus had enough on his plate sorting internal affairs, independent of any growing concerns about Cyrus. It is not hard to imagine a growing sense of unease in Babylonia. Anyone paying attention, when considering Cyrus' conquests of the territories east, north, and northwest of the Babylonian Empire, would have reasonably wondered if Babylonia was next.

Indeed, such concern did occasionally manifest in the sources. As discussed in the last chapter, the Nabonidus Chronicle recorded Cyrus and his army's crossing the Tigris en route to Anatolia in April 547. In the same passage, the chronicle also noted the presence of Nabonidus' son, the crown prince Bel-shar-uṣur, and a Babylonian army stationed at an outpost called Dur-karashu along the bank of the Euphrates northwest of Sippar. The chronicle recorded this event in context of the death of the queen mother, Nabonidus' mother Adad-guppi. The presence of family in the region (i.e., Bel-shar-uṣur) seems straightforward enough. But what matter would impel an army to be stationed in northern Babylonia at that time? A plausible explanation is that this force was a safeguard, or a warning, to Cyrus, who was crossing what the Babylonians likely considered their territory, the old Assyrian heartland.[3] Whether Cyrus respected Babylonian feelings on the matter is unknown to us, though his actions suggest that he did not. From his perspective, the road to Anatolia went that way, and Cyrus may have welcomed the opportunity to visit some of his family's roots, as it were, from the time when Arukku was a guest, or hostage, of the Assyrian court.

Details on the Persian-Babylonian war itself are sparse. A passage from the Nabonidus Chronicle is the linchpin for our information about the conquest and its aftermath, including Cyrus' peaceful entry into Babylon, and that will be considered in due course. The Greek tradition did not preserve much detail, so we may dispense with that first.[4] Herodotus' detailed, if inaccurate, account of the layout of the city of Babylon, and some of the purportedly solid gold colossi therein, has fueled ongoing debate about whether the well-traveled author had ever seen the place. Some of his account is, by his own admission, based on hearsay. While at times differentiating Assyrians and Babylonians, he also consistently conflated them. His rendition of Cyrus' conquest of Babylon dedicated much more time to the legendary queens Semiramis and Nitocris, especially Nitocris' extensive building works in Babylon itself.[5] Herodotus called Nabonidus Labynetus; a son of the aforementioned Nitocris and a father who was also named Labynetus. Not coincidentally, where their information is sketchy, Greek authors often displayed a certain lack of creativity in Near Eastern kings' genealogies.

In his terse account of Cyrus' conquest, however, the literary Herodotus shined. One of his favorite themes was the Persian kings' transgressions of rivers and other natural boundaries. Such transgressions were epic acts of hubris in Greek eyes: the Persian kings placing themselves as equivalent to divinity by their reordering of the natural world. Darius I did this when he bridged the Bosporus in the 510s; more well known is Xerxes' crossing of the Hellespont en route to invade Europe in 480. Cyrus set the stage for these momentous events by diverting two rivers during his Babylonian campaign alone. The first occurred on the march to Babylon, as Cyrus approached a river named Gyndes, near the city of Opis. As Herodotus told it, one of Cyrus' sacred white horses charged into the waters and drowned before it could swim across. This infuriated Cyrus, who paused his march on Babylon for several months in order to punish the river: he had his army split the river into 360 channels, so that "even women would be able to cross it without getting their knees wet." The engineering feat in itself was not unheard of, but remarkable in its scale, plausible in its own right if not traceable in the archaeological record.[6]

Herodotus' account of the conquest of Babylon itself echoed that of his account of the taking of Sardis. This is probably not a coincidence for a matter about which Herodotus clearly had little information. In his version, there was first a pitched battle outside the walls—inexplicably, the Babylonians challenged the Persians in the open field, even though they were well prepared for a long siege. The Persians were victorious and thereafter took the city by storm after a short siege of its supposedly impenetrable walls. This was done by diverting a river for the second time on this campaign, in this case diverting the Euphrates into a nearby lake.[7] Once the Persians were in the city, Herodotus' version adds only some curious editorializing about the Babylonians' missed opportunity of trapping the Persians. He then finished the sequence with another remark on Babylon's sprawl: the city was so large that those in the center of city, celebrating a festival, were completely unaware of what was happening until the Persians fell upon them. In conjunction with that unlikely scenario, Herodotus emphasized that Cyrus' maneuver was unexpected; that bit, at least, fits the wider theme, across many sources, of Cyrus' ingenuity. The surviving excerpts of Ctesias' *Persica* offer no information about Cyrus' Babylonian campaign. Xenophon's *Cyropaedia* jumbled all of Cyrus' campaigns together, accomplished while Cyrus was still effectively a Median prince. In the particular case of Babylon, Xenophon cast the war as against the Assyrian king.

As is readily discerned, these accounts are not very helpful in tracking the actual course of events, for which we must return to Near Eastern sources. When the Nabonidus Chronicle touched on Persian affairs again in 539, the Persian-Babylonian conflict was *in medias res*. The terse account covered a lot of ground, with several broken or difficult-to-read passages. It is worth relaying in its entirety, despite its sporadic cadence in English translation. Parentheses indicate explanatory glosses or alternate translations.

Until the end of the month Ululu (mid- September) the gods of Akkad [. . .] from everywhere were entering Babylon. The gods of Borsippa, Cuthah, and Sippar did not enter (Babylon). In the month Tashritu (late September–early October), when Cyrus did battle at Opis on the Tigris against the army of Akkad, the people of Akkad retreated. He carried off the plunder and defeated (or killed?) the people. On the fourteenth day Sippar was captured without a battle. Nabonidus fled. On the sixteenth day, Gobryas, governor of Gutium, and the army of Cyrus entered Babylon without a battle. Later, after Nabonidus retreated, he was captured in Babylon. Until the end of the month, the shield of Gutium (meaning armed troops from the Zagros Mountains) surrounded the gates of Esagil. There was no interruption (of rites) in Esagil or the (other) temples, and no (ritual) date was missed. On the third day of the month Arahsamna (late October), Cyrus entered Babylon. The ceremonial-vessels were filled before him. Peace was imposed upon the city. The proclamation of Cyrus was read to all of Babylon. He appointed Gobryas, his governor, over the leading officials in Babylon. From the month Kislimu to the month Addaru (late November to late March), the gods of Akkad whom Nabonidus had brought to Babylon returned to their places. On the night of the eleventh of the month Arahsamna (early November), Gobryas died. In the mon[th Addaru?] the king's wife died. From the twenty-seventh of the month Addaru to the third of the month Nisan (late March, year 538), there was a mourning period in Akkad. All of the people bared their heads. On the fourth day of Nisan, when Cambyses, son of C[yrus], went to the temple of Nabu, the official of the temple of Nabu, who . . . [. . .] When he (presumably Cyrus) arrived, in Elamite attire, he took the hand of Nabu [. . .] [sp]ears and quivers he picked up(?) [. . .] and with the crown prince to [. . .] . . . Nabu to Esagil . . . before Bel and the son of B[el . . .]

The passage requires some commentary. Modern translations of it often differ in significant details, owing to the frequent gaps, concise phrasing, and nuanced vocabulary of the text. For example, after his victory at Opis in 539, Cyrus defeated, or killed (even "slaughtered" in some translations), the Babylonian army, or (in some translations) the Babylonian people. The translation chosen obviously colors the tenor of Cyrus' victory. Interpretation of Cyrus' actions may take different turns based on how certain Akkadian words are translated in context.[8]

The passage begins with the removal of various city's gods (i.e., their cultic statues) to Babylon, a measure initiated by Nabonidus as a precaution against an imminent Persian attack. After his victory, Cyrus and his agents recast the same act to be considered impious, spun otherwise as Nabonidus forcibly having removed the divine statues from their homes. Cyrus trumpeted his return of the gods to their own cities and spared no effort in vilifying Nabonidus, as will be discussed further subsequently. The Chronicle specifically noted that the gods of Borsippa, Cutha, and Sippar did not enter Babylon, but it did not indicate why. The notation excluding those cities from the sequence invites speculation. Did Borsippa, Cutha, and Sippar, incidentally quite close to Babylon, not see the need to send their cultic statues to the capital? Or perhaps they had gone over to Cyrus? It was explicitly noted that Sippar was taken without a fight.

There was at least one major battle, cited in the passage. It occurred near Opis on the Tigris River, roughly 42 miles north and east of Babylon, two or three weeks before Babylon fell. It is clear that this victory paved the way for the takeover of the entire region. Gobryas and the army subsequently entered Babylon first, to secure the city. This Gobryas (the Hellenized version of the name written in Akkadian as *Gubaru*) was clearly an important figure in the victory. Read literally, it was his troops who guarded Babylon's main sanctuary, Esagil, the temple of Marduk, so that no important rites or ceremonies were missed. Gobryas was subsequently appointed governor of Babylonia but, as noted in the passage under discussion, died almost immediately thereafter. This same Gobryas has been connected to the Gobryas of Xenophon's *Cyropaedia*, a Babylonian governor spurned by his king who voluntarily went

over to Cyrus and enabled his victory. The trouble with such identification is that there were several prominent men named Gobryas
in the sources. Another Gobryas was prominent just a few years
later as satrap of Babylonia and Across-the-River (the region sometimes translated into English as "Trans-Euphrates"). That region
was Cyrus' revamped administrative territory that encompassed
Mesopotamia and the Levant, that is, approximating the territory of the Babylonian Empire. Perhaps the same, or yet another,
Gobryas was father-in-law to Darius I and a key player in that king's
accession seventeen years after Cyrus' conquest of Babylon. The
identification of, and possible connections between, these men is
yet debated.[9]

Thus, when Cyrus entered Babylon on October 29, 539, Gobryas
and others had paved the way. Better put, Cyrus' plan, preparations,
and the victory at Opis had paved the way. We will return to Cyrus'
triumphant entry into Babylon and other arrangements for the
newly conquered territory at several places in what follows. The
last few lines of the section of the chronicle quoted above also war-
rant mention here. Just before the Babylonian New Year (roughly
mid-March on our calendar), Cyrus' wife Cassandane died. Thus,
the moment of one of Cyrus' greatest triumphs, in which their son
Cambyses was also closely involved, was tinged with great sadness.
The day after the official period of mourning ended, Cyrus, with
Cambyses at his side, partook in one of the most momentous trap-
pings of Babylonian kingship: the *akitu* (New Year) Festival. The
chronicle in previous sections pointedly noted that the *akitu* festival was not celebrated for several years while Nabonidus was absent. Its reintroduction with a foreign conqueror coincided with
an intentional return to normalcy, at least with regard to the traditional festivals and cultic rites. In this instance it included an
official coronation of Cyrus in the temples of Nabu and Marduk,
accompanied by Cambyses, who was crown prince. That Cyrus (it
appears) wore Elamite attire during this sacred festival, presumably dressed in the accoutrements of the king of Anshan, was a

testament to his heritage and offered concurrent symbolism: new rule, but one upholding the old traditions, in Babylon.

When Cyrus took Babylon, Nabonidus had fled but was captured. His subsequent fate the chronicle did not reveal. Similarly, in the Cyrus Cylinder it is noted only that Nabonidus was delivered to Cyrus. Several external traditions suggest that Cyrus spared Nabonidus, whether out of magnanimity or for some other purpose. Such an act was not unknown in previous Mesopotamian tradition, and it fits Cyrus' image. Another Babylonian text—the so-called Dynastic Prophecy, written during the Seleucid period after the fall of Alexander's empire—indicated that Nabonidus was exiled. That tradition, coincidentally or not, finds echo in what was a close-to-contemporaneous account. According to Berossus, the defeated Babylonian king gave himself up before a protracted siege and received territory in Carmania (modern Kerman, in southern Iran), where he eventually died.[10]

Cyrus' Babylonian Royal Inscriptions

It is time for a closer look at Cyrus' inscriptions from Babylonia, those commissioned by Cyrus and his agents. A more systematic treatment is warranted to assess their contents, significance, and historical ramifications. Cyrus likely commissioned dozens of royal proclamations, in multiple copies, following long-standing Mesopotamian models. But there are extant only three of these standard royal inscriptions from throughout Babylonia: the Cyrus Cylinder from Babylon and two short display inscriptions from the cities of Uruk and Ur, both found in multiple copies. Another curious, but important, text, the so-called Verse Account of Nabonidus, will also be discussed below. This text as well as the already-referenced Nabonidus Chronicle contain the name Nabonidus in their modern labels, because they deal primarily with events from his reign that presaged Cyrus' conquest.

Cyrus Cylinder

The most famous of Cyrus' inscriptions, justifiably, is the so-called Cyrus Cylinder, our most important documentary source for Cyrus, alluded to several times already in this book (Figure 1.1). It was discovered in 1879 by Hormuzd Rassam and is housed in the British Museum. The text is inscribed on a clay barrel cylinder, roughly 10 inches long and 4 inches thick. Its shape is typical for a foundation inscription of the type used in Mesopotamia for centuries, of which we have hundreds of examples from scores of kings. The text was composed by a scribe well-versed in Babylonian norms, but it also manifests innovative elements in its structure and its presentation.[11] The cylinder's main themes included the very traditional ones of divine selection and the restoration of order. The language is what we call Standard Babylonian, a dialect of Akkadian, common to both Assyrian and Babylonian royal inscriptions as well as literary texts of the mid-first millennium BCE. The physical structure and arrangement of the Cyrus Cylinder combine specifically Babylonian elements—the use of contemporary (i.e., not archaized) Babylonian script—with an Assyrian variation: the text runs along the long axis, not in separate columns along the short axis, as standard in most Babylonian cylinders. Figure 4.1 shows the British Museum's representation of what the cylinder's text would like in tablet form if it were unrolled.

Foundation inscriptions were dedicated to the gods and deposited as an offering within the foundation, or walls, of temple sanctuaries. One frequent assessment of such texts, then, is that they were written solely for the gods. This is true enough as applied to the interred version of the inscription, although these texts also speak to future kings who might uncover them in the course of restoration or rebuilding work. However, and importantly, it is understood that the information contained in these inscriptions was also distributed and proclaimed in other ways. Two fragments of a tablet also in the British Museum, tablet fragments that are not part of the Cyrus Cylinder itself, have been identified that recorded

Figure 4.1 Photo of the Cyrus Cylinder as if it were unrolled.
© Trustees of The British Museum.

essentially the same inscription as the Cylinder. These fragments provide welcome testimony that the Cyrus Cylinder was not a unique copy of the inscription. Royal inscriptions in general involved a lot of time and effort and were of fundamental ideological importance. In other words, finding evidence for additional copies of the Cyrus Cylinder, while an unusual instance of confirmation, is not at all surprising.[12] The Cyrus Cylinder thus represents a public message that may have been proclaimed in Aramaic, the spoken lingua franca of the time; for that matter, the proclamation was probably made in multiple languages.

While any public proclamation may not have been a word-for-word rendering of what was inscribed on the Cyrus Cylinder, it is reasonable to assume that its essence was similar, if not the same. Every bit has significance both for the contemporary events and for Cyrus' incorporation of traditional motifs. A full translation of the Cylinder is given in Appendix B, with a short summary as follows. The previous king Nabonidus was inept, impious, interfered with the sanctuaries, and was indifferent to the burdens he imposed upon the people of Babylon. Cyrus was the divinely chosen one to stop these outrages, the one who would correct the systemic wrongs of the previous regime and would reinstitute the proper forms. Marduk led Cyrus to victory to restore peace and harmony, especially the reinstitution of divine offerings and normal workings of his cult. Further, Cyrus was a king of a long-standing dynastic line, and thus legitimate royalty as well. Cyrus would restore the abandoned, age-old sanctuaries and return the gods (the divine statues) to their proper places therein, with appropriate veneration. Displaced peoples would be allowed to return home. The new king Cyrus, blessed by the gods, would restore the entire city. When Cyrus, accompanied by Marduk, entered Babylon without a fight, a new era had begun. Nabonidus was removed, and the people rejoiced. "All the people of Babylon, the entirety of Sumer and Akkad, nobles and governors, they bowed before Cyrus, they kneeled, they kissed his feet. They rejoiced in his kingship, and their faces glowed." Of course, it was not just Babylon that was renewed. From that center, like rays emanating from the sun, Cyrus corrected other wrongs elsewhere as well. He restored order out of chaos. This is a foundational idea of universal empire, one adapted from the Assyrians (though older than they) and developed further by Cyrus and his successors.

One of the righted wrongs was discussed in an example above. Nabonidus had removed the divine statues from other cities to Babylon for their protection, so told from Nabonidus' side of the story. But that, of course, was entirely backward, as Cyrus told it: Nabonidus' action was an affront against these very gods. Political spin was hardly a new phenomenon. Cyrus celebrated the return of these statues to their proper cities, along with the restoration of their age-old temples that (in truth or not) had been neglected by Nabonidus and were in need of repair. Indeed, the Babylonian term *zanīnu*, literally the "provisioner of the temples," was one of the most important Babylonian royal epithets, applied in the Cyrus Cylinder to both Cyrus and Cambyses.[13]

The Cyrus Cylinder's text is also notable for its many allusions to Babylonian literary tradition. These are still in the process of being appreciated by modern scholars, but to the inhabitants of Babylon, who were now Cyrus' subjects, some would have been obvious. Other, erudite references to Babylonian literary works—what we would term intertextuality—might have been only appreciated by scribal specialists. As one example, Babylon was "saved from hardship" by Cyrus, a rare Akkadian phrase borrowed, exactly and purposely, from a passage referring to how the god Marduk saved the other gods from destruction in the Babylonian Creation Epic. The Cyrus Cylinder was a literary composition as well as a royal proclamation.[14]

The theme of universal dominion will be explored in more detail in the next chapter, so a few words must suffice here on how Cyrus expressed himself within a standing tradition. The formal titles that Cyrus adopted—King of the World, Great King, Strong King, King of Babylon, King of Sumer and Akkad, King of the Four Quarters—were the same used by Nabonidus, the only Babylonian king to have used this particular formula. Nabonidus and Cyrus both echoed Assyrian usage. The seventh-century kings of Assyria

Esarhaddon and Ashurbanipal styled themselves in the same way, the only marked difference being "King of Assyria" substituting for "King of Babylon."[15] If Nabonidus consciously cultivated an Assyrian model, it is fair to ask if Cyrus was consciously echoing Ashurbanipal or copying Nabonidus. The former certainly applied, perhaps both possibilities did. Nabonidus was also the only Babylonian king to explicitly name Assyrian predecessors, Ashurbanipal among them, though his motivation to link himself to Assyrian kings remains obscure. The last Babylonian king's fixation on Harran may be viewed not just because of devotion to the moon god but also because of his family's origins. Nabonidus' father may have been Assyrian, or in Assyrian service there.[16]

Cyrus invoked Ashurbanipal directly in the Cyrus Cylinder. Cyrus referred to an inscription of that king deposited in the same area where Cyrus placed his: "An inscription with the name of Ashurbanipal, a king who preceded me, I examined in its midst." This could be the very Ashurbanipal inscription, in multiple copies, that Ashurbanipal dedicated to Marduk regarding his restoration work on the same wall that Cyrus mentioned, the Imgur-Enlil of Babylon.[17] An important question to consider in our discussion of Cyrus, though, is: Why Ashurbanipal? Ashurbanipal was indeed one of Assyria's most powerful and most infamous kings, a standard-bearer in later traditions' remembrances and reconstructions of the Assyrian past. As evident throughout this book's treatment, Ashurbanipal's Assyria contributed directly and indirectly to Cyrus' imperial model, his new capital of Pasargadae, and the Achaemenid Empire's organization.

But there were scores of kings who made restorations and left foundation deposits in Babylon for centuries before Cyrus, who, like Nabonidus, was also fascinated by earlier kings, all the way back to Sargon of Akkad almost two millennia previous.[18] Cyrus' mention of Ashurbanipal was a conscious choice that fit Cyrus' predisposition. In other words, Ashurbanipal was invoked not only as a model for a king claiming the mantle of universal empire but

THE CHOSEN ONE 97

also as a connection (re)claimed to his own family history. Cyrus the Great's uncle Arukku spent time at the Assyrian court at the height of the Empire (see Chapter 1). Cyrus' forebears among the royal family of Parsumash thus had direct exposure to the Assyrian ideological system in full bloom. One may imagine the formative impact this had on a nascent Persian kingdom in the late seventh and early sixth centuries, from which the Achaemenids eventually descended. Indeed, one does not need to imagine it. The evidence substantiates in no uncertain terms the magnitude of the Assyrian model's impact on the Cyrus and the Achaemenids.

Royal Inscriptions from Uruk and Ur

Stamped brick inscriptions found in the southern Babylonian cities of Uruk and Ur are the only other royal display inscriptions extant from Cyrus. Unlike the Cyrus Cylinder, these inscriptions were not foundation deposits but stamped on baked bricks used in construction and restoration.[19] Although short, these inscriptions are important, not least because there are so few of these inscriptions preserved from Cyrus. Four copies of Cyrus' stamped brick inscription have been found from the Eanna temple complex at Uruk.[20]

One copy of the Uruk inscription, excavated by K. Loftus in 1850, is housed in the British Museum. Three other copies were excavated by a German team in the 1920s, but their whereabouts are unknown.[21] The British Museum copy, Figures 4.2a and 4.2b, is badly defaced, and Cyrus' royal epithet in the first line is illegible; thus, that restored epithet is in brackets in the following. The inscription then emphasized Cyrus' concern for maintenance of important temples and his lineage:

I am Cyrus, [king of lands], the one who loves Esagil
and Ezida, the son of Cambyses, strong king.

Figure 4.2a Brick stamp inscription of Cyrus from Uruk, BM 90731.

Figure 4.2b Hand drawing of Cyrus' brick stamp inscription
from Uruk by G. Smith, 1873, *Transactions of the Society of Biblical
Archaeology*, vol. II, after p. 148.

The Ur brick stamp inscription is much better preserved, and two copies have been found; see Figures 4.3a and 4.3b. One copy is housed in the British Museum and the other in the University of Pennsylvania Museum of Archaeology and Anthropology. Its elegant orthography and archaizing signs situated Cyrus in a long line of rulers who built and restored the temple of the moon god, Nanna-Suen, where the inscription was found. That fact alone, likewise with Cyrus' inscription found at the Eanna complex in Uruk, is important. Cyrus' work, and record of work, done at sanctuaries such as these was expected of a proper Babylonian king.

Figure 4.3a Brick stamp inscription of Cyrus from Ur, courtesy of the Penn Museum, B15348.

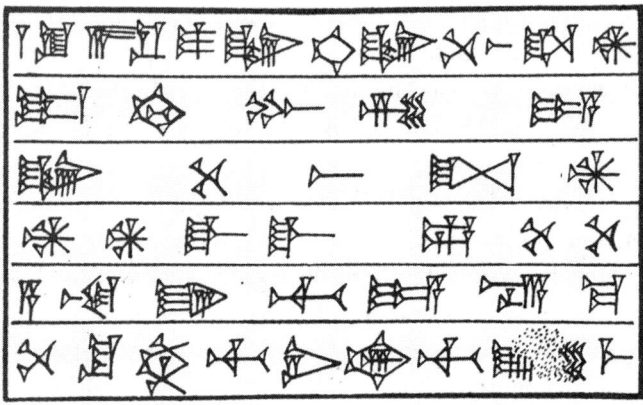

Figure 4.3b Hand drawing of Cyrus' brick stamp inscription from Ur, Gadd 1928, Plate XLVIII, Nr. 194.

Cyrus, king of the world, king of Anshan, the son of Cambyses, king of Anshan. The great gods have delivered into my hands all the lands, and I caused the land to live in peace.

This inscription reiterated Cyrus' lineage, along with the titles "King of the World" and "King of Anshan" (as in the Cyrus Cylinder). With the notable exception of the title "King of Anshan," Cyrus here again relied on traditional Assyrian and Babylonian phrasing, especially with regard to the gods' support of his rule. The gods granted all the lands (plural) to Cyrus; this was also standard phrasing. The formula "I caused to live in peace" (Akkadian *šubti nehti ušešib*) referred to the establishment of peace and security. It, too, is traditional, found as early as the Old Babylonian period, and it recurs throughout Assyrian and Babylonian inscriptions. The phrase is applied in a variety of ways, frequently to describe the settlement of people in their homes and of gods in their sanctuaries; it is used in just that way in the Cyrus Cylinder: "I caused all the lands to live in peace," referring in the standard way to the establishment of peace for all the lands, emphasis on the plural.

In the Ur brick phrasing, after the gods have delivered "all the lands" to Cyrus, rather unusually, Cyrus emphasized the peace and security of one land (singular). In scores if not hundreds of iterations of the formula by previous kings, the plural is used in both parts of the formula.[22] It is hazardous to make too much of one reference in one inscription, but read literally from lands, plural, to one land, there is a slight but potentially significant variation on the typical expression of universality that claims dominion over lands. Much has been made in modern scholarship of how Darius I and his successor often referred to the unification of lands (plural) into one land, or one earth.[23] In consideration of the Ur brick inscription's phrasing, it appears the idea was not new with Darius. In other words, Cyrus' vision may have been both a variation of an age-old formula as well as the literal truth.

Cyrus was of course genuinely concerned with representing himself as a king in the Assyrian and Babylonian mold, as one might expect for a new conqueror of an ancient civilization. It was Cyrus' job to make the invasiveness of a new order (i.e., his rule as a foreign king) minimally so. Observance of traditional forms, rites, and expectations was a critical part of smoothing the transition, this is evident in the narratives of both the Cyrus Cylinder and the Nabonidus Chronicle. The Uruk and Ur display inscriptions manifest the same concerns. Even more so, these inscriptions situated Cyrus in a long line of rulers, who built and restored parts of the Eanna temple complex at Uruk and the temple of Nanna-Suen at Ur—in both cases the continuity is traceable to king Naram-Sin more than a millennium and a half previous.[24] Beyond the exceptional use of the title "king of Anshan," and of course the extent of his power, Cyrus was almost indistinguishable from his Mesopotamian predecessors in his use of selected royal titles and epithets. That of course was not an accident.

The Verse Account (of Nabonidus)

One other, quite curious, Babylonian text from Cyrus' reign must be noted here as well. The so-called Verse Account was, in essence, a one-sided lyrical dispute, composed shortly after Cyrus' conquest (Figure 4.4). Its purpose was a poetic *damnatio memoriae* of the last Babylonian king Nabonidus and his reign. The extant copy of the tablet, in five columns, is quite damaged, making it very difficult to interpret. Its tone is clearly negative, a pejorative and even sarcastic take on Nabonidus' accomplishments. For example,

Figure 4.4 The Verse Account of Nabonidus, BM 38299.
© Trustees of The British Museum.

Nabonidus' piety in restoring temples, especially those of the moon god Nanna-Suen, was recast as impiety against the primary god of Babylon, Marduk, and his sanctuaries. Nabonidus' skill and wisdom, trumpeted in his own inscriptions, were turned on their head in the Verse Account, wherein he was belittled as a moron and a madman. Not only was Nabonidus himself vilified, but his legacy was also attacked. A surviving stela of Nabonidus (Figure 4.5) is notable for its blank area where an inscription would normally

Figure 4.5 Stela of Nabonidus, BM 38299.
© Trustees of The British Museum.

be found. This is interpreted as verification of the Verse Account's claim that Nabonidus' monuments were erased.[25] Cyrus' effective smear is echoed in modern treatments of Nabonidus that, not coincidentally, trend toward the negative.

Despite its different tenor, the Verse Accounts was likely composed as a direct analog to the Cyrus Cylinder. Its structural framework runs parallel to the Cylinder, though the Verse Account appears to have contained more details on Nabonidus' cruelty, neglect, and impiety: "he put the nobles to the sword . . . he blocked the road for the merchant . . . he performed an unholy act . . . he planned foolishness." Some scholars look to the portrayal of the madman Nebuchadnezzar portrayed in the Book of Daniel as a conflation with Nabonidus, this unflattering portrayal perhaps finding its origins in Cyrus' Babylonian inscriptions.[26] Though much of the Verse Account's negative portrayal is a literary device, the dichotomy between Nabonidus' emphasis on the moon god and the pushback by the powerful Marduk priesthood seems to reflect a real tension; that is to say, it was not simply a propagandistic device *post eventum*. Several scholars maintain that the support of the Marduk priesthood is the root cause of Cyrus' peaceful entry into the city and the capture of Nabonidus. That is not a stretch, but no doubt Cyrus' hard-fought victory at Opis a couple weeks beforehand had a lot to do with it as well. Columns three and four of the Verse Account are almost entirely lost, but in the last column—set early in Cyrus' new reign—the Persian king has restored order, adopted the title "King of the World," and received tribute from other kings who were now his subjects. Cyrus reinforced his newfound place in Babylonian tradition through his promotion of the normal: support of the Babylonian established order with Marduk as preeminent.

A Time of Transition

One result of Cyrus' conquest of Babylon was the return of Judean exiles who had been deported to Babylonia after Nebuchadnezzar's sack of Jerusalem in 587–586, during that king's series of campaigns to solidify Babylonian control over the whole Levant.[27] The return of these exiles to Judah and Jerusalem, and the refounding of the temple, make it no surprise that Cyrus received such glowing press in the Hebrew Bible. That phenomenon is useful to consider hand in hand with the Babylonian inscriptions just discussed and will be expanded upon in Chapter 5. While it is often claimed (or implied) that Cyrus himself, in the Cyrus Cylinder, explicitly ordered the return of the Judeans to their homeland, that was not the case. Specific information about the return of Judean exiles stems from their own tradition. The Cyrus Cylinder in the passage that follows gave specifics *from* where exiled gods and peoples were returned but only in general terms *to* where they went, that is, to their homes, wherever those may have been.[28] And the freed peoples themselves were never explicitly identified.

> From [Babylon?] to Ashur, Susa, Akkad, Eshnunna, Zabban, Meturnu, Der, as far as the border of Gutium, the sanctuaries on the other side of the Tigris that had been abandoned for a long time (alternate translation: "had been established long ago") I returned the gods who dwelt there to their places, and I made them take up residence forever. The whole of their peoples I assembled, and I returned them to their homes.

Judeans were never explicitly mentioned in the Cylinder, but it is a natural assumption that they were included in the general proclamation. The passage contains the formulaic, if important, expression: the return of gods (cultic statues) and people to the short list of places (and perhaps not complete because of a break in the text) explicitly mentioned above, which were north or east of Babylon.[29] This passage is understood to manifest a more general phenomenon of the right to return for deported populations or refugees from earlier Babylonian conquests. Its context has thus been justifiably juxtaposed with the more expansive Judean tradition, specifically the prophecy given in Isaiah: "(The Lord) who says of Cyrus,

'He is my shepherd, and he shall fulfill all my purpose'; saying of Jerusalem, 'She shall be built,' and of the Temple, 'Your foundation shall be laid.'"[30]

The backdrop for these momentous events was tension in the Babylonian post-exilic community, the Judeans who were forcibly deported to Babylon by Nebuchadnezzar II in the early 580s and their descendants. Put simply, with Cyrus allowing the Judeans in Babylon to return to Jerusalem, who would be in charge there? By Cyrus' time, these people had lived in Babylon for almost fifty years. Among them were Zerubbabel, the grandson of Jechoniah (Jehoaichin), the last king of Judah. There was tension between the descendants of the house of David and the returning priesthood who would be in charge of the new temple.[31] More to the point in our treatment, there is continued debate about the wider ramifications of this event, which spurred the refounding of the Temple of Solomon. The Book of Ezra contains notice of a proclamation by Cyrus, found during the time of Darius I in the archives of Ecbatana, that authorized the rebuilding of Yahweh's temple in Jerusalem:

> In the first year of Cyrus the king, Cyrus the king issued a decree: "Concerning the temple in Jerusalem, let it be rebuilt, the place where sacrifices are offered and burnt offerings are brought . . . let the cost be paid from the royal treasury."[32]

How much of the proclamation is historical is difficult to say, and opinions vary widely. In any case, there is no traceable action of the temple's rebuilding itself until Darius I's second year, based on information from the books of Zechariah and Haggai. Thus, it has been posited that the proclamation itself may have been anachronistically attributed to Cyrus' time, since it coincides with the positive picture presented elsewhere of the Empire's founder. There is much to be said for connecting these special privileges to Cyrus, whether out of his magnanimity or strategic calculation, or both.

What better agents of Cyrus' benevolence than those freed from bondage and then supported to re-establish their own traditions and temple? The territories of the Levant have always been disputed area, and whether Cyrus yet had any firm plans, he was well aware of the last major kingdom outside his current dominion: Egypt. The return of the Judean exiles provides just one example how Cyrus solidified his rule, as he remade the provincial system.

5

The Imperial Project

The great gods have delivered into my hands all the lands,
and I caused the land to live in peace.
—Cyrus the Great, brick inscription from Ur, lines 4–6

Before we consider various aspects of Cyrus the Great's imperial
program through an ideological lens, it is worth introducing here
some of the more mundane aspects of his rule over a now sprawling
territory. Babylonia in particular sheds light on these matters,
not only because of the continuity of documentation therein but
also because of Cyrus' reliance on their—and by extension the
Assyrian—systems of ruling large territories. Put as a question:
How did Cyrus do it? Any study of the Empire's administration
starts of course with the king, whose power was absolute. Cyrus
and his successors were the focal point of a sophisticated nexus of
bureaucracy and personal relationships by which the Empire was
ruled.

(Re)Ordering the World

Once Cyrus had taken Babylonia, his mission was twofold: to integrate his reign with Babylonian tradition as well as to integrate
Babylon and its territories with the burgeoning empire of his
previous conquests. Cyrus did not leave a list, not that we have
found anyway, of his administrative organization of his empire.

His successors did, though, and the list of territories that Darius I relayed in his Bisotun Inscription is generally understood to be the realm he inherited (one way to put it) upon taking the throne, or in other words, the extent of the Empire as of 522 BCE.

> Darius the king proclaims: These are the peoples (lands) that came into my possession. Through the power of Auramazda, I was their king: Persia, Elam, Babylonia, Assyria, Arabia, Egypt, those of the sea, Lydia, Ionia, Media, Armenia, Cappadocia, Parthia, Drangiana, Areia, Chorasmia, Bactria, Sogdiana, Gandara, Scythia (Saka), Sattagydia, Arachosia, Maka; in all twenty-three peoples (lands).[1]

This list serves as a touchstone for the regions that Cyrus conquered over the course of his three decades as king, not including Egypt, which was added by Cambyses. As has been noted, but cannot be emphasized enough, this was a stunning accomplishment (see Map 3). The list also throws into sharp relief how much contemporary detail, from Cyrus' own reign, that we lack in order to appreciate fully this historic shift. The exact boundaries of the territories within Cyrus' empire are generally impossible to define, unless concurrent with natural phenomena such as major rivers.

It is not always clear whether a particular term in the Bisotun list referred to a group of people or the land in which they lived, or both. For example, even to most Persian governing elites, the Greeks—living in hundreds of independent city-states in Anatolia and Europe—were mostly indistinguishable, and they were labeled generically by the Old Persian word *Yauna*, a rendering of the word "Ionia." During Cyrus' time, that term was understood to refer to the Greeks of western Anatolia (i.e., primarily Ionia) whom Cyrus conquered in conjunction with his overthrow of Croesus, since the Persians had not yet crossed into Europe with their armies. Subsequent lists from Darius and Xerxes differentiated types of the fractious Yauna (i.e., the discrete Greek city-states), but as Persian reach lengthened, there were too many of these barbarians to keep straight.

Thus, geographic markers were applied, for example, distinguishing the Ionians who lived in the sea (islanders) from those who lived across the sea, whose exact location is not specified: from Parsa this was somewhere far beyond the horizon. Some Ionians were even identified by the type of hat they wore. The Scythians were also at times differentiated by their taste in hats or their use of a particular beverage called *haoma*, a drink associated with later Zoroastrian ritual contexts. One wonders if these rather simplistic descriptions of both Greeks and Scythians might reflect an element of disdain for the masses of uncivilized peoples living on the fringes of the Empire. The Persians supposedly placed a value on their subjects based on proximity to the core, and Herodotus' take on the Persians ethnocentrism fit perfectly: the Persians esteemed least those who lived furthest away.[2]

The most basic, if oversimplified, way to describe Cyrus' administration of conquered territories was the addition of another layer of authority, in this case the king's absolute authority, over regional rulers and local institutions. Satraps were, literally, the "protectors of the kingdom," appointed from members of the extended royal family, Persian elite, or local dynasts allowed to remain in power under Persian auspices. The word "satrap" comes from the Greek word *satrapeia* that translates into English as "satrapy," and the satrap (the term derived ultimately from the Old Persian *xšaçapāvan*) may be considered equivalent to the governor of a province, one level below the king.

The stereotypical laissez-faire approach of the Persian administration, referenced in many modern treatments, has a superficial truth to it: as long as the peace was maintained, tribute and commerce continued to flow, and the king's directives followed, all was well. But such a portrayal belies the organizational acumen and rigor as manifested, for example, by the various archival sources such as those from Persepolis. As we have seen, local officials may have been retained but became subordinate to the satrap. In Babylonia, for example, many of the governors (called in Akkadian a *šakin ṭēmi*) of the individual city-states remained native Babylonians, often from prominent families associated with the major temple complexes. Under Nabonidus, these officials were responsible to a "governor of the land" (a *šakin māti*). This was the situation the Nabonidus Chronicle described in the context of Cyrus' appointment of Gobryas, discussed earlier. Under Cyrus' reorganization, the territory of the Babylonian Empire came to be called "the province (satrapy) of Babylon and Across-the-River" (Akkadian *pihat Babili u eber nari*).[3]

Other officials were added to the mix, such as royal secretaries and military personnel, directly appointed by and responsible to the king. After Cyrus' defeat of Croesus, the local officials who were given important positions, such as Pactyes, were balanced by Persian appointees as well, in this case one Tabalus, who (almost literally) held down the fort when Pactyes rebelled, until help could arrive.[4] These royal appointees helped maintain consistent and reliable communication with the king, and they served as a tangible reminder to whom the satrap owed his position. Greek sources contain many examples of a satrap's deference to the king in matters of foreign affairs, in response to one or another Greek city-state's or ruler's request for a change in policy. It is easy to pass off such deference as satrapal equivocation, but the realities of the royal hierarchy suggest otherwise: important decisions were made by the king.

Cyrus' empire included sophisticated administrative systems inherited from Babylonia, Elam, and Assyria that stretched back from his time almost two thousand years. Extant Babylonian archives that spanned the sixth century give insight into the continuity, in rule of Babylonia at least, from the Babylonian kings to Cyrus. Two small caches of Elamite legal and administrative texts, dating from the later seventh or early sixth centuries, found at Susa testify to the continuity of administrative practices within Iran as well. The texts contain individuals of Persian name and some

Persian loanwords that testify to the dispersal of Persians through the region in many different contexts, part of the overarching Elamite-Persian ethnogenesis that served as the backdrop and the foundation for Cyrus' rise. A much more compelling example of early Achaemenid administration comes from the reign of Darius I, the Persepolis Fortification Archive (PFA), which was introduced previously in our discussion of Cyrus' daughters Atossa and Artystone. An interesting feature of the numerous worker-groups tracked in this archive was the range of their ethnicities. Arabs, Bactrians, Babylonians, Egyptians, Elamites, Ionians, Thracians, among several others, are mentioned, workers who were called *kurtash* in Elamite.[5] Some of the Achaemenid royal inscriptions— for example Darius I's so-called foundation charter from Susa (DSf)—associated specific ethnic groups with specific materials or craftsmanship, an inclusive manifestation of the Empire and its diversity. Cyrus, as we have seen, conquered no shortage of peoples, and several defeated populations may have been subject to deportations, such as the Lydians deported to Nippur referenced earlier.[6]

The Roads Go Ever On

The functioning of such a sprawling empire, even in its nascent stage under Cyrus, demanded reliable communications between center and periphery. Once again, we must rely on later sources to appreciate the full structure, but Cyrus laid the necessary groundwork. This system finds echoes even today. Engraved on the Post Office building at Eighth Avenue and Thirty-third Street in New York is the maxim: "Neither snow nor rain nor heat nor gloom of night stays these couriers from the swift completion of their appointed rounds." That inscription is an adaptation of a passage in Herodotus about the Persian messenger system, a sort of "Persian Pony Express," that runs as follows:

There is nothing mortal that travels faster than these
messengers . . . for as many days as the whole route there are
horses and men stationed, one horse and one man set for each
day. Neither snow, nor rain, nor heat, nor night hinders them
from accomplishing the course laid before them as quickly as
possible. After the first one finishes his route, he delivers the
instructed message to the second, the second does likewise to the
third; from there in rapid succession down the line the message
moves.[7]

The most famous of the roads used by these messengers, though
it was only one of many, was what Herodotus called the Royal Road
from Susa in Elam to Sardis in Lydia. This was one of many roads,
to all corners of the Empire, that converged in Parsa as a nexus. The
Susa-Sardis route ran roughly 1,500 miles and took a journey of
ninety days. But royal dispatches could move much faster, a relay
system with fresh horses and messengers at each staging post, cut-
ting the travel time significantly. Individuals or groups on state business carried a sealed document (Elamite *halmi*) that allowed access
to supplies or provisions en route to their destination. The Elamite
term *pirradazish*, translated "fast messenger," occurs numerous
times in the Fortification tablets, and refers to just such a system. Of
course, rivers and larger waterways also served as important routes.
One example is the "canal of Gubaru," one of an elaborate system of
canals throughout Babylonia, mentioned in several Babylonian administrative texts dating from Cambyses onward.[8]

The Persian Army

Persian rule was backed up by the potential as well as the real application of force. Territory once gained must be held to the king's law.
That the Persians were able to conquer and retain so much territory for so long testified to their army's effectiveness. While Cyrus'

campaigns were mostly expansionist, there are examples, such as the revolt of Pactyes after the Lydian conquest, that demonstrated the consequences of rebellion or recalcitrance. We have little in the way of descriptive sources for the Persian army, its organization or size, especially under Cyrus.

Persian military forces were drawn from all areas of the Empire, members of the professional corps as well as conscripts levied for local action or for major campaigns. Emphasis on horses and horsemanship in several sources suggests the importance that Cyrus placed on cavalry. The term in Old Persian for "army," the word *kāra*, may also be translated as "people," which results in confusion in modern translations. That phenomenon applied not only to the Persians; for example, the Babylonian word *ummānu* is another term that may also be translated as "army" or "people" depending on context.[9] In ancient times, a city's populace might often be called to war, and the troops' effectiveness differed widely depending on training and equipment available—and that varying by socioeconomic level. The general phenomenon is easier traced among the better-known circumstances in Greek city-states, wherein Athens, for example, the male populace was militarily organized by socioeconomic level: from the lower strata who supplied rowers for the fleet, to the more prosperous forming the armored infantry, to the elites who constituted the cavalry.

Levied troops did not have the same sort of armor or weaponry as those corps that formed what we would call a standing army. From Babylonia, we can assess how military forces were conscripted. Military obligations accompanied grants of land, arranged by what is called the *haṭru*-system, *haṭru* being the Akkadian word for "bow." This system is traceable through the Neo-Babylonian period, already well established by Cyrus' time, and he continued it. The amount of land granted to each person was commensurate with that person's socioeconomic status and, thus, the amount of services expected in return. The system was land-for-service: grants of land were given by the crown in return for services on demand.

Grant holders, or tenants, often relinquished the supervision of the estates to managers from prominent families, what we might even term business firms, one example being the Murashu family from the later fifth century.[10]

Greek sources frequently refer to the (usually exaggerated) numbers of the Persian army or the variety of its contingents. But these sources are neither clear nor consistent with regard to the makeup of the army or its tactics. For the better-documented periods starting from Darius' and Xerxes' forays into Greece in the early fifth century, the perspective is usually the same: heavily armed Greek infantry in phalanx formations were superior to lightly armed Persian infantry. It is difficult to sift the realities of individual battles from this general picture, which also obscures the diversity in both sides' forces, heavy- and light-armed. In Cyrus' time at any rate, whenever it may have been put to the test (for example, in western Asia Minor), the Persians, with very few exceptions, were victorious.

The backbone of the Persian army consisted of an elite, permanent corps, the so-called Immortals, which numbered 10,000 soldiers, according to Herodotus. Whenever one of their number died or was wounded or ill, another would take his place, so the number of the battalion always remained 10,000. Herodotus noted that the Immortals—by Xerxes' time anyway—were conspicuous for their gold bracelets and other prestige items. These are frequently mentioned in conjunction with Persian officers and nobles, a phenomenon that also fed Greek stereotypes of Persian effeminacy, but in their own (Persian) context they were highly prized markers of honor and status. An inner core of the Immortals, numbering 1,000, may have been the king's select bodyguard. This would have represented the cream of the Empire's elite, socially and militarily. This force was commanded by the *chiliarch*, a Greek word meaning "commander of 1,000," perhaps from an Old Persian word *hazarapatish*.[11] The chiliarch was clearly a high official in the army and at the court, where he regulated access to the king.

Herodotus offered a vivid account of the vast and diverse forces of the imperial levy. This was purportedly the full army and navy of Persians and their subjects, the vast forces that Xerxes arrayed against Greece before his invasion in 480. Herodotus also named many of the commanders, an elaborate depiction of the peoples of the Empire with descriptions of their clothing and equipment. For example, Persians and Medes were arrayed in felt caps, colored tunics over scale mail, trousers, wickerwork shields, and a variety of weapons; Scythians wore a particular type of upright headgear, and like many eastern Iranian contingents carried bows, battle axes, and dagger. In this lengthy passage Herodotus provides important descriptions for the ethnography of the Persian Empire, and the genealogical connections among the extended Persian royal family and the elites.[12] It has often been remarked that Herodotus' entire portrayal better describes a parade than a battle array. Nonetheless, it appears to have typified the diversity of peoples and weaponry that the Persian commanders had to weld into an effective fighting force. Cyrus would have faced this problem at a fundamental level, in light of his rapid conquests—with what must have been initially composed of Persian, other Iranian, and Elamite forces—and the incorporation of levies from then-conquered peoples. Cyrus did not campaign at sea; though his conquest of the Phoenician cities would have gained him access to warships, these formed the core of a navy integrated with the other armed forces under Cambyses.

A Unifying Ideology

With the conquest of Babylon in October 539, Cyrus controlled, by far, the most expansive empire to date. With the exception of Egypt, no known civilization lay beyond his reach. The peoples of far Europe, of northwestern and central Africa, of the Central Asian steppes, of the Indian subcontinent, and of the Far East were either unknown to Cyrus or not yet subjects of attention. But the

Empire was not yet at its maximum extent, and Cyrus himself was not done with campaigning. The foundations he laid—military, political, and cultural—had enormous impact on the histories of the Middle East, Central Asia, and Europe.

This section further explores how Cyrus consolidated and methodized his rule through an expansive royal ideology, one eclectic in its adaptations, intentional in its function, and distinctively Persian in its manifestation. As part of how Cyrus' imperial imagination was translated into practical application, it is also important to consider how the work on his new capital at Pasargadae gave insight into his priorities. Cyrus was clearly more than a great conqueror, he had a long-range vision.

The Achaemenid Empire's imperial ideology, as expressed in both text and image, has often been portrayed in modern scholarship as static. At the height of the Empire, its staying power and consistency may be considered such—this is a matter of semantics—but such an interpretation does not do justice to its sophistication and effectiveness. In any case, that debate is better set later than Cyrus; the imperial vision was necessarily dynamic over its first decades, as the system evolved. For many expressions of the imperial messaging, there is a great deal of material extant from Cyrus' time. In addition, evidence from Assyria, Babylonian, and Elam at their heights, as well as evidence from later in the Achaemenid period (especially the reign of Darius I), has a lot to tell us. Though this is a common refrain by now, without a definitive blueprint available, by necessity some of Cyrus' intentions must be extrapolated.

The parallels between Achaemenid and especially Assyrian ideologies of kingship and imperialistic expression are pervasive, beyond the truism that the king was the focal point of the Empire. It is not a coincidence that the Assyrian legacy loomed large in Cyrus' endeavors. In both systems, the main component of such was the centrality of the king in a universal empire: favored by and representative of (if not the creation of) the gods, a moral force as conqueror, and a just ruler. Cyrus the Great tapped several traditions, but Assyrian influence remained prominent from the beginning. This was not only because Assyria had been the imperial model par excellence, if now superseded by Cyrus, but also for other reasons, as will be discussed.

Royal ideology is a more complex phenomenon than a list of titles, but that is the place to start. In doing so the Cyrus Cylinder and his other inscriptions discussed in the previous chapter must be revisited in some of their particulars. Continuity of royal ancestry was an essential part of the formula in Assyrian and Babylonian kingship, and the Persians thought so as well. That Cyrus' forefathers were also kings was critical, that Cyrus was of an "everlasting line [literally 'seed'] of kingship." The phrasing is traditional, and it formed the backdrop for Cyrus' adoption of grander titles of royal dominion: King of the World, Great King, Strong King, King of Babylon, and King of the Four Quarters. The titles Great King, Strong King, and King of Babylon were all straightforward enough. Cyrus was already king of Persia (modern Iran) and Anatolia (modern Turkey, Armenia, and Azerbaijan), with the Babylonian Empire (modern Iraq, Syria, Jordan, Lebanon, and Israel) now another jewel in Cyrus' crown.

Those three titles were bookended—encompassed, if you will—by titles indicating totality: "King of the World" (Akkadian *šar kiššati*) and "King of the Four Quarters" (*šar kibrāti erbetti*).[13] Continued use of these titles was both standard practice and also deeply meaningful within a broader perspective of ideological sentiment. That the ideological symbolism was conjoined to the actual extent of Cyrus' conquests made the symbolic real, more meaningful, and truly formidable. In the history of empires, Cyrus represents a watershed moment.

The centrality of direct rule, or an acknowledgment of the king's superiority, over vast territories was often expressed as an extension of the cosmic order. That was certainly the case with Achaemenid ideology, adapted especially from the Assyrian model and shaped to Persian principles. An imperialistic imperative was also found in epithets of Cyrus' Elamite predecessors, who literally styled themselves *likume rišakka,* "expander of the realm." The concept of universality manifested even in the dating formula of mundane Babylonian administrative texts via the title "king of lands" (Akkadian *šar matāti,* often written logographically LUGAL KUR.KUR), the formula adopted into Old Persian as well, *xšāyaθiya dahyūnām.* While Assyrian and Babylonian models generally emphasized rulership over a plurality, by the time of Darius I this sentiment was complemented by, often combined with, a literal sense of rule over one world, a unity: "one king of many, one lord of many."[14] Cyrus' potential role in this evolution is not to be overlooked, as discussed in Chapter 4.

The king was the sun around whom all else revolved. The Persian king's physical stature, costume, and regalia were all carefully managed to highlight his august position.[15] Xenophon's descriptions in the *Cyropaedia* captured well the essence of the royal presentation, part of carefully choreographed appearances to command respect and to invoke awe. Greek authors frequently referred to the physical splendor of the Persian king, the king's subjects even overcome by it, such as this from Xenophon: "And when they saw him, they all prostrated themselves before him . . . they were overcome by his power and his splendor, because Cyrus appeared so great and so good to look upon." This was tantamount to the aura that the Babylonians experienced in the presence of Cyrus ("their faces glowed"), as described in the Cyrus Cylinder. The aura, and mainly the power that it both implied and manifested, has a long history in Mesopotamian and Elamite traditions. It signified the close connection between king and divine, what may be described as a shared essence.

In Mesopotamian tradition, this shared power was termed in a variety of ways, but its most forthright expression was the *melammu,* an Akkadian word that is often translated to the effect of "fearsome radiance" or the like. But a single translation does not do the phenomenon full justice to the term. The *melammu* was often associated with radiance, but, more important, it was always associated with power: frequently in martial contexts, but also manifested in exceptional physical capabilities, sheer might, or the projection of a force that overwhelmed anyone in contact with it. In some Assyrian representations the king could apply this force to destroy enemies. The phenomenon carried over into succeeding periods as the Persian *fravashi* (Avestan *xvarnah*). It is a complex subject, its manifestations and its ramifications still being debated.[16] This aura would accompany, protect, and enhance the king in any royal role but be fully evident during formal contexts, such as court or ritual ceremonies, in which the king wore full regalia.

When Cyrus and Cambyses partook of the New Year Festival (*akitu*) in late March 538, that Cyrus wore Elamite attire—presumably his formal garment as king of Anshan—was remarkable for several reasons, though there is much missing in our knowledge of that sequence. It is easier to discuss the Achaemenid court in its mature form, especially as the Greeks viewed, or imagined, it. Ancient sources refer in general to Cyrus' striking good looks and stature, which would have been amplified more so when he donned his full, ceremonial regalia. Xenophon's depictions of the king in majesty in the *Cyropaedia,* even if they may hit close to the mark for Cyrus, were in the main Hellenized renderings of the Achaemenid court under later kings, particularly that of Xerxes and his successors. The king's robe and accoutrements marked him from others; this included special headgear, for example a type of crown called in Greek the *kidaris*. The Roman author Quintus Curtius Rufus described the Persian king's elaborate attire: a purple tunic interwoven with white, a gold-embroidered cloak, and a gold belt from which he often wore a special dagger. The king and members of the nobility also frequently donned false beards and are portrayed with such in the iconography, a practice that was very old in Mesopotamian traditions. The king's beard was generally longer and more elaborate than others. Cyrus mixed styles and added innovations to cultivate a uniquely Persian vision.[17]

Greek sources reveled in a Persian court replete with excess and effeminacy. Their portrayals were likely an intentional misreading of the pageantry and costumes that were integral to the king's presentation as something more than human, akin to divine. As an extension of these same sources' projected dominance of the women and eunuchs in the court context, they delighted in other aspects of shocking behavior: various forms of excess (sexual or otherwise) and violent caprice, a direct counter to the ideological messaging described above. While it is not a stretch to envision instances of despotic behavior in any absolute monarchy, it is difficult to discern fact from fiction in many of these accounts. Further, Greek authors—many of whom lived in territories controlled by, and were formally subjects of, the Persian Empire—were aware of the official, ideological messaging, and their writings often played against it. Interestingly in those portrayals, we rarely find the stereotypical negativity attributed to Cyrus. When it is found (e.g., his hubris against rivers as described in Herodotus), it is even more rarely amplified, as though ancient authors of all nationalities held him in grave respect. In other words, Cyrus was rarely the object of scurrilous gossip or innuendo, in direct contrast to every one of his successors.

More Territory, More Capitals

Cyrus' rapid conquests and the necessities of organization required him to do practically everything at once. He was no doubt one of history's most effective multi-taskers. Through his conquests he acquired several important cities, three of which retained their previous status during the Achaemenid period: Babylon, Median Ecbatana, and Elamite Susa (see Map 3). Babylon and Susa were centuries-old cities, roughly 200 miles away from each other on the Babylonian alluvium. Susa was the city most often named in Greek sources from the fifth and fourth centuries BCE, but the reason for that is not clear, for example, whether it was the capital at which the kings spent most of their time, or it was simply the horizon of most Greek experience. Cyrus himself was frequently on the go, and the main capital was, in essence, wherever the king happened to be. It may thus be better to refer to these cities as royal power centers, rather than as capitals per se.

Later Achaemenid kings' courts were also itinerant, perhaps a carryover from their ancestors' semi-sedentary, pastoral origins. Kings and their entourages moved from one capital to the other as much for the climate as for other reasons, such as the king's required involvement in certain rituals. Susa or Babylon in the low-lying plains appealed during the winter; Ecbatana in the mountains was attractive during the summer. Three of Cyrus' capitals straddled the Zagros mountain chain—his new capital Pasargadae in Parsa, Susa in Khuzistan, and Ecbatana in Media. Pasargadae was not complete by the time he died; his successors Cambyses and Darius I finished it. The later capital of Persepolis, the remains of the terrace essentially an Achaemenid museum in stone, was a project initiated by Darius I; beyond the occasional comparison it lies beyond the scope of this book. Babylon was the focus of much of the previous chapter. A few more words are dedicated here to Ecbatana and Susa, as a brief segue before the main focus on Pasargadae.

The Median capital Ecbatana (modern Hamadan) remains an inhabited city in which no large-scale excavations are feasible. Little is known about it from Cyrus' time. Herodotus' imaginary description, which included battlements plated in silver and gold, is generally not taken seriously as a description of the city.[18] Xenophon's idealized reconstruction of Cyrus' youth had the future king raised there, at the Median court, but that bit of Xenophon's portrayal is fanciful. In the Nabonidus Chronicle's terse account of Cyrus' conquest of Asytages, Agbatana (the Babylonian name for Ecbatana) was noted only for its having been looted. The city's location along the major east-west trade route in northwestern Iran (the forerunner of the Silk Road) attests to its strategic importance, but with so many questions swirling around the organization of the Medes in Cyrus' time, it is difficult to say much beyond that it was Astyages' home, and by extension, the Medes' most important center.

Cyrus' relationship with Susa is similarly obscure, as neither the archaeological nor documentary records have provided many clues. The Assyrian king Ashurbanipal dedicated a lot of clay (i.e., in writing his annals) to his devastation of the city in 646, the reading of which leads one to believe that nothing would ever live or grow there again. That, of course, was hyperbole: the city was a major center during Achaemenid times, with sporadic but compelling evidence testifying to its renewal before that. Excavation results allow a glimpse of the city during the Neo-Elamite period that preceded Cyrus, but precious little is understood of the critically formative period. Whether any Elamite kingdom based there was conquered by Cyrus himself or one of his forebears remains in the realm of conjecture. A passage in Herodotus, echoed by later writers, indicated that the king would drink only (or at least preferably) of water from the River Choaspes, probably to be identified with the modern Karkeh which flowed near Susa. Whether the king did so for purported health benefits, the usual interpretation, or for some ritual purpose is unknown.[19]

Another reason Susa does not often enter discussions about Cyrus the Great is that there is no evidence for major Achaemenid-period works there before Darius I, who expended a great deal of resources and money there. Several of Darius' royal inscriptions testify to his building activities at Susa and demonstrate the site's importance, especially his great palace and the adjoining *apadana* (an Old Persian term often translated "audience hall"). One text in particular, found in multiple copies, took a page out of the Assyrian playbook in relaying the diversity of subject peoples contributing— not that these work groups had much choice—in the construction and embellishment of the city. The particulars were often closely connected to peoples' geographic origins; for example, Bactrians and Sogdians from the northeast brought gold and lapis lazuli, respectively. This range also portrayed an idealized vision of empire: multiple peoples from multiple lands contributing toward one project, one goal. The evidence for stone-toothed chisel workmanship, marking the presence of Lydian and Ionian stone-cutters laboring at Pasargadae, has been much remarked upon in the modern literature. Darius utilized the same in his work at Susa, "The stone columns that were worked here were from Elam . . . the masons who crafted the stone were Ionians and Sardians."[20] Cyrus did not leave us similar documentary testimony, or, rather, we have not found it explicitly recorded in an inscription, but his plan and work at Pasargadae took the same approach.

Pasargadae

Cyrus founded a new capital with aspirations that matched his new world empire. Pasargadae (Elamite *Batrakatash*) is situated within the Dasht-i Morghab, which translates to the "Plain of the Waterbird." Thus stems the site's modern name, Morghab, located in an elevated valley in the northern part of Fars, on the main route between Isfahan and Shiraz. It is approximately 50 miles east-northeast of Anshan and approximately 23 miles north-northeast of Persepolis. The site of Pasargadae is one of the most elevated in that region, roughly 6,200 feet above sea level, and there has as yet been found no indication of previous settlement there. The site's plan is still not fully appreciated, and current maps do not reflect the full scope of the settlement and activity; see Figure 5.1a for a recent site map. Pasargadae was founded as an expression of Cyrus' vision of universal rule, but it was not completed before his death. Construction continued at least a decade into the reign of Darius I. Pasargadae was in effect constructed around a park: a large, formal garden measuring roughly 1,000 feet per side (see Figure 5.1b). This park was bounded on its northwestern and southwestern edges by free-standing, multi-columned buildings. Modern excavators have

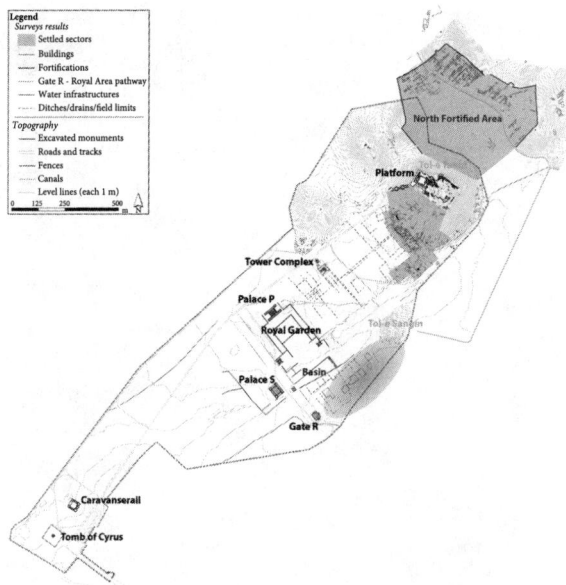

Figure 5.1a Site plan of Pasargadae, after Gondet et al. 2021. Courtesy of Rémy Boucharlat and Sébastien Gondet.

termed these buildings palaces, which may be misleading as to their actual function in Cyrus' day. Nonetheless, the labels are retained, as they are standardized in the modern literature.

Available site maps suggest the site was a collection of monumental buildings distributed over a wide area, but there remains much work to be done there. Pasargadae has long held fascination, even after its initial association with Cyrus was lost. For example, travelers' accounts from the late fifteenth century onward reveal that the famous Tomb of Cyrus had been identified frequently, and curiously, as the tomb of the mother of Solomon, the Madar-i Suliman.[21] Pasargadae's importance persisted throughout the Achaemenid period, although as a palace and administrative center it was eclipsed by Persepolis. One example of Pasargadae's lasting import, an extension of Cyrus', is in a report by the Greek writer

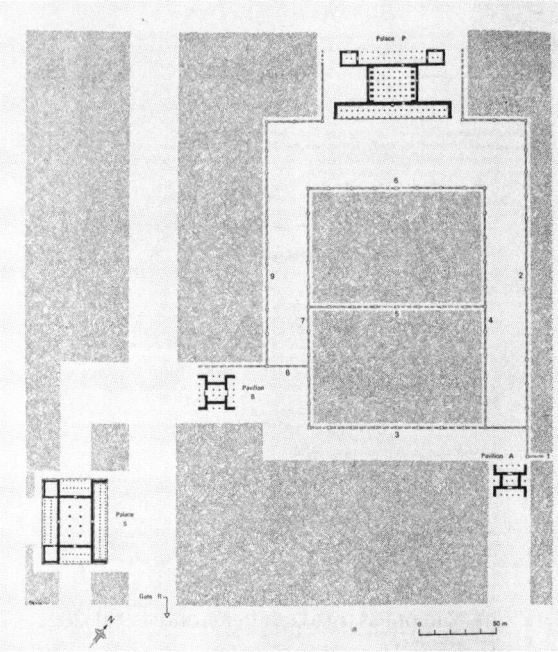

Figure 5.1b Schematic drawing of Royal Garden precinct. Courtesy of David Stronach (Stronach 1978, Figure 48).

Plutarch, who described an important royal coronation ritual that was held at Pasargadae into the fourth.[22] The rite, overseen by Persian priests, involved the newly crowned king entering the sanctuary of the warrior goddess (Iranian Anahita) and donning the garments that Cyrus wore, before he himself became king. The new king then ate a cake of figs, some bitter leaves of terebinth, and drank a bowl of sour milk. Plutarch implied that there was more to the ritual, unknown to outsiders. The significance of these foods and their consumption in this context is unclear—perhaps a reminder of earlier, humbler days—but the setting at Pasargadae and link with Cyrus are telling. The ritual was clearly meant to establish the new king's connection with, and continuity from, the first ruler of their empire.

There are other indicators of the site's importance in later traditions. Herodotus, in his list of the six Persian tribes, described the Pasargadae tribe as the noblest, a distant echo of the city's site and significance. Ctesias set Cyrus' climactic battle against Asytages there. The Greek geographer Strabo also relayed the site's importance to Cyrus:

> Cyrus held Pasargadae in honor, because there he defeated Astyages the Mede in the final battle, transferred the rule of Asia to himself, founded a city, and built a palace as memorial to his victory.[23]

Archaeological work at Pasargadae has revealed the grandeur of the site, though the excavated remains make up only a portion of the whole settled area, focused on the central garden area as alluded to above. While the use of stone-working techniques from western Anatolia and the use of the toothed stone chisel have been used to establish approximate dates for the building on the site, there have been no archives yet found that allow precise chronological demarcation of its stages of construction. The site continues to astonish in many ways. Its incorporation of stone monuments and sophisticated hydraulic features have no known precedent in Fars, though the Persians found inspiration from their imperial predecessors in Assyria, Babylonia, and Elam.

Cyrus' far-ranging conquests exposed him to many cultures and influences, and he was a quick study. It has become clichéd that the early Persian kings and their advisors were masters at adoption and adaptation, to create something new and uniquely Persian. But the repetition of that fact must not be allowed to diminish its import, and Cyrus must take pride of place in these developments. What is even more striking about Pasargadae is the apparent lack of defensive fortifications. It must be emphasized that this phenomenon, or lack thereof, applies to the central quadrant, the so-called Royal Garden area. The site as a whole has not yet been sufficiently explored to draw definitive conclusions.[24] Nonetheless, for a man who spent so many years sacking cities, this is a striking juxtaposition.

Tomb of Cyrus

For centuries before its proper identification, the tomb was associated with the mother of Solomon. This was a curious connection to the ancient king and, in Islamic tradition, prophet, but not an uncommon one, as will be seen in discussion of some other monuments from the site subsequently. Seventeenth-century European travelers remarked on the tomb's popularity as a shrine, especially among women who would visit it in all kinds of weather to pray for fertility. Situated on the southwestern periphery of the site, about a half mile from the central complex, the Tomb of Cyrus is a remarkable monument (Figures 5.2a and 5.2b). It consists of a six-tiered plinth, on which rests a gabled tomb chamber with a sloped roof. In the words of the excavator, David Stronach, "The setting of the tomb is masterly. It stands apart from all other monuments, dominating the southern half of the Morghab plain. Its position is such that it attracts the eye from almost any vantage point."[25] The tomb is plain but elegant, its lack of ostentation matches characteristics of Cyrus' own personality as relayed in a variety of testimonies examined so far in this book. The structure's massive stonework and smooth surfaces project dignity, simplicity, and strength. The base of the plinth measures roughly 44 × 40 feet, and the entire structure is roughly 36 feet high. The tiered design calls to mind not only the stepped pyramids of Egypt but also, and more directly, the ziggurats (temple towers) of Mesopotamia and Elam. Tombs with similar tiers have been found elsewhere in Fars and even in Lydia and western Anatolia. Its cella with gabled roof finds parallels with Anatolian structures, Urartian as well as Phrygian and Lydian. Since the dates of Anatolian analogs are

Figure 5.2a Tomb of Cyrus from the west. Courtesy of David Stronach (Stronach 1978, Plate 21).

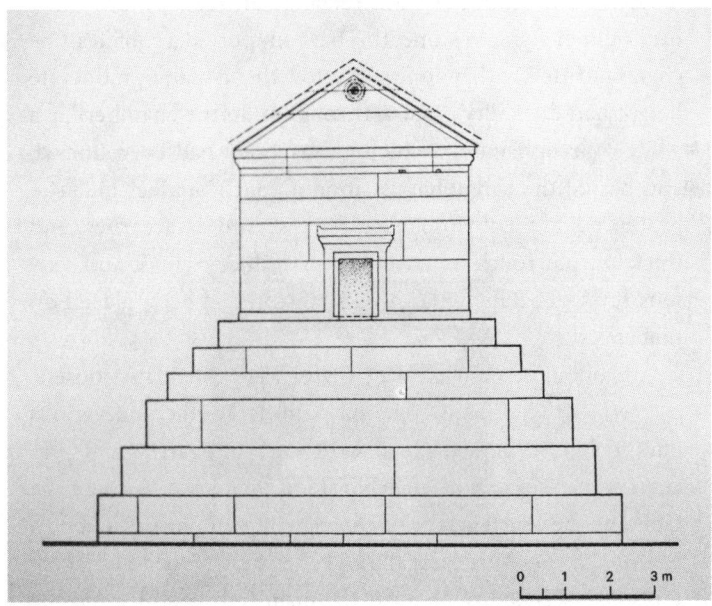

Figure 5.2b Drawing of Tomb of Cyrus. Courtesy of David Stronach (after Stronach 1978, Figure 13).

uncertain, it is unclear whether Cyrus and his builders drew inspiration from them, or vice versa.

The tomb is unmarked by any surviving inscription, though several ancient writers commented on the tomb and an accompanying inscription. The longest of these testimonies is from Arrian's *Anabasis*, describing Alexander of Macedon's visit to the spot. Arrian based his account on that of Aristoboulos, one of Alexander's officers who was present with Alexander at the site in the year 330 BCE, 200 years after Cyrus' death.

> The desecration of the tomb of Cyrus son of Cambyses (I), which was found ruined and ransacked, distressed Alexander, as Aristoboulos reports. Cyrus' tomb was in the royal park in Pasargadae. A grove of many kinds of trees had been planted around it.
>
> The grove was irrigated, and deep grass had grown in the meadow. The tomb itself was rectangular in shape and had a base built of squared stone; this base supported a roofed stone chamber fitted with a door so narrow that a man of moderate height had difficulty passing through it. In the chamber lay a golden sarcophagus in which Cyrus' body had been buried, and beside the sarcophagus stood a couch, its feet made of beaten gold; a Babylonian tapestry served as a carpet, and thick purple robes as coverlets. A military cloak and various tunics of Babylonian workmanship had been placed on that couch.
>
> Aristoboulos reports that there were Median trousers, garments dyed in blue, some of them dark, others of various hues, collars of linked metal, scimitars, and earrings of precious stones set in gold. A table stood there, and between the table and the couch lay the sarcophagus containing Cyrus' body. Within the enclosure, near the ascent leading to the tomb, there was a small chamber built for the magi who had guarded the tomb even in the days of Cambyses, son of Cyrus. The office of

guardian passed from father to son, and the king used to provide these guardians with a fixed daily allowance that included a
sheep, wheat flour, and wine, and a horse each month to sacrifice
to Cyrus.

The tomb had an inscription in Persian characters that read,
"You there! I am Cyrus son of Cambyses, who founded the
Persian empire and reigned as king of Asia. Do not begrudge me
my monument." Alexander had made up his mind to visit the
tomb of Cyrus should he conquer the Persians and he now found
that everything in it had been carried away except the sarcophagus and the couch. . . . Aristoboulos reports that he himself was
ordered by Alexander to restore Cyrus' tomb to its original condi-
tion; to deposit in the sarcophagus as much of Cyrus' body as had
been preserved and to replace the lid; to repair everything that
had been damaged; to spread the couch with garlands; to repro-
duce item by item everything that had been placed in the tomb; to
re-create its ancient arrangement; to obliterate traces of the little
door, partly by plastering it with clay; and to stamp the clay with
the royal seal.[26]

The usual caveats must be recalled about the transmission (i.e.,
accuracy) of this material in the ancient sources, but the passage
contains much of interest. The emphasis on the tomb's placement within a royal park matches the importance of these parks
to Cyrus. The emphasis on materials of both Babylonian and
Median craftsmanship highlighted the traditions of two of Cyrus'
immediate imperial predecessors. The provisions allowed for the
magi (priests) caretakers and guardians of the tomb are of the
sort recorded in the Persepolis Fortification tablets of goods for
other tombs in the region.[27] No evidence of an inscription, in Old
Persian or otherwise, has been discovered in modern times. The
inscription relayed by Arrian, especially the title "King of Asia,"
has no ancient Near Eastern parallels; that bit reads as a Greek
construct.

Gate R

The so-called Gate R (Figure 5.3a) is part of the central complex, sometimes called the palace precinct. It served as one of its entry points, along with the remains of those structures termed in the literature Palace P and Palace S (see Figure 5.1b). These three focal points are all at least 600 feet from each other, a fact that spurred several interpretations that the site was laid out like a nomadic camp. In actuality, this spacing was planned and utilized for the large gardens, the park that beautified and conceptually linked the buildings of the precinct. Gate R is also notable in that it contains the only relief from Pasargadae that was preserved almost in its entirety: the winged figure, often called a guardian genius in the modern literature.

Gate R was a free-standing, rectangular building roughly 93 × 83 feet in dimension that consisted of a large main room with small

Figure 5.3a Remains of Gate R from the west. Courtesy of David Stronach (Stronach 1978, Plate 41).

anterooms just off the north and south doorways. Gate R's two main doorways are estimated to have themselves been 30 feet in height. The height of the interior columns is estimated to have been at least 52 feet, but these are no longer extant beyond the column bases (socles) and a few fragments. The main room was a hypostyle hall, an open-air hall with a roof supported by the two rows of four columns, as shown in the plan of Figure 5.3b. This arrangement finds antecedents in structures from Median sites and from Hasanlu in northwestern Iran, but, as with the other Pasargadae monuments, is notable here for its composite character: a blending of eastern and western styles and building techniques. Perhaps based on comparisons with Xerxes' gate at Persepolis, Ernst Herzfeld's investigations in the 1920s determined the outer

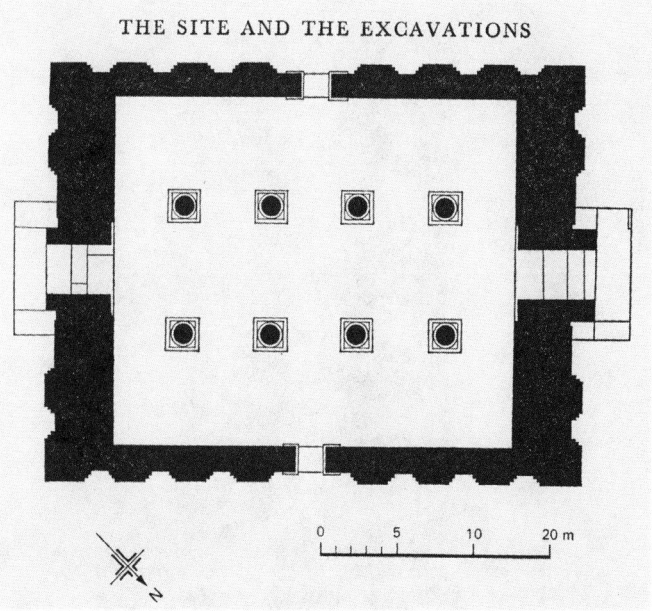

Figure 5.3b Plan of Gate R. Courtesy of David Stronach (after Stronach 1978, Figure 24).

entrance was flanked by a pair of winged bulls, but the fragments have never been published.

The winged figure from Pasargadae is one of the most significant surviving sculptures from the early Achaemenid period, a microcosm of the imperial plan (see Figures 5.4a and 5.4b). It represented elements of several of the major traditions incorporated under the Persian aegis—an alternate perspective than, for example, portrayals of the individualized peoples on the later Persepolis reliefs, but a version of the same message: universal empire. It is stunning in its execution, symbolism, and internationalism. Integrating an Assyrian-styled posture and wings, an Elamite robe and hairstyle, and an Egyptian crown, the winged figure is a hybrid, an internationalizing construct of a sort otherwise not extensively known during the Achaemenid period.

Figure 5.4a The winged figure from Gate R. Courtesy of David Stronach (Stronach 1978, Plate 44).

Figure 5.4b Drawing of the winged figure from Gate R. Courtesy of David Stronach (after Stronach 1978, Figure 25).

There were originally at least four such figures, of which only a single one survived, from the eastern door jamb of the northeast doorway of Gate R. This figure's significance remains enigmatic: whom and what was the winged figure meant to represent? If the figure was intended as a symbolic amalgam of a young empire, the fact that similar representations are not widely known is striking. Is the dearth of similar imagery an accident of archaeological preservation? Was the figure itself an experiment that failed to take elsewhere? Or was the figure representative of something unique to Cyrus or to his capital, Pasargadae?

The inclusion of the Egyptian headdress is curious, since Cyrus did not conquer Egypt. Modern commentators have noted the same Egyptian motif commonly used in Levantine contexts, thus reflective of Cyrus' rule of these regions. It seems likely there was

more to it. The winged figure was completed during the time of
Cambyses or even Darius I, when Egypt was part of the Empire.
Whether one assigns it to the reign of Cyrus, Cambyses, or Darius
has major ramifications for its interpretation. Drawings of the
figure from the nineteenth century show a copy of an inscription
(CMa) above it, "I am Cyrus the King, an Achaemenid," as illus-
trated in Figure 5.4c. This inscription, and its complement CMc,
are believed to have been installed during Darius I's time, and it is
important for our understanding of his program that incorporated
Cyrus into his own dynastic inheritance; this is discussed further
in Appendix C. It is an odd inscription in a number of ways beyond
its placement: scholars have hesitated to characterize it as a label for

Figure 5.4c Drawing of winged figure from Gate R as seen in the early
nineteenth century, with inscription still extant, by Sir Robert Ker
Porter, *Travels in Georgia, Persia, Armenia, Ancient Babylonia*, Vol. I,
1821, opposite p. 492.

the figure shown, particularly since the same inscription, in five extant and several additional copies presumed, was found elsewhere at Pasargadae and not always associated with a figure. Nonetheless, its function as a label is hard to resist outright, and, in any event, one cannot help wondering to what extent the figure's placement itself at Gate R was deliberately suggestive, if not explicitly significant or signifying.

The suggestion of the figure as a "mythologized Cyrus" ought to be considered a distinct possibility, not just from the perspective of its placement at the gate or of a cult offered to deceased kings but also as to its significance as a literally larger-than-life representation of an Achaemenid king: a figure more than just the intermediary between king and god but one who partook of the divine sphere. The intersecting symbolism seems unlikely to be a coincidence, regardless of whether the Pasargadae figure was commissioned by Darius as part of his own program, or whether Darius adopted the same gesture for his own relief sculptures at Bisotun and Naqsh-i Rustam.[28] Though the full significance of any shared symbolism among these images remains to be discerned, it is possible that the figure (alongside the other imagery discussed in this chapter) represented yet another instance of a deliberately evoked ambiguity mediating the space—and at times when there was no space— between royal and divine.

Palaces S and P

The structure that modern excavators labeled Palace S, also called the Audience Hall, lies approximately three-fourths of a mile northeast of the Tomb of Cyrus, roughly halfway between Gate R and Palace P. It was a rectangular, hypostyle hall surrounded by columned porticoes on all sides. The main hall consisted of two rows of four columns each, while each side portico also had two rows of columns. Fragments of some the capitals indicate their animal form—on parallel with capitals at Persepolis later; at Palace S these included at least two types of lions (one horned), bulls, and horses. The one intact column indicates a height of at least 43 feet for the column itself; through the 1960s it was adorned with a stork's nest, as shown in Figure 5.5a. This is in marked contrast to a cut into one side of the lower column, evidence of an attempt to topple it.

Of the original eight stone rectangular columns (*antae*) flanking the four porticoes (Figure 5.5b), only three damaged ones remain. Through the mid-nineteenth century each still had a copy of the trilingual CMa inscription; today only one, the southeast portico, remains with the inscription intact (Figure 5.5c). The four entrances of the main hall were adorned with Assyrian-inspired

Figure 5.5a   Palace S remains from the north, with stork's nest on column. Courtesy of David Stronach (Stronach 1978, Plate 50b).

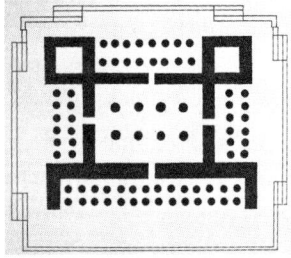

Figure 5.5b   Palace S schematic. Courtesy of David Stronach (after Stronach 1978, Figure 27b).

Figure 5.5c Palace S, top of anta with CMa inscription from the southeast portico. Courtesy of David Stronach (Stronach 1978, Plate 64a).

reliefs, now mostly lost. Nonetheless, based on the Assyrian parallels the remains are readily identifiable as an *ugallu* (a lion-demon), a smiting-god figure, an *apkallu* (a fish-man, associated with legendary Mesopotamian sages), and a bull man, as shown in Figure 5.5d and Figure 5.5e. However, these were not simple copies of Assyrian reliefs. Modifications to the arrangement of the figures in the Pasargadae reliefs differ in some important aspects, as for example, the pairing of the bull man and fish-garbed figure is not evident in Assyrian examples.[29] Since none of the Pasargadae reliefs is completely preserved, the extent of the Persian modifications is uncertain, as is how they fit into a wider ideological program.

The structure called Palace P (Figure 5.6a) is roughly 250 × 138 feet in size. It included a rectangular hypostyle hall with five rows of six columns, a long portico with two rows of twenty columns, and a shorter portico with two rows of twelve columns; see Figure 5.6b

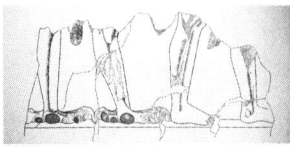

Figure 5.5d Drawing of relief fragments from Palace S: lion demon and smiting god(?). Courtesy of David Stronach (after Stronach 1978, Figure 34).

Figure 5.5e Relief fragment from Palace S: bull man and *apkallu*. Courtesy of David Stronach (Stronach 1978, Plate 59).

Figure 5.6a Palace P portico, looking southwest. Courtesy of David Stronach (Stronach 1978, Plate 69a).

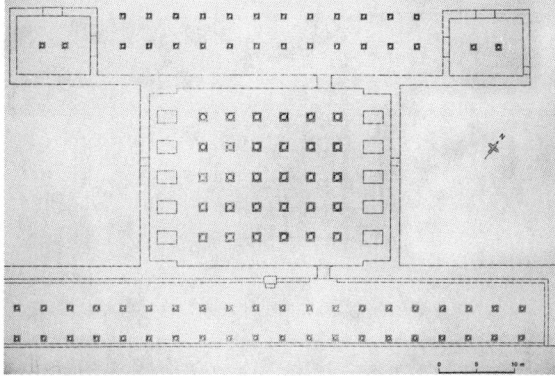

Figure 5.6b Schematic plan of Palace P. Courtesy of David Stronach (Stronach 1978, Figure 41).

for the plan. The designs on the column shafts closely paralleled the same from the Persepolis Treasury, one of many architectural similarities that connect Darius I's later capital with Cyrus'. Only one anta of Palace P survives, on which is also inscribed a copy of the CMa inscription roughly 20 feet above the floor .

Surviving relief fragments from the two doorways that join the central hall to the two porticoes suggest the same scene in four versions, in each of the two jambs of each doorway. Only the lower parts of the figures survive: the king, followed by an attendant, leaving the main hall. Both figures wear the pleated robe associated with Persian court garb; similarly, the king bears a scepter and is engraved at larger scale than his attendant—again, anticipating what became typical in Achaemenid portrayals. On the right-hand jamb of the northwest doorway the partial Akkadian and full Elamite versions of the inscription CMc survive: "Cyrus the Great King, an Achaemenid," inscribed on balancing oblique folds of the robe (see Figure 5.6c). An Old Persian version is assumed to have been inscribed above those, but it is no longer extant. On the facing jamb, only the beginning of the Akkadian version survives.

Figure 5.6c   Relief fragment from Palace P, right-hand jamb of northwest doorway showing Cyrus and an attendant. Courtesy of David Stronach (Stronach 1978, Plate 80).

Paradise Found, the Royal Garden

The structures called Palace S and Palace P were remarkable in their design as open buildings with four-sided access. The distance between the main structures seems odd at first but becomes comprehensible when the layout is considered as a park. The structures' elegant colonnades and deep porticoes were at home in the intentionally park-like setting and served as entrances to what has been called the Royal Garden, a setting that recalls at least in parallel the famous Hanging Gardens of Babylon that—in one version of the story—Nebuchadnezzar built for his Median wife.[30] The Pasargadae gardens would have included a variety of trees, flowers, and other sorts of vegetation, so that the structures would have been nestled within, or viewed from, a lush setting: a powerful testament to the planning and vision that went into this project. It has become clear that Pasargadae, or at least the central quadrant of it, was not meant to be an urbanized setting, nor did it become one later. David Stronach's extensive work there in the 1960s, and more recently that of Rémy Boucharlat and his team, allow a special look into Cyrus' master plan and its implementation. Cyrus' engineers harnessed the nearby Pulvar River, roughly a half mile from Pasargadae's center, the water necessary for the site's lifeblood. Construction of a canal from the Pulvar was likely the very first act at the site, which, as far as can be determined, had not been occupied previously. Further, evidence has been found for dams along the Pulvar. At least two of these dams date to the Achaemenid period; they are of high-quality, polished stone masonry (the same sort found within Pasargadae), which makes sense in light of the necessity of regulating the volume of water entering the canal and water courses. A well-watered and lush landscape, striking already in an otherwise semi-arid area, depended on the season and river flow.

The water courses of the Royal Garden alone, not counting any other waterworks, are estimated to have run more than 3,600 feet. Stone-lined channels with dressed upper surfaces, either flush or just above the surrounding ground level, were intentionally exposed to view and, thus, part of one's experience of the site. Two pavilions (labeled A and B in the plan of Figure 5.1b, one at the southeast corner and the other near the southwest corner, along with the structure called Palace P appear to have served as the formal points of entry. It is worth reiterating that the modest but elegant structures described above were notably placed at the edges of the central gardens, an arrangement that reveals that the gardens themselves were the main feature. Geomagnetic surveys have revealed a large trapezoidal pool, fed by the canal, that measured more than 650 feet in length and 160 feet in width, and was roughly 5 feet deep. Sluice gates testify to the pool's utilitarian value also in regulating the water.

The Persians were renowned for their parks and gardens, called in Old Persian *paradayadā*. Considering the plan of Pasargadae's

Royal Garden, it seems plain that Cyrus was the source of this renown. Subsequent Achaemenid kings and elites made their creation and preservation a priority, not just in the main capitals but in the provinces as well. The Old Persian word *paradayadā* (Elamite *partetaš*) is understood as the origin of the Greek word *paradeisos*, hence the typical English translation "paradise" for these large and elaborate parks, but the original word's translation and meaning are disputed. The garden setting makes one confident that the beauty and tranquility of the place—a "pleasant retreat," as some modern scholars translate *paradayadā*—was clearly meant to be emphasized.

Cyrus' construction of his capital entirely around, in effect, just such a *paradayadā* testifies to that fact. A bit over a century after Cyrus, Artaxerxes II copied this approach when he built at Susa a huge, new palace complex (covering roughly ten acres) set among lavish gardens; the Old Persian inscription reads, "By the grace of Auramazda, I built this palace in my lifetime as a *paradayadā*."[31] These "pleasant retreats" could vary in scale and were not proprietary to the king. In fact, similar works by satraps and other elites throughout the Empire indicate that the custody or ownership of a *paradayadā* was a marker of sophistication and imperial prestige. Greek literature contains several mentions of them. Xenophon recorded an anecdote of Cyrus the Younger giving a tour to an astonished Spartan general of the former's own *paradeisos* near Sardis, which, Cyrus made sure to note, he himself frequently worked to beautify it.[32]

The Zendan and the Tall-i Takht

Much work remains to be done at Pasargadae to better understand the site and its significance. Two structures highlight this. The first is a tower roughly 275 yards to the northeast of the central complex, the so-called Zendan-i Sulaiman ("Prison of Solomon"), or the

Zendan for short (Figures 5.7a and 5.7b). The structure is a square, tall tower (roughly 46 feet in height), buttressed at the corners, with three rows of false windows on three sides of the building. The structure's purpose is still debated, along with that of its close analog, the so-called Ka'bah-i Zardusht ("Cube of Zoroaster") at Naqsh-i Rustam, the burial site of seven Achaemenid kings from Darius I onward, near Persepolis. Posited explanations for both structures include a fire temple, an annex or accompaniment of the royal tombs, or a place of other religious or ritual significance.

The second example is the Tall-i Takht (called Takht-i Marar-i Sulaiman, "Throne of the Mother of Solomon"), labeled "Platform" in Figure 5.1a, on the northern edge of Pasargadae (Figures 5.8a and 5.8b). Remains there indicate several courses of brick for an

Figure 5.7a The Zendan, northwest façade. Courtesy of David Stronach (Stronach 1978, Plate 96a).

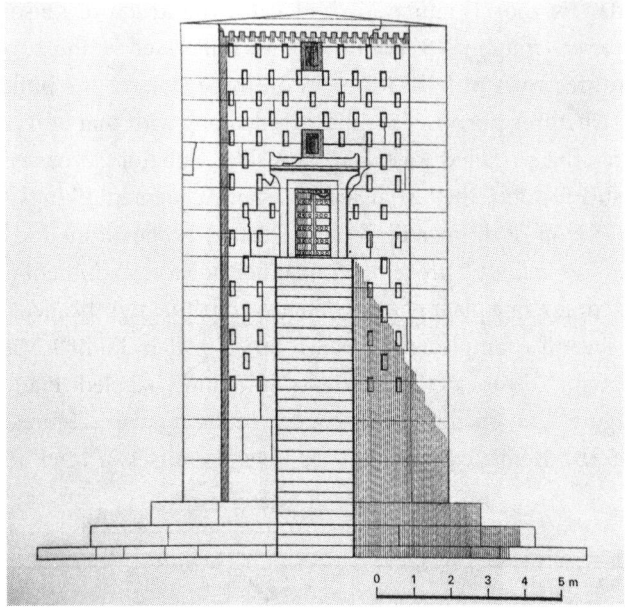

Figure 5.7b Drawing of the Zendan, reconstruction of northwest elevation. Courtesy of David Stronach (Stronach 1978, Figure 57).

elevated palace, presumably Cyrus', that was never finished, so its purpose and function remain a mystery. The names of many of these structures stem from the Sasanian or early Islamic periods, when their Achaemenid origins had been mostly forgotten. Instead, people of the time associated the impressive remains with Zoroastrian tradition or the ancient prophets, and legends associated with Solomon were quite popular.[33]

Exit Pasargadae

No residential quarter has yet been excavated in the area. Some of the small finds discovered thus far, however, give flavor to the

Figure 5.8a The remains of the Tall-i Takht as seen from the southwest. Courtesy of David Stronach (Stronach 1978, Plate 3a).

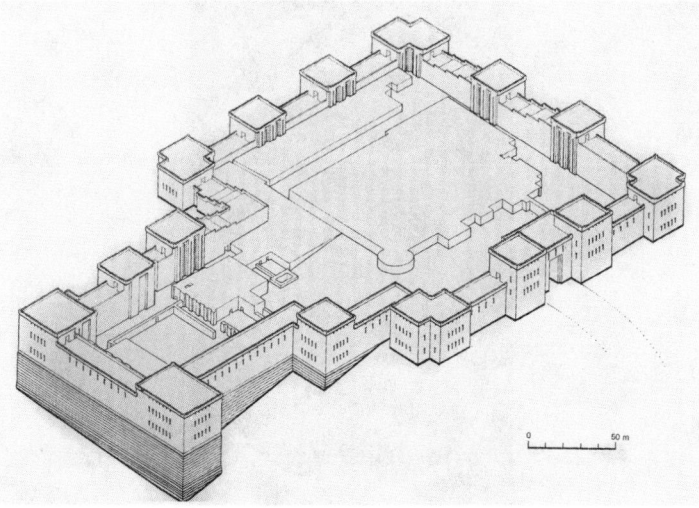

Figure 5.8b Drawing of reconstruction of the Tall-i Takht. Courtesy of David Stronach (Stronach 1978, Figure 75).

occupancy of the site, such as ibex-headed bracelets of a common type (found at multiple places from the Achaemenid period) and several elegant, fine-mesh, golden earrings (Figures 5.9a and 5.9b). Last but certainly not least among such finds is a fragmentary alabaster vessel with the partial cuneiform inscription "King of Babylon" (*šar Bābili*, Figure 5.9c). This sort of find allows ample room for speculation. Was this a commemorative piece for the new king of Babylon, Cyrus, after his conquest of Nabonidus? Or was it inscribed for one of Cyrus' successors, all kings of Babylon as well? Or was it a trophy from Cyrus' conquest itself, perhaps belonging to a previous king of Babylon or member of his court?

Other finds from the site lend themselves to wider discussions. A prominent example is the significance that should (or should

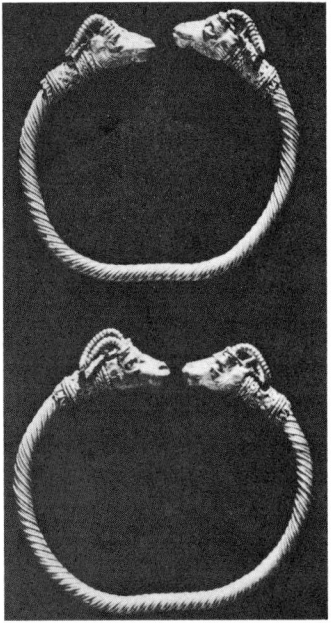

Figure 5.9a Ibex-headed bracelets from Pasargadae. Courtesy of David Stronach (Stronach 1978, Plate 147a).

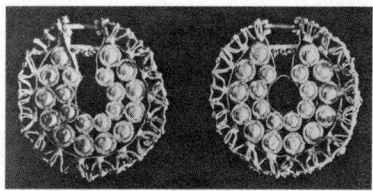

Figure 5.9b Gold earrings with sixteen freestanding rosettes from Pasargadae. Courtesy of David Stronach (Stronach 1978, Plate 149a).

Figure 5.9c Alabaster jar fragments with remains of cuneiform signs reading "King of Babylon." Courtesy of David Stronach (Stronach 1978, Plate 167d).

not) be attached to elaborate rosette patterns found in many places at Pasargadae, which has engendered much discussion in the modern literature. From Cyrus' tomb, the remains of a lower half of a raised disc discovered on the apex of the triangular gable over the cella's doorway is a unique feature in Achaemenid sculpture, as reconstructed in Figure 5.10. The sculpture represents a small, central rosette of twelve petals, surmounted by a larger rosette of twenty-four petals, and these aligned with the points of twenty-four rays of the outer register. Its prominent place on an otherwise

Figure 5.10 Reconstruction of probable form of rosette from the Tomb of Cyrus. Courtesy of David Stronach.

mostly unadorned monument reasonably suggests a symbolic meaning, but what it might symbolize is open to debate.

Among the fragments from the Zendan's broken doorway, one includes three rosettes on a roughly 1.5-foot, white limestone fragment each containing a thin, pointed sepal between each of the twelve petals, as diagrammed in Figure 5.11. Rosettes also appear upon the robes of the winged figure and other reliefs. It is uncertain when to read significance into their appearance on sculptures: always, sometimes, or never? Rosettes were common decorative elements, certainly not just at Pasargadae. Exemplars

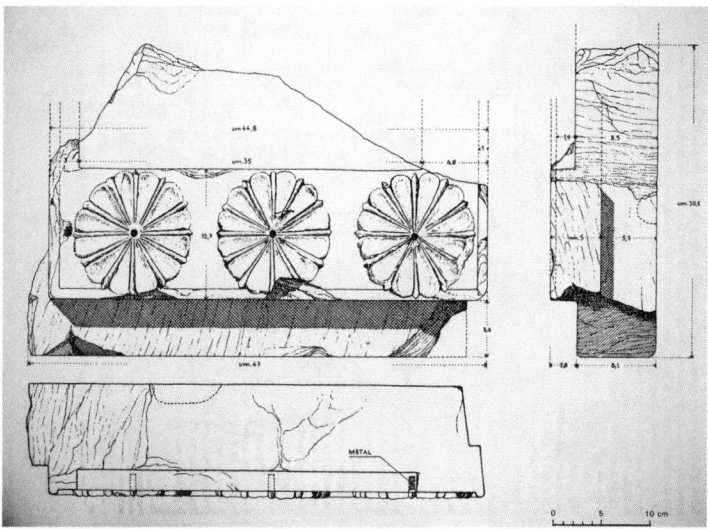

Figure 5.11 Drawings of rosettes on a white limestone fragment, probably from one of the Zendan's door leaves. Courtesy of David Stronach (Stronach 1978, Figure 64).

from Assyria are often without sepals, those used in the west (e.g., Ionia and Greece) with sepals. Both types are found in Achaemenid contexts and, again, it is not always evident whether their use was decorative, symbolic, or both.

Two free-standing plinths at the western end of the enclosure termed the Sacred Precinct, just less than a mile northwest of the Royal Garden area, have also inspired much discussion and multiple interpretations. They are most frequently considered as platforms for fire altars. They both stood initially 7–10 feet high, and the southern one has a surviving staircase; see diagrams in Figure 5.12. Several commentators have noted that fragments from the platforms share similarities with the fire altars portrayed in the tomb reliefs at Naqsh-i Rustam showing the kings' communion with Auramazda.

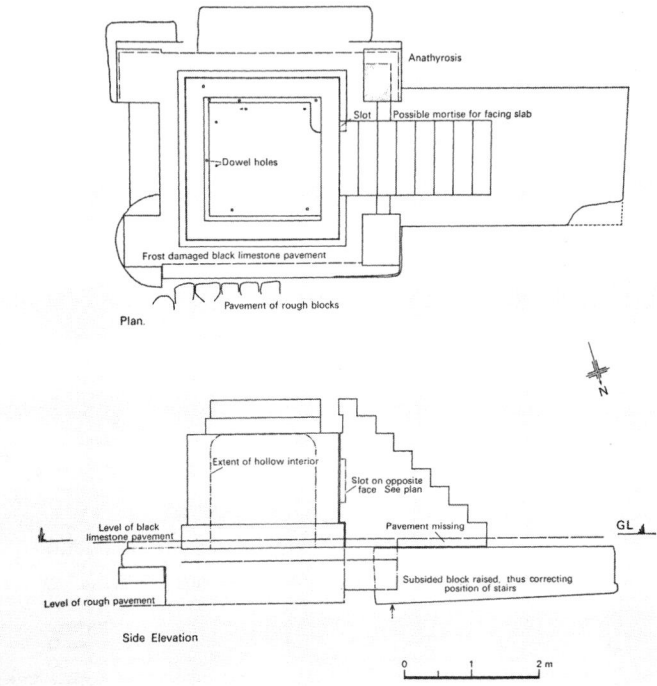

Figure 5.12 Drawing of the Sacred Precinct plinths, plan, and elevation. Courtesy of David Stronach (Stronach 1978, Figure 70).

Cyrus the Polytheist

Where academic discussions of the preceding often intersect is the question of Cyrus' religious proclivities, both with regard to his role as king and with regard to his personal beliefs. Many modern scholars have suggested that Cyrus was an adherent of Mithra, the sun god, in light of numerous connections with the sun god mentioned by ancient authors. That may be, but even if so, it seems unlikely to be the end of it. The literature of these debates is wide-ranging with regard to both its scope and its quality.[34] In a polytheistic society, it is doubly difficult to pin down an individual's personal beliefs, unless he or she has left a direct and explicit record of them. Cyrus did not. As discussed in the previous chapter, Cyrus allowed and encouraged the worship of other gods. Further, he consciously linked himself to them within their indigenous traditions, for example, Yahweh in Judah and Marduk in Babylonia. Cyrus desired to be recognized within these belief systems for purposes of legitimacy. Among the ramifications of Cyrus' efforts toward such, it certainly allows modern interpretations to infer Cyrus' tolerance of other beliefs. That seems a given. In a polytheistic system, especially in the ancient Near East, it is difficult to view otherwise.

In modern scholarship, Achaemenid kings are often described as Zoroastrians, primarily because of the ubiquity of Auramazda (a normalization from the Old Persian spelling of the more commonly used "Ahuramazda" or "Ahura Mazda") in the royal inscriptions from the time of Darius I. This may be an apt characterization on the surface—especially if one focuses only on the ideology as expressed in the royal inscriptions—but it is oversimplified and one that does not do justice to the variety of evidence. Scholars instead have taken to term the system as espoused in Achaemenid royal inscriptions as Mazdaean (emphasizing Auramazda) rather than Zoroastrian per se. Zoroastrianism is an age-old religion that did not reach its peak until the Sasanian period (c. 250–700 CE), and it was not static. Based on teachings of the prophet Zoroaster (the Greek name of Zarathustra), over time Zoroastrianism became strongly dualistic, a phenomenon detectable in Darius I's emphasis on the truth and antipathy against the Lie, as Old Persian *drauga* is often translated into English and, indeed, capitalized as an anathema. Darius' worldview thus closely paralleled Zoroastrian dualism as manifested in the cosmic struggle between Auramazda and Ahriman (also called Angra Mainyu). Thus, while the evidence from Darius I's reign is easy to discuss in its connections to Zoroastrian beliefs, for Cyrus it is not.

The date of Zoroaster himself is also still debated, with estimates ranging from c. 1800 to the sixth century BCE. Zoroaster's relevance to Achaemenid history as a living person is dependent on one's assessment about when he lived. The early dating is based on Zoroaster's surviving hymns, the *Gathas*, and their presumed age based on linguistic analysis of the words in their Indo-Iranian context; written copies date centuries later than the hymns are assumed to have been composed. The late date for Zoroaster stems from a Greek tradition that dates Zoroaster 258 years before Alexander the Great. That 258 years can be measured in various ways. It has been taken to mean 258 years before Alexander's birth, or 258 years before his overthrow of the Persian Empire. To add to the mix, or perhaps better worded, to take away from it, for many scholars questions about the of date of Zoroaster are nonstarters. Some doubt that Zoroaster ever existed, that he was a literary creation (or amalgam) lending credibility to an evolving belief system. A central problem in establishing a mid-first-millennium historical context for the Zoroastrian scriptures, the much later compilation of the Avesta, is that none of it contains any clear reference to the Medes or the Achaemenid Persians.

However one defines a Zoroastrian stream of tradition, the Achaemenid kings were instrumental in shaping it. Instead of forcing the Achaemenids into a preconceived Zoroastrian system, consider rather the Achaemenids' foundational impact on a still nascent and evolving tradition—thus the adjective Mazdaean, rather than Zoroastrian, as noted above. Dating Zoroaster to 258 years before Alexander's overthrow of the Persian Empire, which has achieved acceptance by many scholars, placed him in the early sixth century. This would make him a rough contemporary with Cyrus the Great. This author will leave the question of Zoroaster's dating open, as certainty on the matter is not currently possible, and any such a dating has enormous consequences. For example, such a chronological schema would throw into greater relief Cyrus' dynastic origins within the geographic focal point of the Elamite-Persian ethnogenesis and the clearly Mazdaean inclinations of Darius I and his successors. But such dichotomies, while useful in general overviews, oversimplify the complex interplay among Elamite, Iranian, and Mesopotamian traditions that were manifested in western Iran in the sixth and fifth centuries BCE. The documentary record from within a generation of Cyrus' own time, especially as manifested in the Persepolis Fortification Archive, has demonstrated beyond doubt the state-sponsored support of a multitude of deities. This included not only Iranian gods but even privileged (in quantitative terms) Elamite gods, at least in the immediate region of Persepolis. Well over a dozen Iranian, Elamite, and Mesopotamian deities were worshipped in the core of the Empire, testimony to the continuity and compatibility of several traditions.[35] Auramazda is attested in the Fortification documents as well. Viewed simply from that archive's perspective, and measured only quantitatively, Auramazda was a seemingly minor deity. This phenomenon serves as a useful reminder—and powerful juxtaposition—to the unique and compelling prominence of Auramazda in the corpus of royal inscriptions. An important corollary to this is that the PFA offers overwhelming evidence that the Achaemenid kings' emphasis on Ahuramazda did not displace older or local gods.

It is beyond doubt that Darius I's emphasis on Auramazda was effectively a new phenomenon in the extant record. Auramazda was ubiquitous in Darius' inscriptions, a powerful indicator of Darius' Iranian sensibilities. The Elamite scribe(s) of the Bisotun Inscription differentiated Auramazda as "the god of the Iranians." The gloss in the Elamite version, even though omitted in the accompanying Old Persian and Babylonian versions, suggests, as does the entire inscriptional corpus, that Auramazda may have been a relatively recent introduction to western Iran, at least among its non-Iranian (i.e., Elamite) inhabitants.[36] When one considers the geopolitical context, that all these elite Persian families and clans were well intertwined by the mid-sixth century, it seems reasonable to assume that if Cyrus was not a Mazdaean on the same plane as Darius, he was certainly familiar with, and comfortable with, its tenets. Among other indications, it is useful to recall here that he named one of his daughters Atossa, in origin an Avestan name: *Hutaosā*.

The disparate threads are impossible to reconcile at present. To conclude this section, it may be helpful simply to reiterate the hurdles to solving this puzzle: the lack of Cyrus' own written testimony from Iran, the uncertainties with regard to the date of Zoroaster and the Gathas, the complete lack within early Avestan tradition of identifiable geopolitical markers, and so on. That debate will continue. It was not only Cyrus' achievements on the battlefield that were fundamental to a lasting empire. His judgment and acumen were likewise, as manifested in his successful integration of various belief systems, his vision of an inclusive and encompassing ideology, and his (literally) foundational contributions to a new world capital. These left powerful legacies both for this immediate successors and for posterity, as we will see in the next chapter.

6

Legacies

No one among the Persians would ever compare himself to Cyrus.

—Herodotus 3.160

Among foreign peoples even now, it is spoken and sung that Cyrus was most handsome in person, most generous in spirit, most dedicated to learning, and most desirous of glory, so that he endured any danger and undertook any work for acclaim.

—Xenophon, *Cyropaedia* 1.2

Cyrus' legacy began in his own lifetime, as exhibited by multiple testimonies throughout this book. His status of course loomed quite large among his successors, as the opening quotes to this chapter reveal. Cyrus' death and its various retellings fed the legend even in antiquity.

The Death of Cyrus

Babylonian documents indicate that Cyrus died sometime in August 530. Cambyses was recorded as king in these same sources by the end of that month. These bureaucratic records, or contracts, were written on clay tablets and examples have been found from several sites throughout Babylonia. Since they were not designed to include tendentious political statements, they were not royal inscriptions, they are considered reliable guides on chronology. The records were marked by month and year of the current king's reign, sometimes including a specific numeric date. However, such documents rarely, if ever, provided any context for the king's passing or his successor's accession. In other words, while these documents afford some precision on *when* Cyrus died, they offer no details on *how* or *where* he died.

As is clichéd by now, the Greek traditions form the basis of the narrative. Before the extant versions of Cyrus' death are surveyed, a brief review of his career is in order. There are significant gaps in our knowledge of Cyrus' reign, c. 559 to August of 530. The first several years are almost a complete blank in the historical record. It seems reasonable to place Cyrus' marriage to Cassandane and the birth of Cambyses in this period (i.e., the early to mid-550s), if not before. Cyrus must have spent the early years of his reign both expanding and consolidating his power within Iran, endeavors that would have included alliances (some via diplomatic marriages) or conquest, or both. Whether Cyrus planned his early moves with an eye toward future expansion, or was reacting to external events, cannot be ascertained. If Cyrus' early conquests were reactive, he became swiftly adept at capitalizing. Cyrus had conquered Media by 550/549, Lydia by the mid-540s, and Babylon in 539. Of these three, only the conquest of Babylon may be dated with any precision: Cyrus entered the city on October 29, 539.

There are scattered and contradictory references in later Greek sources to Cyrus campaigning in the east and northeast, what became the provinces of Carmania, Drangiana, Areia, Arachosia, and Gandara—modern Afghanistan and Baluchistan. But the chronology and even sequence of these episodes are uncertain. After the conquest of Lydia, Herodotus noted that Harpagus devastated "lower Asia" while Cyrus himself did likewise to "upper Asia": a vague descriptor that could refer to a lot of places beyond the Anatolian plateau. The eastern territories were no doubt of greater import to Cyrus than Greek Ionia, the conquest of which was delegated to Harpagus. Herodotus had emphasized the great importance of campaigns against Babylon, Egypt (which ultimately fell to Cambyses), the Bactrians, and the Scythians. It is during one or more of these campaigns that Cyrus founded several cities and fortresses beyond Pasargadae, one legacy of several empire builders throughout history. The largest of these appears to have been Cyropolis along the Jaxartes (see Map 3), a city about which nothing else is known beyond allusions in authors describing Alexander the Great's campaigns.[1] It is safe to assume that Cyrus made more than one journey into these regions, whether at the head of an army or with a large entourage tantamount to an itinerant court, as later Achaemenid kings did.

Greek authors situated Cyrus' death while he was on campaign in the extreme northeast; our main sources are once again Herodotus and Ctesias. It will not surprise the reader that their accounts differed in important details—in fact, they differed in essentially all details except the campaign's general direction and that Cyrus died from a wound in battle. Herodotus asserted that he has relayed the "most plausible" (Greek *pithanōtatos*) version of the different stories about Cyrus' death. We do not know on what criteria Herodotus based his judgment to vet the stories of Cyrus' end, but Herodotus' remark is an important reminder that there was more than one story in circulation. That may also be juxtaposed with Herodotus' similar comment about Cyrus' life story, that he had relied on those Persians who would tell him the truth more so than those whose purpose was to glorify Cyrus' achievements.[2]

Herodotus set Cyrus' death during the campaign against the Massagetae, a Scythian people who lived beyond the Araxes, usually identified with the Jaxartes, the Syr Darya in modern Kazakhstan; see Map 3. It is a Greek cautionary tale on the limits and consequences of hubris, to which even Cyrus was answerable. The tale—and not only Herodotus' version of it—also tapped into Greek mythology of the Amazons, a legendary race of warrior women, so the usual caveats must be applied to assessment of a compelling story. The

Massagetae were ruled by a widowed queen, Tomyris, whom Cyrus first attempted to wed, perhaps seeking a diplomatic victory through a dynastic marriage. When rebuffed, Cyrus turned to the military option. As part of the campaign, Cyrus bridged the Araxes—Herodotus used the verb "to yoke" (Greek *zeugnunai*), as one would oxen—with pontoon bridges that even included towers. This was a major feat of engineering that anticipated Darius I's crossing of the Bosporus to battle the European Scythians and Xerxes' crossing of the Hellespont to invade Greece. It also anticipated a key component of Cyrus' and his successors' legacy in later traditions.

In Greek literature, these acts of subjugating natural phenomena, in this case bodies of water, were highly symbolic. They were violations of the natural world, and the negative consequences that come from surpassing boundaries were a stock theme of imperial overreach. In other words, these engineering marvels were not simply impressive works to get the king and his armies where they needed to go. In Greek literary terms, they were acts of profound hubris: the transgression of natural boundaries put the kings on the level of gods, a dangerous path.[3] One wonders how much Cyrus viewed the impressive operation simply beyond getting from point A to point B. Regardless, Tomyris warned him to stay within his territory or pay the price.

In council with his advisors, Cyrus instead took the advice of none other than Croesus, who by this point in Herodotus' narrative had become a "wise advisor," another one of Herodotus' favorite literary devices. Croesus was thus still hanging around the court, popping up at sometimes surprising moments—from a cynical view, whenever useful for Herodotus' narrative—to dispense sage(?) advice. Croesus here may perhaps be considered rather a "wise guy," who advised Cyrus that if he did not attack, not only would the Massagetae pursue him and overthrow his empire—which seems a bit extreme in itself—but also that Cyrus would lose face to a woman. That, of course, could not be borne. The literary context is ironic on several levels, primarily a nice touch in that it was Croesus' own decision to cross a river and engage Cyrus that led to his own disastrous defeat.[4] This is great stuff, but also, again, difficult to disentangle from literature and legend.

And there is more. Before battle commenced, Cyrus dispatched his son Cambyses homeward, with Croesus in tow, with the explicit command that Croesus be treated kindly. Herodotus left unsaid that this was done so that Croesus could advise (plague?) Cambyses later in the narrative. At the appropriately ominous time after Cyrus had crossed the bridge—that is, transgressed the boundary—Cyrus then had a dream foretelling him of the rise of Darius. In the dream, Darius appeared as the figure-in-winged-disk, an important symbol in Achaemenid ideology that is usually identified as the god Auramazda in close communion with the king, for example, as shown in Figure 6.1 and Figures C.1 and C.2.[5]

Figure 6.1 Top register of tomb relief from Naqsh-i Rustam showing king (Darius II) and the figure in the winged disk. Courtesy of the Oriental Institute of the University of Chicago.

Herodotus himself was undoubtedly familiar with this symbol; the winged disk image figured in a variety of Achaemenid sculptures, from monumental reliefs to cylinder seals. In this anecdote the Greek historian presented it both as a harbinger of Cyrus' end and as a repurposed symbol of Achaemenid dominion, the wings overshadowing (as per Herodotus' description) both Asia and Europe. Not one to ignore divine messages, Cyrus dispatched Hystaspes, Darius' father who was one of Cyrus' generals, back to Parsa to forestall any perceived threat. Thus, in this version of the story Cyrus sent back home the crown prince, an important advisor, and a high-ranking official—along with an indeterminate number of troops with them—before what Herodotus also termed the largest battle ever fought to that time.

The Persians' initial victory over the Massagetae, who were led initially by Tomyris' son Spargapises, was thanks to another stock theme in Greek literature: a trick. The trick here involved a drunken banquet. The Persians laid out a great feast and then feigned a retreat. When the Massagetae raided their camp, their entire force became drunk on the wine "abandoned" by the Persians. The Persians returned, killed many of the Massagetae, and captured the rest. Among the prisoners was Spargapises. Tomyris demanded Spargapises' return with the threat that otherwise she would give Cyrus his fill of blood, since Cyrus seemed ravenous for it. Cyrus in any event did release Spargapises upon the latter's own request, but Spargapises immediately committed suicide before the question of what would happen to him was even posed. When Cyrus was killed in the subsequent engagement, Tomyris was true to her word: she cast Cyrus' head into a container filled with blood, an ignominious end for the great conqueror. The staying power of this story was demonstrated when, in the early seventeenth century, the Flemish artist and diplomat Peter Paul Rubens envisioned the scene in one of his paintings (Figure 6.2). Cyrus in the end faced retribution for his hubris. And, although Herodotus never explicitly said so, it was implied: Croesus had his revenge.

Figure 6.2 Queen Tomyris and the Head of Cyrus. Oil painting by Peter Paul Rubens (1577–1640).

National Trust Photo Library / Art Resource, NY.

Ctesias' account of Cyrus' end is similar to Herodotus' only in the setting of a far-flung location. Cyrus campaigned against the Derbices, who were ruled by a certain Amoraios. Surviving details are sparse.[6] During the battle, in which Amoraios' force was supplemented by war elephants, Cyrus was wounded and taken from the field. A large cavalry force led by Cyrus' ally, the Scythian Amorges, rushed to Cyrus' aid and compelled the enemy forces to retreat. Cyrus died from his wound shortly thereafter, but not before making arrangements for the succession. Cambyses was named king.[7] Cyrus' other son, whom Ctesias called Tanyoxarkes— named Bardiya (or Barziya) in Babylonian texts and Smerdis in Herodotus—was named governor of the Bactrians, Chorasmians, Parthians, and Carmanians, whom he freed from tribute. Their half-brothers, Spitakes and Megabernes, Amytis' sons by her first husband Spitamas, were made satraps of other provinces. Cyrus then commanded all of them to obey their mother and to maintain friendly relations with Amorges. This deathbed last will and testament is echoed in Xenophon's *Cyropaedia*, but therein Cyrus, the epitome of the philosopher-king, died in peace, surrounded by family and friends. Xenophon granted his Cyrus the time and opportunity to reflect eloquently on his life, his achievements, arrangements for his burial, and expectations of his sons regarding the succession, among other matters.[8]

Reality and Imagination

Most Greek writers held complementary views of Cyrus as a model of impeccable behavior, wisdom, and judicious good government. In effect, he became the idealized philosopher-ruler. Xenophon certainly regarded Cyrus as such, and we see similar indications in Plato. For example, in an often-quoted passage in the *Laws*, Plato lauded Cyrus' generous inclusiveness and insightfulness. Regardless of how much of these portrayed characteristics were grounded in reality, and it seems quite a bit, they formed the basis for the generally positive image of Cyrus that survived in later traditions.[9]

Xenophon's *Cyropaedia* is perhaps the most important text for crystallizing Cyrus' legacy, at least in Western traditions, a work cited several times already in this book. It is certainly the most admiring of our extant sources for Cyrus, which is itself a compelling statement in light of Cyrus' overall positive press. It is also the least useful for historical reconstruction. Xenophon identified Cyrus as the son of Cambyses and Mandane, as did Herodotus, but the similarity in treatment ended there. In Xenophon's version, Cyrus spent his entire youth in Astyages' court, raised as a prince. There is no Sargon Legend, the switched-at-birth or humble origins folktale, in Xenophon's story. Cyrus was born and raised as a presumptive heir of Persia, also ultimately succeeding his uncle as king of the Medes. In the *Cyropaedia*, this uncle was Xenophon's fictional Cyaxeres, Astyages' son, and Cyrus' inevitable succession to the Median throne was accomplished peacefully through marriage to Cyaxeres' daughter.[10] Xenophon, in essence, cleaned up various loose ends evident in Herodotus' and Ctesias' accounts, meaning that if any of what Xenophon knew or gleaned of the historical Cyrus did not fit Xenophon's literary aims, it was ignored. But Xenophon's point was not to write a historical work.

Xenophon's idealized representation of Cyrus' life and reign is thus often impossible to reconcile with the historical record. Xenophon certainly had a lot of experience with Persians, and although the setting of his *Cyropaedia* is mostly fictional, it is a work mined rather for information about Persian customs and culture. The Cyrus within the *Cyropaedia* was a fictionalized one, regardless of how much Xenophon's version echoed the historical Cyrus, the "real Cyrus" if the phrase may be used. It is to be reiterated that the "real Cyrus," with regard to the man's personality and outlook, is unattainable based on our current sources. While not unimportant, it is not those features—which we would obviously welcome if available—that contribute to Cyrus' import in the historical tradition.

Xenophon's Cyrus the Great was modeled on Xenophon's contemporary, Cyrus the Younger, called so to distinguish him from his great-great-great-grandfather who is the subject of this book. The younger Cyrus died about 40 miles north of Babylon, at the Battle of Cunaxa in 401, having led an army of Greek mercenaries in an attempt to overthrow his brother, the king Artaxerxes II. That Cyrus fit into Xenophon's mold of the ideal king and served as a model for Xenophon's Cyrus of the *Cyropaedia*. After the defeat at Cunaxa, the remaining Greek forces' march homeward, with Xenophon as one of the leaders, was immortalized in another of his works, the *Anabasis* (often translated to the effect of *The March Up Country* or *The Return of the 10,000*). Therein is found a paean for Cyrus the Younger, worth quoting even in excerpts:

[Cyrus the Younger was] the man most kingly and worthy to rule of the Persians born since Cyrus the Elder, as agreed by all those known to have intimate knowledge of him. First, while still a child and being educated along with his brother and the other boys, he was considered to be the best of all in everything . . . most respectful among his comrades, more obedient to his elders than those inferior in rank to him. Next, he was the greatest lover of horses and best at handling them. They judged him to be keenest to learn and practice the arts of war, the use of both bow and javelin. When he reached the right age, he was most fond of hunting and putting himself at risk when facing wild animals. Once, when a bear charged him, he did not run away, but grappled with it and was dragged off his horse; he was wounded, and still had the scars, but eventually killed it. . . . He thought it most important that when he made a treaty or agreement or any promise, that he always kept his word. The result was that the cities trusted him and went over to him. . . . It was also obvious that if anyone did him a good or bad turn, he tried to outdo him. Some even reported a prayer of his, that his life might be long enough to outdo those who had done him well or ill in recompense. . . .] However, all agree that he particularly honored those who were good in war. . . . Whenever he noticed someone ready to face danger, he made him a commander of the area he was subjugating and later rewarded him with other gifts too. Like that, the brave became very wealthy, while the cowards were only deemed worthy to be their slaves. Consequently, there were many ready to face danger, when they thought that Cyrus would notice them. Further, if a man was plainly trying to demonstrate his uprightness, he did everything to enable him to live more prosperously than those who were greedy for unjust gain.[11]

The preceding excerpt is in the main a Hellenized, and far more expansive, version of the traits and qualities prized by the Achaemenid kings themselves. We do not have Cyrus the Great's own words for this, but the idea is distilled by Darius I in one of his tomb inscriptions, in which he summarized his own physical and mental capabilities, along with the importance of just rule, all the things appropriate to the proper exercise of kingship. After several lines extolling his righteousness and intellectual discernment, Darius continued:

> Moreover this is my ability, that my body is strong. As a fighter I am a good fighter. At once my intelligence stands in its place, whether I see a rebel or not. Both by intelligence and by command I then regard myself as superior to panic, when I see a rebel just as when I do not see (one). . . . As a horseman I am a good horseman. As an archer I am a good archer, both on foot and on horseback. As a spearman I am a good spearman, both on foot and on horseback. These are the skills that Auramazda has bestowed upon me and I have had the strength to bear them. By the grace of Auramazda, what has been done by me, I have done with these skills that Auramazda has bestowed upon me.[12]

A related example is found in the final chapter of Herodotus' history, a Persianized version of the Greek motif that from soft lands came soft men.[13] No surprise, Cyrus was the hero of the anecdote. To the suggestion that the Persians, now preeminent among nations, could leave Parsa and choose or take any region they wished in which to live, Cyrus responded with a cautionary note. The Persians' home territory made them who they were, and to emigrate to a "softer" (i.e., easier) land would risk their losing the advantages—toughness and martial superiority—that their own harsher environment gave them, and instead of ruling others they themselves would become ruled. Cyrus' argument of course won the day.

The qualities that Xenophon saw in Cyrus the Younger served as a template, and these were transposed upon the already-sterling reputation of Cyrus the Great, thus portrayed in the *Cyropaedia*. But regardless of the factual accuracy of the comparison, the Cyrus of the *Cyropaedia* was in the main Xenophon's vessel to explore questions of leadership and good government. These themes were ongoing conversations among Greek writers of the Classical period, and any study of the *Cyropaedia* ought first to be considered in that context. Cyrus was a natural choice as an exemplar for such a topic, by Xenophon's time already well over a century had passed since Cyrus' death—and his legacy made him both a respected and admired figure even among the Empire's enemies and rivals. Cyrus had become both ideal ruler and ideal father figure to all his subjects, free and slave, a categorization that recalls Herodotus' famous maxim that the Persians regarded Darius as a merchant (Greek *kapēlos*), Cambyses as a despot (Greek *despotēs*), and Cyrus as a father (Greek *patēr*).[14]

Xenophon applied this portrayal of Cyrus in his other works as well, a template for discourses on political philosophy. Another example of this occurred in his *Oeconomicus*, a treatise on estate (and life) management. Cyrus' imperial organization was referenced by Socrates in that work as the model for an effective estate-holder, to explore how virtue and restraint are necessary moral foundations of both successful household and empire, further juxtaposing the equally important (and noble) arts of war and of cultivation.[15] Xenophon's portrayal of Cyrus the Great, and the popularity and staying power of this positive image of Cyrus perhaps did more than anything else to burnish Cyrus' legacy. Put another way, to understand the portrayal of Cyrus in the Western tradition, it helps immensely to understand Xenophon, or, at least, Xenophon's philosophy and worldview as distilled through his characterization of Cyrus.

Cyrus the Great's legacy looms large in the biblical tradition as well, as touched on briefly in Chapter 4. Cyrus was a savior figure, literally a messiah ("anointed") figure in Isaiah:

> Thus says the Lord his anointed, to Cyrus, whose right hand I have grasped to subdue nations before him and ungird the loins of kings, to open doors before him so that gates may not be

closed. I will go before you, and level the mountains, I will break in pieces the doors of bronze, and cut asunder the bars of iron. I will give you the treasures of darkness and the hoards in secret places, that you may know that it is I, the Lord, the God of Israel, who calls you by your name.

The passage quoted above viewed in Cyrus a new David, who five centuries earlier ruled the Judean kingdom at its height in the Levant. Isaiah prophesied that Yahweh would take Cyrus by the hand and lead him to victory over all nations. This is, of course, reminiscent of Marduk and Cyrus in the Cyrus Cylinder: "Marduk caused him (i.e., Cyrus) to take the road to Babylon, and like a friend and companion he walked at his side."[16]

Isaiah also proclaimed, in a similarly prophetic vein, the appearance of Yahweh's chosen servant who will bring justice throughout the earth, "a light to the nations." This passage also resonates with the message of the Cyrus Cylinder. More directly, it parallels the explicit mention of Cyrus in subsequent chapters: he fulfilled the prophetic word; he restored Judah, Jerusalem, and the temple; and he brought glory to Yahweh.[17] However, the "chosen servant" in that passage is not identified, and biblical scholars debate the servant's identity in these and related chapters within Isaiah. Prophetic contexts are inevitably vague and opaque. Nonetheless, this is compelling stuff, certainly as read within the confines of the Judean tradition but even more so when considered on parallel with the Cyrus Cylinder. Also as part of the mix, the date of composition of Isaiah, as is the case for much of the Hebrew Bible, is much debated. Most consider the mention of Cyrus the Great as the terminus post quem. Several elements of the text suggest a date of composition within the Achaemenid period, if not during the reign of Cyrus himself, though the earliest surviving manuscript dates centuries later.

Cyrus' victory and the dispensations granted to the Judeans fit well within a rubric of an overarching, tolerant approach— regardless of motive or belief system. Among specialists, Cyrus' motives for returning deported gods (cult statues) and people are generally understood as practical as they were altruistic—they could be both.[18] We would not expect royal inscriptions like the Cyrus Cylinder to dwell on the negative, or on any harsh measures in the conquest and imposition of order. For example, recall that the Persian-Babylonian battle at Opis was not mentioned in the Cyrus Cylinder, and we would not know about it save for the brief but important reference in the Nabonidus chronicle.

In the Cyrus Cylinder, instead, Cyrus' peaceful entry into Babylon was highlighted—a peaceful entry that would not have been possible without the previous work of military force. It is nonetheless noteworthy that, while both Cyrus' Assyrian and Babylonian predecessors included in their display inscriptions many examples of royal beneficence, there is also no shortage of explicit and specific references to wrath, retribution, and destruction. One has to look hard for instances of such attributed to Cyrus, even in external traditions. Arguments from silence are always fraught, but it is difficult to consider this lack of negative portrayals—across multiple traditions—as being without significance.

Recalling Cyrus: Alexander III of Macedon

Cyrus' achievements and legacy shaped the course of world history for the next two centuries. His impact on his Achaemenid successors, his own descendants through his daughter Atossa, has been noted numerous times throughout this book. Starting in 334, the Achaemenid Empire faced the one existential threat it failed to quell, that of the invasion of Alexander III (the Great) of Macedon. Alexander himself went to great lengths to emulate the Empire's founder. Both the Empire's genesis under Cyrus and its fall to Alexander were seminal events, but for different reasons.

Cyrus appeared seemingly out of nowhere, when he conquered much of the known world from the 550s to 530s BCE. Of course, "out of nowhere" is a relative assessment: the modern perspective is deceptive from limited data and uncertain chronologies, as evidenced in previous chapters. Subsequent conquests by Cyrus' successors brought Egypt, Libya, the Sudan, the Indus Valley, and parts of southeastern Europe under Achaemenid territorial control, making what was, already under Cyrus, the largest empire to date even larger. These discrete areas and kingdoms had never before been one territorial unit, one that persisted in its essentials for more than 200 years. Debate will persist how effectively the far-flung peripheral territories were held—to what extent, for example, typical Scythians or Ionian Greeks considered themselves as subject to the Achaemenid king—but that is not of concern herein.

Alexander campaigned throughout the eastern satrapies and into India in the 320s, and it took him a decade to bring this sprawling territory under his control. Unlike Cyrus, Alexander captured an administratively unified unit, no mean feat to conquer and to hold, but in the end his was an ephemeral achievement. Upon his death in 323 this empire splintered into the so-called Hellenistic kingdoms: Antigonid Macedonia, Seleucid Greater Mesopotamia, and Ptolemaic Egypt, along with several small kingdoms in Anatolia and elsewhere. There are few extant records from the time of Alexander himself, despite the fact that he was well prepared to record his own historical importance. He made sure several chroniclers accompanied him on his eastward expedition. These accounts of his generals and staff, lost to us, were tapped by later writers such as Arrian (writing in the second century CE) and Quintus Curtius Rufus (writing in the first century CE), among others, and it is upon these later writers that the history of Alexander is based.

Alexander venerated Cyrus' memory. The lengthy passage from Arrian quoted in the previous chapter demonstrated the regard and concern that Alexander expressed for the tomb of Cyrus and its maintenance. Alexander's disbursements of Persian court garments and accoutrements to his elite guard, the Companions, and other followers as marks of prestige followed the example of Achaemenid rulers, who themselves were renowned even in later periods for their largesse. The honors that Cyrus granted to the Persian women for their role in the battle against Astyages were continued by Alexander. In the *Cyropaedia*, Cyrus was consistently generous, particularly so before his death. Even if Xenophon took creative liberties in specific words and actions, he was well aware of the customs through his association with Cyrus the Younger, and it is hardly a stretch to imagine their origins with Cyrus the Great. An extensive section on Cyrus' disbursal of gifts to several prominent followers and officials ended with the important reflection that not only were the king's gifts of the highest quality, but also they were instantly recognizable. Only the king could give certain tokens, and these of course signified the utmost honor.[19] When the universal monarch gave a token of esteem, people were meant to notice.

Alexander modeled his rule in the newly conquered territories of the Persian Empire on the Achaemenid system, by necessity. During the course of his campaigns, he did not have the time or inclination to reinvent the wheel, and for that matter the Achaemenid governing apparatus and its institutions had worked effectively for two centuries. There are several examples how Alexander modeled his ruling persona on Cyrus in particular, because of the status the Persian Empire's founder had in the tradition. A fine example may be found in a comparison of the respective kings' entries into Babylon after their Mesopotamian conquests. Alexander victoriously entered Babylon in 331 BCE, in the same month, October, that Cyrus did 208 years earlier. Accounts of the historians Arrian and Quintus Curtius Rufus, which emphasized the joy greeting Alexander, have been put forward as examples of the despised rule of the Persians, but this in the main is a misnomer. While there was periodic resentment, resistance, and rebellion against Persian rule, the stereotype of Persian despotic rule has staying power only from that single perspective: applicable in some cases, but not as a general rule.

Alexander's entry into Babylon as a choreographed performance was not much different than that of Cyrus, whom the Babylonians greeted with joy and shining faces.[20] These portrayals were stylized, of course. One might compare the circumstances of Alexander and the Persian king Darius III with Cyrus and Nabonidus. If one were to swap out the respective names in the relevant sources, one would discover consistency and conformity in the program. In other words, Alexander's victorious entry into Babylon, like Cyrus', should be viewed as the voluntary surrender of the city, amid ritualistic acts, as signaling an orderly transfer of power. That same phenomenon had occurred several times in the *longue durée* within Near Eastern traditions. An earlier example still is the Babylonian conquest in 710 by the Assyrian king Sargon, whose example Cyrus himself followed. Cyrus also entered Babylon without a fight, the reception a carefully choreographed entrance that belied the violence that preceded it.

Arrian's and Quintus Curtius' accounts of Alexander's entry into Babylon were unsurprisingly quite different in origin and in form from Babylonian accounts of Cyrus' entry. Although the Greek and Latin accounts record what was in its essentials the same phenomenon, they were neither indigenous nor contemporary, and they were also part of narrative histories. Beneath their own stylized approach, they nevertheless reveal the same pattern. Alexander's victory at Gaugamela in 331, and Darius III's withdrawal to Ecbatana, left the way to Babylon open and undefended. The Persian commander Mazaeus delivered the city to Alexander after negotiations assured a peaceful transition. By extension, a traditional reception was arranged for Alexander, one that hearkened back to Cyrus and his Babylonian and Assyrian predecessors. Alexander's entry into the city likewise culminated in Alexander's due respect to the Babylonian god Marduk (Bel) and his temple. This continuity, or renewal, is even more interesting when considered in light of the fact that many of the Babylonian rituals involving the king seem to have gone into abeyance by the time of Xerxes' reign (486–465), an intentional downplaying by that king of Babylon's geopolitical importance to the Achaemenids.

One of our few contemporaneous sources for Alexander's victory stems from the Babylonian astronomical diaries. The label is applied to a series of texts in which Babylonian scholars recorded astral phenomena for their careful record-keeping, often noting important political, military, or cultic activities that coincided with the celestial observations. In one entry of a diary for the year 331, Alexander is labeled "King of the World" (Akkadian *šar kiššati*), the same royal epithet Cyrus himself claimed in the Cyrus Cylinder.[21] Cyrus' adaptation of this title, as we have seen, was neither incidental nor accidental. It was a conscious choice that enveloped tradition, prestige, and power. Similarly, its application to Alexander implied continuity of tradition despite a change of dynasty.

Subtle but Formidable Remembrances

Cyrus' legacy certainly did not end with the Empire's fall. Among the Achaemenids' successors in Iran, though, it can be harder to track in later periods. After Alexander, some Hellenistic rulers in the east Mediterranean were still keen to claim links to Cyrus and the Achaemenids, which bolstered their own dynastic or territorial claims. For example, Mithradates Eupator of Pontus in the first century BCE claimed descent from both Cyrus and Darius in his paternal line.[22] Cyrus' imprint was felt also in the Roman tradition, not only among authors of the time writing about Alexander, as discussed in the previous section. Allusions to Cyrus—his lifetime more than 500 years removed at the time of the Roman Empire's height during the first century—generally were of two types: either specific references to the historical Cyrus or to Cyrus as a literary figure, the latter mainly (but not exclusively) based on Herodotus' anecdotes or Xenophon's model.

As is evident, equating the Greek tradition's Cyrus with the "real" Cyrus is a challenge. One impetus for the staying power of Cyrus' memory in Roman times was the very phenomenon of their own debt to the Greek tradition. Many Roman authors arrogated the cultural and literary inheritance of the Greeks, who by the first century BCE were Roman subjects, and by which point the Romans' only serious rival was the Parthian Empire. One consistent motif involved, in essence, history repeating itself. To wit, the Romans identified themselves with the lionized, stylized role of Greeks had who cast themselves as a bulwark against Achaemenid Persian imperialism and oppression a few centuries earlier. In Greek literature, this applied to any of the imperial activities of Cyrus and his successors, but especially to Xerxes' invasion of Greece in 480–479. For the Romans, the Achaemenid Empire thus became a literary analog for the Parthian Empire.[23]

Put another way, it was common for the Romans to allegorize their rivalry with Parthia in terms of, and identification with, the previous era's west-east (i.e., Greek-Persian) antagonism, one that was writ so large in the Greek experience that the Romans inherited. That is a simplistic description for both periods, of course, but it served its purposes, especially when cast in literary and thematic terms. A key difference must be emphasized, especially as it pertained to Cyrus' reign. The Greeks of western Anatolia (Ionia) were under Cyrus' direct rule, and remained subjects of the Achaemenid Empire.[24] Subsequently, while the Ionian Greeks were often a security problem and occasionally a threat to the Achaemenids' western holdings, with regard to resources, cohesion, and the ability to project military force, there was no comparison to the scale of Cyrus' power or, by extension, to the scale of the Roman-Parthian dynamic. The fifth- and fourth-century Greeks were not unified or focused enough, even at the height of Athenian or Spartan power, to provide any true threat to the core of Achaemenid power. This did not change until the mainland Greeks were forcibly unified by Philip II of Macedon in the 330s and combined with the already-extensive manpower of the Macedonians and their subjects in southeastern Europe. From these came the forces that Philip's son, Alexander, led eastward.

So, although the Roman-Parthian dynamic was much different on a geopolitical scale, historical memory of Cyrus and the Achaemenids remained ever-present, a rich source to be tapped. Cyrus the Great served as an allusion, and at times an illusion, a figure of foundational historical import to whom Parthians, or their successors the Sasanians, might be compared or referenced. For example, the Roman satirist Horace referred to the Parthian king Phraates IV as sitting on the throne of Cyrus. Tacitus, Herodian, and other writers referred to Parthian claims of territories previously held by Cyrus and the Persians, sometimes including Alexander in the mix as well. The Romans may have considered such claims rhetorical, but the Parthians and Sasanians likely thought otherwise. References to Cyrus within Roman contexts situated him with great conquerors and founder-figures of the past. Justin compared the first Parthian king Arsaces' place among the Parthians with Alexander among the Macedonians, Romulus among the Romans, and Cyrus among the Persians.[25]

Cyrus was a touchstone as a purely literary figure as well. Cyrus and his successors remained great object lessons, even when the historical details were conflated or outright wrong. Ammianus Marcellinus named both Cyrus and Darius (I) as great warrior kings whose hubris brought them to bad ends, a lesson straight from Herodotus. But Ammianus' historical credibility was not helped when he placed Cyrus' march against Tomyris and the Massagetae, located east of the Aral Sea (see Map 3), as crossing the Bosporus instead of the Araxes. Roman images of Cyrus—especially those not directly applied to the geopolitical Roman-Parthian rivalry discussed above—echoed Greek renderings of Cyrus popularized by Xenophon, Herodotus, and, to a lesser extent, Ctesias.

For example, in the mid-first century CE, Valerius Maximus relayed several stories of dream visions from Herodotean tradition, including that of Astyages' dream about his daughter Mandane foretelling the birth of Cyrus. Suetonius had Julius Caesar wishing for a quick death, Caesar explicitly referencing Cyrus' drawn-out affair—as relayed in Xenophon—as one to be avoided. The orator Cicero explicitly recalled Cyrus several times through his intimate knowledge of Greek literature. For example, Cicero referenced Xenophon's distillation into Cyrus the qualities for ruling a just empire, the Latin *imperium*. In another context, Cicero noted jocularly that he was prepared for any threat from the Parthians because he had read the *Cyropaedia*. Cyrus was referenced by Cicero frequently as a model of impeccable character, solemn dignity, and fundamental courtesy.[26]

Tracking Cyrus and his successors in later Iranian traditions is, somewhat surprisingly, a more difficult job than doing so in Greek and Roman ones.[27] Cyrus and the Achaemenids are effectively absent from the *Avesta*. The *Avesta* presents a related but distinct Iranian historical tradition, one different from that crafted by the Achaemenid dynasty that left such an imprint in the Western tradition. In a similar vein, with few exceptions scholars have not found Cyrus or any obvious imprint of the Achaemenids in the later *Khwadāy-nāmag* (Book of Lords, compiled in the seventh century CE but mostly lost) or in the *Shahnameh* (written by Ferdowsi, c. 1000 CE). The *Shahnameh* especially has been mined for echoes of the Achaemenids; somewhat ironically, it represents Alexander in a favorable light, as a descendant of two kings, each named Dara, referring to Darius I and to Darius III. Despite the paucity of explicit references to Cyrus himself in this later tradition, there are many potential parallels. One example is the similarity in theme between the accounts of Cyrus' rise and that of the Sasanian king Ardashir's. Another is manifested in the person of the heroic king Kai Khosrow of the *Shahnameh*, who was raised by a shepherd, as was Cyrus in Herodotus and Ctesias.[28]

Nonetheless, it is curious that Cyrus was not prominent in these later ancient and medieval traditions. Scholars continue to grapple with this peculiarity. Cyrus was also surprisingly absent in the imperial programs of both Parthians and Sasanians, whose models hearkened back to the Achaemenid one. At least by way of explicit mention of its kings, the entire Achaemenid dynasty seems almost forgotten. One reasonable theory for this phenomenon is that the Parthians and Sasanians, especially the latter, aligned their dynastic traditions with the different traditions as preserved in the *Avesta*. This makes sense for a dynasty whose national religion was Zoroastrianism. Also notable is that Sasanian Iranism (the idea of *Ērānshahr*), rooted in Zoroastrianism, precluded the development of an integrative imperial ideology of the sort established by Cyrus and the Achaemenids.[29]

Conclusions: New Out of Old

In the later nineteenth century, the late Qajar period in Iran, Achaemenid motifs and representations became popular in a variety of media—bas reliefs, textiles, ceramics—sculptures especially inspired by the remains of Persepolis. This was perhaps inspired by the rediscovery of Old Persian (and other languages written in cuneiform scripts) and the intense new interest in the Achaemenids as heard through their own voices.[30] Cyrus the Great himself perhaps commands more attention in the present day than he did at any time since the height of the Achaemenid Empire. It is appropriate to close this book as it began, with discussion of the Cyrus Cylinder. Cyrus' legacy, even when not obvious, never went away. It roared back into visibility in 1971 with a celebration of Iran's 2,500th anniversary, sponsored by Shah Reza Pahlavi, who connected himself and the modern nation-state of Iran in a direct line to Cyrus the Great. The Shah invoked Cyrus directly:

> O Cyrus, Great King, King of Kings, Achaemenian King, King of the Land of Iran! I, the Shahanshah of Iran, offer these salutations from myself and from my nation. At this glorious moment in

the history of Iran, I and all Iranians, the offspring of the empire, which thou founded 2,500 years ago, bow our heads in reverence before thy tomb. We cherish thy undying memory, and at this moment when the new Iran renews its bond with its proud past . . . Cyrus! Great King, King of Kings, Noblest of the Noble, Hero of the history of Iran and the world! Rest in Peace, for we are awake, and we will always stay awake.[31]

In conjunction with these celebrations, the Shah also arrogated the Cyrus Cylinder as the so-called first charter of human rights. A replica of the Cylinder was gifted to the United Nations, with great ceremony, where it remains on display (Figure 6.3).[32] This

Figure 6.3 Replica of the Cyrus Cylinder displayed at the United Nations building, New York.

UN photo by Michos Tzovaras, courtesy of United Nations Photo Library.

is a remarkable example of an ancient legacy applied to a modern ideology.

The Cyrus Cylinder itself is, as we have seen, a foundational text, literally a foundation inscription from Babylon. While the document is vitally important in our understanding of how Cyrus portrayed himself as king to a primarily Babylonian audience, it has little to no bearing on his attitude toward human rights. This is not least because what moderns mean by the shorthand phrase "human rights" is nebulous, but also because it is an idea that did not exist in antiquity per se, or at least not the same way the concept is understood today.[33] The magnanimity that Cyrus displayed to the captive populations held in Babylonia was described in formulaic language from the Mesopotamian tradition of royal inscriptions—even if Cyrus likely did all the things as advertised—and the inscription must be first considered from the perspective of how that formulaic language situated Cyrus in a long-standing tradition.

The fact that Cyrus in the Cylinder—and in a myriad of other sources from different times and different places—received almost universally good reviews understandably makes one inclined to believe in his exceptionalism as a leader and ruler. The reader has thus far made it through several chapters testifying to that very fact. Indeed, the relevant section of the Cyrus Cylinder that referred to return and restoration focuses mainly on divine sanctuaries (temples), and people are referenced only generally.[34] The general allusion could apply to several peoples and ethnic groups; the ambiguity in phrasing is not accidental. As one example, the return of Judean exiles (the so-called Babylonian diaspora), the descendants of those deported from Jerusalem upon its destruction by Nebuchadnezzar II in 587/586, is not explicitly mentioned in the Cylinder. But it was no doubt part of the process, as discussed in Chapter 4. Cyrus was lionized in their tradition just so, and it is no wonder. To those Judeans, and others freed from Babylonian captivity, Cyrus was indeed a liberator. This action went beyond any question of "human rights" (again, however that is to be defined for the ancient Middle East), even if that was a desirable byproduct. And though Cyrus himself must be considered exceptional, the Cyrus Cylinder in and of itself does not confirm any unusual or remarkable aspects of a ruler of Babylon that were not claimed by other Babylonian, Assyrian, or Elamite monarchs who had preceded Cyrus and left their own, quite similar, testimonies, often in the same places: temple sanctuaries, city walls, and other structures built or restored under royal directive. The Cyrus Cylinder's exceptional elements—within the genre of royal inscriptions—that point to what may be termed herein Cyrus' personal touches were also discussed in Chapter 4. Coupled with the array of other testimonies about Cyrus, these in toto demonstrate the exceptionalism and genius of this man who created the world's first geopolitical hyperpower.

In consideration of the modern attention lavished on Cyrus as a paragon of human rights, now effectively part of his modern legacy, it is worth considering how this concept was manifested in antiquity. Such considerations in ancient times were not relayed in wording that may be translated as something akin to "human rights" but rather in the parlance of justice. There is an extensive documentary tradition in Babylonia and Assyria (among other traditions), and from that it is easy to discern that justice was a fundamental concern of their kings. For example, thirteen centuries before Cyrus, the Babylonian king Hammurabi—he of the famous law code—called himself "king of justice" (Akkadian *šar mišarim*). The Akkadian word for "law," *dīnu*, finds its complement in Old Persian *dāta*, and the evidence for the Achaemenid Empire as a rule-bound environment in both Near Eastern and Greek sources is extensive.[35]

It was the king who was the ultimate arbiter of justice, but this did not mean that justice was arbitrary. Although the sources indicate several instances of royal caprice, such caprice was considered even in antiquity as *in*justice. A famous anecdote in Herodotus had the

Persian royal judges put on the spot by the king Cambyses' query as to whether there was a law prohibiting the king from marrying his sister. The judges split the difference by responding that they could find no law advocating such, but they also told Cambyses that the law allows that the "king can do as he pleases."[36] In other words, though the king's power was absolute, there were checks on that power. To consider how this system worked within the Empire's administrative bureaucracy, one must look beyond the literary record. And, of course, the maintenance of justice in local contexts would still have been informed by local traditions.

Babylonian administrative records contain abundant examples of prosecution of cases of theft and other criminal behavior. Litigants had various means of seeking redress for wrongs, and cases that could not be decided at the local level—via smaller assemblies of local officials or judges—often ended up before the governor.[37] Cast at an ideological level, the king's role in the maintenance or dispensation of justice was necessarily described in general terms. In other words, references to abstract justice abound, though the king's personal involvement in the day-to-day application is not so easily tracked. With Darius I's and Xerxes' inscriptions, the emphasis on justice was pitched in terms of Mazdaean dualism: opposing the Lie and rewarding the truth, balancing the interests of both the mighty and the weak, and hearing both sides of disputes.[38]

Cyrus informed his own legacy even before his death, by way of his conquests and his approach to ruling such a large territory over more than three decades. This was, as we have seen in previous chapters, an evolving process that reproduced (or, rather, reimaged) a reliable message of a visionary ruler. This message was manifested in many forms as promulgated by Cyrus himself, and it was disseminated and reproduced over time in various places by multiple authors. Not all these writers were Cyrus' agents, or even his subjects, but the basic portrayal of a brilliant, humane, just, yet commanding figure remains remarkably consistent over time and across a breadth of source material. Cyrus' own concern for justice was described in the Cyrus Cylinder through his care for his people: he "shepherded them with truth and justice." This remains a powerful, and lasting, legacy.

APPENDIX A

On Sources

A discussion of sources is generally not high on the list of exciting reading, yet in many ways it is the most fundamental part of any project. The issue was broached briefly in Chapter 1, but this Appendix includes a longer treatment. There are several reasons Cyrus the Great remains an enigma, and the lack of sources for his life and career is at the forefront of those reasons. To frame the problem, imagine writing, twenty-five centuries removed, a narrative about someone from whom we have almost zero direct testimony, and very little indirect testimony from this person's contemporaries. Further, this project is to be completed from the perspectives of, what amount to in modern parlance, the chronographer, the politician, the historical novelist and mythographer, the priest, the poet, the accountant, and the lawyer. This sounds like an ideal situation in some ways, if detailed accounts survived from each. But they do not. Further, none of the writers knew the subject directly, most lived in other countries and decades (if not centuries) later, and all had completely different concerns in their writings that touched, at times, briefly and indirectly on the subject. With few exceptions, this is the general situation that confronts any modern historian writing about Cyrus the Great.

The information that follows offers a brief overview of complex phenomena, both of the range of documentary source types, how they are interpreted, and how they are cited herein. A history of Cyrus the Great is that of the rise of the Achaemenid Persian Empire and its contemporary milieu. The Empire's scope is reflected in documentary sources from several languages. Those of the core included Old Persian, Elamite, and Babylonian (a dialect of Akkadian), as well as Aramaic, the last the lingua franca of the entire ancient Near East. As may be considered fitting for the Empire's vast scope, the preceding list includes languages from the Indo-European languages family (Old Persian), the Semitic languages family (Babylonian-Akkadian and Aramaic), along with the often-forgotten stepchild that is Elamite: the language of the Persians' predecessors in Iran and used by the early Persians themselves, a so-far-unclassified linguistic isolate. Since Aramaic was usually written on parchment, not much of it has survived from the sixth century BCE, a major loss to any semblance of a complete picture. Several types of Old Persian, Elamite, and Babylonian documentary sources do, however, survive. Monumental and other royal inscriptions commemorated the kings' deeds and broadcast their ideology. Foundation deposits were texts buried as, in essence, pious time capsules that commemorated building or restoration work to temples or other structures. Chronicles recorded cultic, military, and other milestones of kings' reigns. Administrative and economic records recorded various types of contracts and bills of sale and often included helpful chronological markers. All these types of texts present their own challenges in understanding and interpretation, beyond the ever-present—and, indeed, fundamental—challenges presented by their fragmentary states of preservation. Many of the preceding types of documents were recorded on clay tablets or on mud-brick walls (less commonly on stone or precious metals) and, as a consequence, became worn or damaged even in antiquity. Relatively few have survived even partially intact, and in those cases mostly by accident, for example, through having been baked in the flames of destruction. It is rare to find a fully preserved text.

Royal inscriptions are generally the most common sources used to anchor a historical narrative. Types of these proclamations run the gamut from what are called dedicatory inscriptions (i.e., on walls, on gates, on vases, etc., also called "display inscriptions") that relayed name, title, and epithets to longer, substantive accounts that relayed the particulars of a king's accession or military campaigns, often called annals. Some of these inscriptions were buried in walls or foundations during construction or restoration work—termed "foundation deposits" that were allude to previously. Until recently in modern scholarship, these inscriptions were considered to have been for the gods' eyes only, the implication being that the king's subjects or successors would never see them, unless they were encountered during subsequent restoration work. But while the gods and future kings were indeed intended audiences, it has become clear that these carefully crafted vehicles of royal ideology were disseminated via other means, if not as display inscriptions then through oral proclamations, and also distributed in other languages and media, such as Aramaic on parchment, copies of which have not survived.

One example of this, and one of our main documentary sources for Cyrus the Great—and thus one that receives frequent attention in this book—is the Cyrus Cylinder (see Figure 1.1). The descriptor "Cyrus Cylinder" refers not only to the object itself, but also, and more so, to its contents, that is, the text inscribed upon it. The Cyrus Cylinder itself is an object in the form of a classic foundation deposit—a clay, oval, barrel cylinder, this one roughly 10 inches long and 4 inches thick at the center—with forty-five lines of inscribed text. Much of the text is formulaic, nonetheless still important, but it also contains several innovations, and much of historical import, that will be discussed throughout the book. Appendix B contains a translation of the inscription. Fragments of a large clay tablet, not a cylinder, with the same inscription as the Cyrus Cylinder itself confirm what scholars have long suspected: the contents of these inscriptions were proclamations that were read aloud to the citizens of Babylon and other cities. Such cross-referencing, the dissemination in multiple copies and formats, was commonplace. Beyond the king and his agents, who determined the thematic messaging, the inscriptions themselves are works of professional writers (i.e., scribes), and, after all, what writer does not want his or her work read?

For both Cyrus the Great and his son and successor Cambyses, however, there has survived surprisingly and frustratingly little in the way of royal inscriptions. Inscriptions of their successors, some of which will also be referenced herein, were often trilingual, engraved in the respective Old Persian, Elamite, and Babylonian languages. Royal inscriptions found in the peripheral regions of the Empire often included a version of the local or regional tongue; for example, in Egypt Achaemenid royal inscriptions included a version inscribed in Egyptian hieroglyphics, or in some cases were written in Egyptian only. English translations and transliterations of royal inscriptions are accessible still mainly within the specialized literature. The most comprehensive collection of translated sources relevant to Cyrus the Great, and the entire Achaemenid period, is A. Kuhrt, *The Persian Empire: A Corpus of Sources from the Achaemenid Period* (Routledge, 2007), an indispensable resource for the study of this period.

Royal inscriptions are cited herein by standard conventions: abbreviated with king's first initial, superscripted number (for successive kings after the first with the same name), and location where it was found. Lowercase letters differentiate separate inscriptions from the same site. For example, DPe §2 stands for Darius I, Persepolis, inscription e, paragraph 2, and A^2Sd §2 stands for Artaxerxes II, Susa, inscription d, paragraph 1. It should be noted that updated, complete editions of the trilingual Achaemenid royal inscriptions with full commentary—in all their versions, not just Old Persian—remains a desideratum. The Achaemenid Royal Inscriptions online (ARIo) Project is an online resource, aggregated from various translators, where translations of most of the royal inscriptions may be accessed: http://oracc.museum.upenn.edu/ario/index.html. This site is hosted by the Open Richly Annotated Cuneiform Corpus (ORACC: http://oracc.museum.upenn.edu/), an aggregating website for scores of translations of a variety of ancient Near Eastern documentary sources from Sumerian times onward. The Internet site Livius.org also has translations of many of the royal inscriptions and other resources dedicated to the study of Cyrus the Great and ancient Persia (https://www.livius.org/category/persia/) along with materials from several other ancient civilizations.

Beyond the most frequently consulted genre of the royal inscriptions, ancient Near Eastern documentary sources include administrative records, omen queries, astronomical diaries (i.e., records of celestial observations), and royal correspondence between kings and officials. For the last, unfortunately, there is little that survives from the Achaemenid period and even less from the reign of Cyrus. This is not because they did not use such means of communication—they most certainly did—but because such correspondence has not been found. Another critical source for reconstructing Cyrus' times is the so-called Babylonian chronicle series. These chronicles were terse, year-by-year accounts of kings' reigns that recorded major cultic, political, military, or other activities, some of the earliest of what we may call historical (in the modern sense of the word) records.[1] Information from these texts serves as essential chronological anchors for Cyrus the Great's reign.

The nineteenth-century decipherment of cuneiform scripts, starting with Old Persian which opened the path for decipherment of Akkadian and then Elamite, is an engaging story in its own right, traced in a number of works in modern scholarship.[2] While our knowledge of these languages continues to advance, there is still much to learn. It is for this reason—the loss of these languages to history until very recent times—that the study of Achaemenid history has been primarily a construct based on Greek and biblical accounts, on whose traditions the first Persian Empire had an enormous and lasting impact. With the decipherment of various cuneiform scripts, more records from the core of the Empire became accessible. The royal inscriptions, chronicles, and administrative texts described above have revealed new insights and perspectives, as well as important correctives of Greek accounts. As a result, our understanding of Cyrus' times has changed, sometimes dramatically, in the last few decades of modern scholarship.

Nonetheless, there remain a variety of methodological problems and caveats. Royal inscriptions portray matters as the king or his advisors wished the audience to see them, at times a relative reality crafted to fit a representation of a laser-focused, ideological messaging. As such, these materials must be read and interpreted accordingly. The same caveat, of course, applies to all sources, regardless of type or audience. As one example, the Hebrew Bible preserved important information about Cyrus and the restoration of Solomon's temple in the later sixth century, the era after the Babylonian Captivity in which Cyrus' conquest of Babylon enabled a return of many Judean exiles.[3]

These caveats serve as an appropriate segue to another set of sources used to reconstruct Cyrus' life and the early Empire. This material stems from a variety of Greek and Roman authors, especially the Greek authors of the later fifth through mid-fourth centuries BCE. These included mainly Herodotus (the so-called Father of History), Ctesias, and Xenophon, whose works still dominate Achaemenid historiography and on whom we rely for a narrative framework of Cyrus the Great. While some of these sources have the advantage of never having been lost (or their languages forgotten), more often than not their information was based on oral tradition more so than the occasionally traceable documentary or archival source. Further, these writers wrote for a Greek audience, and their aims were as much literary as they were historical.

Herodotus wrote his *History*—the Greek word *historia* initially meant something akin to "inquiry"—in the mid-to-late fifth century BCE. Herodotus was from Halicarnassus in southwestern Anatolia, an area that was conquered by Cyrus and formally part of the Achaemenid Empire. Ctesias wrote roughly a generation later in the late fifth and early fourth centuries BCE. He was a Greek physician from Cnidus, in the same region of southwestern Anatolia and thus also part of the Achaemenid Empire, who served at the court of Artaxerxes II for almost two decades. He was the author of a number of works; citations herein are most often to his *Persica* (roughly translated as "Persian matters"), a monumental work in twenty-three books of which only fragments or summaries preserved in later sources remain. Xenophon of Athens was a slightly younger contemporary of Ctesias, who wrote numerous works dating to the first half of the fourth century BCE. Xenophon's most important work for the subject at hand was the *Cyropaedia* ("the Education of Cyrus"): an idealized, highly stylized, and highly embellished account of Cyrus the Great's life. The *Cyropaedia* tells us a lot about an Athenian officer and aristocrat's imagining of the early Persian Empire, and its novelistic rendering of its founder Cyrus as a prototype of the philosopher-king. Plato likewise cast Cyrus as an ideal ruler; these and related references are discussed in Chapter 6. Xenophon's *Cyropaedia* is far removed from a historical treatise, though still mined for insights into Greek portrayals and attitudes about Cyrus, as well as contemporary Persian customs.

While other authors and sources are cited frequently throughout the book, Herodotus, Ctesias, and Xenophon remain the usual suspects for information about Cyrus' life, especially before he became king. Their reputations, from antiquity to the present, vary widely. While Herodotus' acumen as a storyteller and literary artist is seldom questioned these days, as a historian (at least by modern standards) he has been considered along the entire spectrum from keen observer to naïve dupe, from antiquity to the present. Ctesias' reputation has fared worse: he was generally considered a colossal dunderhead, a pathological liar, or some combination of both. Xenophon strikes modern readers as an aristocratic soldier with a general proclivity to autocratic rule and a concomitant distaste for democracy, an aspiring philosopher with prosaic writing ability. The truth for each, of course, lay somewhere within these extremes.

Citations of the preceding and other major Greek and Roman works follow convention by author, book, and paragraph (or section) number. For example, Hdt. 1.125 refers to Herodotus, Book 1, paragraph 125. Ctesias is cited by fragment number and (if appropriate) letter and, for longer fragments, paragraph (§) number, for example, F8d §32 for fragment (F) number 8d, paragraph 32. Since several works of Xenophon survive, the abbreviated title is also included in the citation, such as Xen., *Cyro.* 8.3 for Xenophon, *Cyropaedia*, Book 8, paragraph 3. Accessible text editions with translation for major Classical authors are published in the Loeb Classical Library series, though many other English translation of Herodotus and Xenophon are available. English translation of Ctesias are far fewer, the main edition now being Stronk 2010.

Translation of the Cyrus Cylinder

There are many translations of the Cyrus Cylinder available in the scholarly literature; two accessible recent translations are Kuhrt 2007a: 70–74 and one posted at Livius.org: https://www.livius.org/sources/content/cyrus-cylinder/cyrus-cylinder-translation/ (accessed October 23, 2020). The definitive scholarly editions of Finkel 2013 and Schaudig 2019a should be consulted for any serious work with this text and its treatment in modern times. The following translation is my own but based on these works. It must be emphasized that the translation provided here is written for the general reader, and it glosses several difficulties in the reading of the sometimes incomplete (or missing) cuneiform signs, as well as understanding of the syntax. The full text of the Cyrus Cylinder is at present unavailable to us. Although much of it is preserved, there are several gaps or breaks where the text is illegible or missing. Its beginning and end remain quite broken, and restorations of these sections can vary significantly; for example, compare the translations for the fragmentary lines 1–7 in Finkel 2013 and Schaudig 2019a.

Brackets in the translation below indicate reasonably confident restorations, based on partial signs or words extant. Ellipses are used to indicate breaks of varying length, in which entire words or phrases are illegible or broken away, and for which restorations would be entirely speculative. Words in parentheses are added to indicate alternate translation or to give context or referents. Throughout the entire text, again not least in areas where the cylinder's clay is fragmented, it is not always clear whether the god Marduk or the king Cyrus is the subject of several grammatical clauses (e.g., in lines 13–14, referents in line 19), even if the sentiment is clear enough, regardless.

Translation

Line 1 [When Mardu]k, king of the whole of heaven and earth . . .

2 . . . his [] . . . laid waste . . .

3 one unsuitable was installed to the lordship of his land (Babylonia) . . .

4 he (Nabonidus) imposed upon them . . .

5 Nabonidus made a counterfeit of the Esagil (Marduk's temple) . . . at Ur and the other sacred cult-centers

6 he implemented unsuitable displays (i.e., improper rites). . . . (In) his daily worship he continually uttered blasphemies.

7 He disrupted the regular (offerings). He established [tainted rites?] within the midst of the sacred cult-centers. He was determined to cease [proper] reverence toward Marduk, the king of the gods.

8 Nabonidus ceaselessly did evil to his city. Daily . . . he unwearyingly wore down his people with an unrelenting yoke.

9 Hearing their complaints, the Enlil of the gods (Marduk) grew extremely angry, and . . . their territory. The gods who dwelt within them abandoned their temples,

10 angered because Nabonidus compelled them (i.e., their cult-statues) into Babylon. Marduk, the august Enlil of the gods, then turned toward their dwellings which had been abandoned (alternate translation: dilapidated)

11 and he turned toward the people of Sumer and Akkad (i.e., Babylonia), who had become like corpses, he relented, he took pity upon them all. Marduk surveyed and considered all the lands,

12 he searched thoroughly for a just ruler, one favored in his heart. Marduk took him by the hand, Cyrus, the King of Anshan, he summoned his chosen one, he named his name to rule over all.

13 He (Marduk) compelled Gutium and the whole of the *umman-manda* (the Medes) to bow at his (Cyrus') feet. All of humankind, Marduk delivered into his (Cyrus') hands,

14 Cyrus assiduously shepherded them with truth and justice. Marduk, the great lord who nurtures his people, joyfully discerned Cyrus' good deeds and his righteous heart.

15 So that he go to Babylon, Marduk spoke to Cyrus. Marduk directed him to take the road there, and like a friend and companion, he walked at Cyrus' side.

16 Cyrus' vast army, bristling with weapons, its number uncountable like the water in a river, marched with him.

17 Without a fight or battle Marduk had Cyrus enter into Babylon, his city, and he saved Babylon from hardship. He delivered Nabonidus, the king who did not revere him, into Cyrus' hands.

18 All the people of Babylon, the entirety of Sumer and Akkad, nobles and governors, they bowed before Cyrus, they kneeled, they kissed his feet. They rejoiced in his kingship, and their faces glowed.

19 All the people joyfully extolled the lord, through whose support they were restored to life, and by whom they were saved from oppression, and they extolled his name.

20 I am Cyrus, King of the World, Great King, Mighty King, King of Babylon, King of Sumer and Akkad, King of the Four Quarters,

21 the son of Cambyses, Great King, King of Anshan, the grandson of Cyrus, Great King, King of Anshan, the great-grandson of Teispes, Great King, King of Anshan,

22 (I am Cyrus) of an everlasting line of kingship, whose reign Bel and Nabu love, whose kingship they desire in their happiness. When I entered Babylon in peace,

23 amidst joy and jubilation I took residence in the royal palace. Marduk, the great lord, established for me my destiny, the one whose vast heart loves Babylon, and daily I carried out his worship.

24 My immense army marched into Babylon in peace, and I did not countenance any menace throughout the whole of Sumer and Akkad.

25 Within Babylon and all its sanctuaries I diligently cared for their well-being. As for the citizens of Babylon [. . .] who, neither in accord with divine will nor their destiny, were forced to bear hardship

26 I soothed their fatigue, I released them from bondage. Marduk was pleased.

27 For me, Cyrus, the king who reveres him, and to Cambyses, my own son, and to all my army,

28 Marduk gave sweet blessings, so that we walked before him safely and happily. [By his] exalted [word,] all the kings who sit on thrones

29 from all corners of the world, from the Upper Sea to the Lower Sea, who dwell in dis[tant territories], the kings of Amurru who dwell in tents,

30 they all brought their weighty tribute and kissed my feet in Babylon. From [Babylon?] to Ashur, Susa,

31 Akkad, Eshnunna, Zabban, Meturnu, Der, as far as the border of Gutium, the sanctuaries on the other side of the Tigris that had been abandoned for a long time (alternate translation: had been established long ago),

32 I returned the gods who dwelt there to their places, and I made them take up residence forever. The whole of their peoples I assembled, and I returned them to their homes.

33 And the gods of Sumer and Akkad, whom Nabonidus removed into Babylon, to the anger of the lord of the gods, by the command of Marduk, the great lord,

34 I returned them to their cellas in contentment, to their pleasing abodes (literally: their "seats of well-being"). May all the gods, whom I restored to their sanctuaries,

35 daily beseech Marduk and Nabu that my days be long, and may they invoke my good deeds. May they say to Marduk, my lord: "As for Cyrus, the king who reveres you, and Cambyses, his son,

36 . . . May they be provisioners of our shrines forever." All the people of Babylon pray for my kingship, and I caused all the lands to live in peace.

37–38 ... Every day I (Cyrus) ordered delivered to [the temple? ...] geese, two ducks, and ten wild doves, in addition to the former offerings of geese, ducks, and doves. I worked to strengthen the Imgur-Enlil, the great wall of Babylon ...

39–41 ... the quay of baked brick on the bank of the moat, which a previous king had bui[lt but not completed] ... on the perimeter, work that a previous king had not completed with his workers, the levy [from his land into] Babylon. ... I built anew and c[ompleted with bitu]men and baked brick. ...

42 ... great [gates of cedar wood], covered in bronze, thresholds and door fittings cast in copper(?), I established at all the gates.

43 ... An inscription with the name of Ashurbanipal, a king who preceded me, I examined in its midst. [I returned it] to its place. ...

44–45 May Marduk, the great lord, grant me the gift of long life ... [and an enduring rei]gn. May I gladden your (Marduk's) heart forever.

Scribal note/colophon, from Cylinder inscription Fragment B1:
[Written and check]ed ... the tablet of Qishti-Marduk, son of [...]

Teispids and Achaemenids

This Appendix offers a deeper dive into the evidence and the attendant schol-arly debates associated with some of the thornier questions about Cyrus the Great's rise, those that are too convoluted to include in Chapters 1–2 without a significant interruption to the narrative. The same caveat occurring frequently elsewhere needs to be applied here: the evidence is incomplete, complex, and open to interpretation. There are several components treated herein that overlap two overarching issues: (1) the extent of territory held by Cyrus and his predecessors before the victory over the Medes and (2) the connections between the family lines of Cyrus the Great and Darius I, who came to power in 522 at the expense of Cyrus' sons. The second issue in particular is a corner-stone of contention in modern scholarship on the Achaemenids. This is mainly Darius' fault, as it were, a statement that is at the same time a backhanded com-pliment: a manifestation of Darius' success in propagating his message of legit-imacy, and his right-to-rule, through cooption of Cyrus' lineage into his own.

A foundational question that motivates this book remains: the enigma of how the regional kingdom of Anshan (i.e., Assyrian Parsumash and Old Persian Parsa) positioned itself under its early rulers—Teispes, Cyrus I, and Cambyses I—as the springboard for Cyrus the Great's world empire. Part of the answer is contingent upon the dynasty's relationships with other Iranian and Elamite groups: the alliances and conquests effected before Cyrus the Great conquered the Medes. As discussed in Chapter 1, the forging of an Elamite-Persian ethnogenesis could not have been a seamless process over the eighth through sixth centuries, as Assyrian letters describing Elamite-Persian friction in southern Khuzistan testify to at least one violent episode. That episode is unlikely to have been anomalous, but the situation cannot be further tracked at present.

It is worth considering the possibility that Cyrus' forebears expanded their reach beyond Fars, including into Khuzistan. These two regions were cultur-ally and politically linked in Elamite tradition for centuries previous, in ideo-logical terms manifested in the Elamite royal title "King of Anshan and Susa" (*sunkik Anzan Šušunka*) used by many late second-millennium kings as well as a few rulers of the first, for example, Shutruk-Nahhunte II of the late eighth century. If Cyrus the Great's forebears were successful in extending their terri-tory, by the time Cyrus the Great took the throne circa 559 he may already have ruled more than Anshan (Parsa) proper, the area roughly concomitant with modern Fars, his family's core territory. This admittedly impressionistic scenario immediately begs several questions, one among them being why Cyrus did not adopt the title "King of Anshan and Susa" as his Elamite predecessors did. But speculating on why Cyrus did or did not do something, speculation no less prefaced on a reconstructed scenario, gives rein to multiple answers, all hypothetical. One such hypothetical answer is that the traditional Elamite title simply did not resonate with Cyrus; in other words, he may not have viewed himself as an Elamite king, at least, not in the same tradition as did Shutruk-Nahhunte II.

Beyond the traditional Assyrian and Babylonian titles co-opted by Cyrus in the Cyrus Cylinder there remains the title "king of Anshan." Other attestations also occur in Babylonian inscriptions. Its first use came when Nabonidus applied it to Cyrus in the Sippar Cylinder. The title accompanied Cyrus at his introduction in the Cyrus Cylinder, when chosen by the god Marduk to succor Babylon, and is the same title attributed to his predecessors. It also is used in the Ur brick inscription as an epithet for Cyrus himself and for his father Cambyses.[1] Thus, the title "king of Anshan" carried an important and, within the extant record, unusual significance. As applied in the Cyrus Cylinder and Ur brick inscription, it is both assertion and acknowledgment that, although he was of a royal lineage, Cyrus could not count himself as descended from a Babylonian royal line—indeed, far from it. Cyrus' use of the title "king of Anshan" seems an odd choice; it is a title that had not been used for centuries and with only a handful of attestations total over a broad swath of time. How should modern historians interpret this phenomenon? Of course, that choice of title need indicate nothing more than that it was who Cyrus was, the king of the region of Anshan—in other words, the title may have reflected nothing more than a geographic descriptor, such as "king of Babylon" or "king of Assyria," an important epithet, but not revealing beyond that simple fact.

But if one reads significance into a ruler's choice of titles and epithets, the search for deeper meaner is hard to resist. To expand on the preceding, the title "King of Anshan" is an outlier in the corpus. With very few exceptions it is not found in Elamite, Assyrian, or Babylonian texts.[2] Scholars have attempted to explain the use of the title as a Babylonian archaism, a common phenomenon in royal inscriptions and especially among Cyrus' predecessors in Babylon, the Neo-Babylonian kings. That is a reasonable assertion but an awkward one in context. When archaisms are used, they have readily identifiable antecedents, often a recasting of much older titles, formulations, or expressions. If "King of Anshan" was meant to be an archaism, it is an unusual choice. Why not, for example, the "King of Elam"? Though the Elamites themselves did not use that title, it was commonly used in a variety of Mesopotamian royal inscriptions and correspondence to refer to kings of that region for centuries previous, with hundreds if not thousands of attestations. There is one extant text, a copy of a prophecy dating to the Seleucid period, that appears to refer to Cyrus just so, as the "king of Elam," but it is an anomaly.[3]

The title "king of Elam" was more versatile, a catch-all epithet that could be understood to refer to the region encompassing both Khuzistan (Susiana) and Fars. It was, in effect, Assyrian and Babylonia shorthand for the formal Elamite title "king of Anshan and Susa" discussed above. An example of its staying power comes from its continued use in Babylonia in a rich textual tradition describing the last time Elamite kings held Babylon, 600 years before Cyrus the Great. The twelfth-century Elamite kings who conquered, sacked, and ruled Babylon for several years—Shutruk-Nahhunte I and his sons Kudur-Nahhunte and Shilhak-Inhushinak—used the title "King of Anshan and Susa" frequently in their own royal inscriptions. During their domination of Babylon, the Elamites removed the statue of Marduk and took it to Elam. This was a traumatic event: anytime a god left his or her city with an enemy, it could only be explained by extreme divine displeasure. In other words, Marduk's anger at his own people resulted in his departure, a rationalization for the Elamite kings' victories as manifested by the god abandoning his or her people. Only the loss of divine favor could explain such a situation, just so in Marduk's anger at Nabonidus and favor toward Cyrus as relayed in the Cyrus Cylinder.

In the twelfth century example, ultimately, the Babylonian king Nebuchadnezzar I (r. 1126–1105) reasserted native authority, and he undertook a successful campaign deep into Elam to recover the statue of Marduk. This sequence left an indelible mark in Babylonian tradition for centuries. There are several copies of texts, dating from the Neo-Babylonian and Achaemenid periods, that preserved the hymns and poems commemorating this event. Rewriting the story of Marduk's wrath and its ramifications, as well as Nebuchadnezzar's glorious campaign that heralded Marduk's return, was a common exercise used in scribal schools for practice writing cuneiform. Students not only heard these stories as part of their oral history but wrote them out to learn their language and its script, an event seared into the national consciousness.[4] These texts refer always to the King of Elam and never to the King of Anshan. These traditions would not have been unknown to Cyrus and his agents.

The standard interpretation for Cyrus' use of the rare title "King of Anshan" is that it was Cyrus' conscious preference. Before he became King of the World, he was King of Anshan. Cyrus himself did not sit with the stylus and inscribe the Cylinder's contents, but it seems a stretch that his preferred title was not used, and even more so that he was unaware of his inscriptions' contents and how they referred to him. Royal inscriptions were often read aloud publicly, probably on multiple occasions, and since these were in effect the king's words it is generally safe to assume that the king had a sense of what those words were, especially with regard to his titles and prerogatives—if he did not dictate the core message himself. A more compelling question may be why Cyrus did not adopt, as did his successors from Darius I onward, the title "King of Parsa," the Old Persian toponym for the Elamite region of Anshan.[5]

Cyrus' lineage and his predecessors' historical milieu have been discussed at some length in Chapter 1. To review briefly, in the only extant genealogy commissioned by Cyrus himself, he names himself son of Cambyses (I), grandson of Cyrus (I), and great-grandson of Teispes, all titled as kings of Anshan. The only other dynastic line preserved from of this period is that of Darius I. Extant evidence from Darius' reign happens to be much richer, and it is to this evidence that we must turn next to apprehend more pieces of this puzzle. The situation requires a great deal of context.

Within two years after he usurped the throne in 522, Darius inscribed a lengthy victory proclamation on the side of Mt. Bisotun (also spelled in English as Bisitun or Behistun, among other variants). Bisotun is roughly halfway between modern Kermanshah and Hamadan (ancient Ecbatana), a sacred and prominent place on a major thoroughfare through the Zagros Mountains. Roughly 200 feet above the road, Darius carved a relief showing himself triumphant over his rivals, who were cast, from Darius' view, as rebels and pretenders; note Figures C.1 and C.2. Each of these rivals claimed kingship during the months after Cambyses' death in 522, when the empire that Cyrus founded threatened to unravel. Each was identified by the royal name he assumed and his ethnicity. Darius, in the long tradition of royal understatement, went to great lengths to describe how he preserved the empire and restored it to its former glory during the time of Cyrus. Those that questioned Darius' legitimacy had compelling object-lessons portrayed on the Bisotun relief, a chain of these bound challengers as shown in the drawing of Figure C.2. Each of them met horrible punishments culminating in a gruesome execution, justified by the magnitude of their crimes against the now-legitimate king, Darius.

The relief also portrayed two unidentified retainers behind Darius holding weapons, but the focus of the relief is upon Darius himself and the figure in the winged disk that hovers above the scene, with whom Darius is in direct communion. This figure-in-disk symbol is usually identified with the Mazdaean (Zoroastrian) god Auramazda. Darius invoked Auramazda dozens of times in the accompanying inscription, divine favor a critical component of any claim to legitimacy. Surrounding the relief on both sides and below it is a trilingual inscription that elaborated the particulars of Darius' legitimacy: his royal lineage and his victories over his rivals at the beginning of his reign—the last, of course, the real marker of his legitimacy. The inscription was recorded in the Elamite, Babylonian (Akkadian), and Old Persian languages, each inscribed with a distinct cuneiform script. There are two copies of the Elamite version, the first to the right of the relief and the second to the lower left, as shown in Figure C.1. The second is a recast of the first, done after the addition of a later rebel king, Skunkha the Scythian, to the relief necessitated the defacement of

Figure C.1 The Bisotun relief and inscription of Darius I, inscribed c. 520 BCE, Mt. Bisotun, Iran.

Courtesy of the George G. Cameron Photo Archive, Kelsey Museum of Archaeology, University of Michigan.

part of the first Elamite version. The Akkadian version is to the left of the relief, and the Old Persian version underneath the relief. Captions in all three languages identify the rebel kings, but not the retainers behind Darius nor the winged symbol. The relief would have been visible from the road, but not the inscription.

This inscription served as the official version of Darius' accession to the throne and for modern scholars a master text for understanding Achaemenid royal ideology. While Darius' assertions in this document must be considered through the lens of royal apologia, his statement that he disseminated the inscription throughout the empire in other languages is both unsurprising and demonstrable. Versions of the inscription have been found in Babylon, in Egypt, and the substance of the narrative informed Greek authors from the western fringes of the empire as well, even if the Greek end product looked dramatically different than Bisotun's initial input. While the study of Darius' reign contains much of interest, the events leading to his accession (the so-called crisis of 522) involve many questions of interpretation and reconstruction, the focus herein will be primarily on what this inscription reveals about Cyrus and his family.[6] While Darius' account at Bisotun is in a class by itself among royal apologia, it too is beholden to centuries of Mesopotamian and

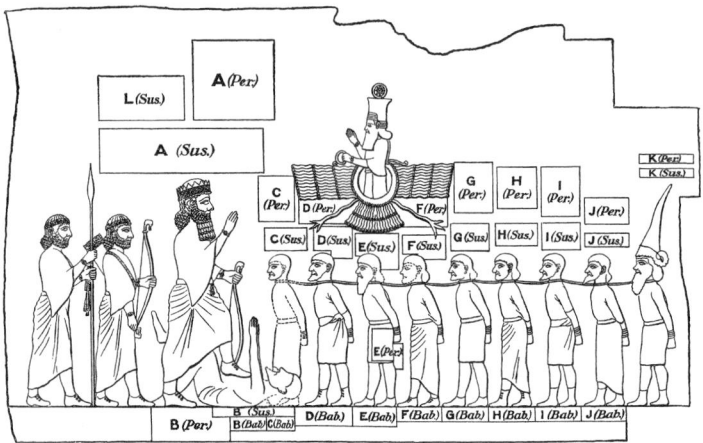

Figure C.2 Drawing of Bisotun relief from L. W. King and
R. Campbell Thompson, *Sculptures and Inscription of Darius the
Great on the Rock of Behistûn in Persia*, London, 1907, Plate XIII.
The capital letters indicate separate inscriptions or labels, and the
abbreviations Per., Sus., and Bab. stand for Old Persian, Susian
(rather: Elamite), and Babylonian (Akkadian), respectively.

Elamite conventions—as well as the precedents established by Cyrus—that
Darius and his agents adopted and adapted to their own use.

   For our purposes here, roughly the first quarter of the Bisotun inscription is
germane, and especially the very beginning of the inscription, in which Darius
relayed his titles and lineage. What follows is a composite translation of the
Old Persian, Elamite, and Babylonian versions of sections §1–4:

§1   I am Darius the Great King, King of Kings, King of Persia, King of Lands,
     son of Hystaspes, grandson of Arsames, an Achaemenid.

§2   Darius the King proclaims: My father is Hystaspes, and the father of
     Hystaspes is Arsames, and the father of Arsames was Ariaramnes, and
     the father of Ariaramnes was Teispes, and the father of Teispes was
     Achaemenes.

§3   Darius the King proclaims: Therefore we are called Achaemenids. From of
     old we have been noble and from of old our line has been kings.

§4   Darius the King proclaims: Eight of my line[7] have previously been kings.
     I am the ninth to hold the kingship. We are nine kings of an everlasting line.

In this inscription Darius traced his own lineage through five generations—Hystaspes, Arsames, Ariaramnes, Teispes, and Achaemenes—and, further, noted that he was the ninth king in an everlasting line. If Darius was the ninth king, who were the previous eight? Darius did not explicitly label his own direct ancestors as kings in this section, though the implication that at least some of them were kings follows in the third section. It is taken for granted that Cyrus the Great and his predecessors were to be included in any accounting of Darius' eight previous kings. With Teispes as the linchpin between Darius' genealogy and Cyrus' as given in the Cyrus Cylinder, that leaves Cyrus I, Cambyses I, Cyrus (II) the Great, and Cambyses II. It remains an open question whether Cambyses II's brother, Bardiya, is to be included in Darius' count. Bardiya ruled for roughly six months in 522, well-attested in Babylonian administrative documents. Later in the inscription Darius effectively discounted him, when he claims that Bardiya had been killed by his own brother Cambyses in secret.[8]

For Darius' proclamation that "eight of my line have previously been kings" there are a lot of candidates, and, thus, an accounting problem. From Darius' given lineage there are Hystaspes, Arsames, Ariaramnes, Teispes, and Achaemenes. From Cyrus' given lineage there are Cyrus I, Cambyses I, and Cyrus (II) the Great himself; the Teispes who was Cyrus' great-great-grandfather being the same Teispes mentioned by Darius. Also should be included Cambyses II and, whether Darius was counting him or not, Bardiya. That makes ten. The impressive and often convoluted ingenuity applied in modern scholarship's attempts to reconcile the discrepancies provides confirmation that academics do not get out enough. One part of the dilemma involves squaring what we know (including, for example, of Bardiya's brief reign in 522) with whom Darius was including in his own accounting. That Darius' and Cyrus' forebears were, of course, contemporaries is not a roadblock. It is well-attested through Near Eastern history that multiple individuals could hold the title "king" at the same time; any number of contemporaneous kings might be subordinate to the "king of kings." Whichever approach is applied tends to involve a lot of hair-splitting, as will be seen further below. A key point in these comparisons is that Cyrus traced his genealogy only to Teispes, three generations removed from himself. Darius' ancestral line included only one common ancestor with Cyrus, that same Teispes, who in Darius' list was the son of Achaemenes.

Because of the discrepancy in how Cyrus and Darius listed their first ancestor in their respective dynastic lists, a movement within the last decade of modern scholarship has gained traction in labeling Cyrus and his line specifically as "Teispid." Use of this label distinguishes the dynastic break heralded by Darius I's accession, emphasized by Darius' emphasis on "Achaemenid." This is an important distinction, but herein the traditional terminology, Achaemenid, has been generally maintained to all the kings of the first Persian

Figure C.3a Detail of the CMa inscription from Palace P, courtesy of
David Stronach (Stronach 1978, Plate 71a).

Empire, from Cyrus to Darius III, to minimize confusion. If the label "Teispid
Dynasty" is to be used, then it should include Cyrus the Great's forebears from
Teispes through Cyrus' offspring Cambyses, Bardiya, Atossa, and Artystone.
The empire that Cyrus founded continued after the death of the last male
member of that line, Bardiya, and was reconstituted, consolidated, and expanded further by Darius I. Darius incorporated the Teispid line into his own
through an implied, combined genealogy with Achaemenes—with Teispes
as the first common ancestor—as well as his completion of the founder's capital at Pasargadae, including and especially the inscriptions in Cyrus' name
proclaiming him an Achaemenid.

The two inscriptions labeled CMa and CMc were briefly alluded to in
Chapter 5's discussion; close-ups of both of them are included here in Figures
C.3a and C.3b. Both are quite problematic in their interpretation. They are
as straightforward in translation as they are not in authenticity. Pasargadae
was not complete when Cyrus died, or even during Cambyses' reign. Darius
I added many finishing touches and, although the issue is at times contested,
most scholars are convinced that he added the CMa and CMc inscriptions
bearing Cyrus' name sometime near the completion of the project in the 510s.
These inscriptions thus remain a linchpin of modern Achaemenid historiography, and the bibliography on this issue is enormous.[9]

CMa: I am Cyrus the King, an Achaemenid
CMc: Cyrus the Great King, an Achaemenid

Read literally, the CMa and CMc inscriptions identified Cyrus an
Achaemenid, of the same heritage as Darius I, whose Achaemenid (from Old

Figure C.3b Detail from the garment of a Palace P relief (see also
Figure 5.6c) with close-up of CMc inscription, courtesy of David
Stronach (Stronach 1978, Plate 83a).

Persian *Haxāmanišiya*) descent was a prominent, and oft-repeated, theme
in his own inscriptions. There are three main reasons scholarly consensus
considers these inscriptions dubious, meaning that they were commissioned
not by Cyrus but by Darius I—done so as one component of Darius' efforts
to link Cyrus' lineage to his own. First, as noted above, construction of
Pasargadae was not completed until well into Darius I's reign; the reliefs and
their accompanying inscriptions were among the final touches inscribed in
the 510s. Second, Darius himself claimed that he created the Old Persian cuneiform script, a claim that itself is controversial but one generally accepted
on the weight of the evidence.[10] Third, as noted above, a comparison of the
genealogical claims made by Darius I does not match up with the one inscription that contains Cyrus' lineage and was commissioned by Cyrus himself: the
Cyrus Cylinder from Babylon, which traces Cyrus' lineage only to Teispes.
Cyrus himself never mentioned Achaemenes, a surprising omission if indeed
Achaemenes resonated in Cyrus' own royal lineage. Faced with a choice of
explaining why Cyrus did not bother to mention Achaemenes or of assuming
that Darius co-opted Cyrus' lineage via Teispes, scholars have generally chosen
the second option, since it gels with other evidence. That Darius made a point
to intersect his and Cyrus' lines was in antiquity a common approach and even
an expectation.

Our other main source in considering this puzzle is Herodotus, for whom
the term "Achaemenid" was a clan designation. In his rehearsal of the Persian

tribes Herodotus noted that all Persian kings came from the Achaemenid clan of the Pasargadae tribe. That attribution was his way of expressing the importance of the label Achaemenid as a dynastic marker, which, although from a different viewpoint, echoed the ideological message of Darius I's royal inscriptions. In one of his most compelling literary set-pieces, Herodotus envisioned a dramatic debate set at the Persian court in the late 480s, where the question at hand was whether to invade Greece. In the course of Xerxes' pronouncements—remember that Herodotus is writing roughly fifty years after the events described—the historian effectively welded Cyrus' and Darius' distinct lineages through Xerxes' proclamation that he will destroy Athens, effectively swearing by his own ancestors: "May I be no son of Darius, son of Hystaspes, son of Arsames, son of Ariaramnes, son of Teispes, son of Cyrus, son of Cambyses, son of Teispes, son of Achaemenes."[11] Herodotus strung the disparate lines together by including an extra Teispes, as shown in Chart 3. It is likely not a coincidence that Herodotus made Darius the ninth king in his line, as Darius himself claimed he was in the Bisotun passage quoted above. We

Chart 3 Royal lines of the early Persian kings as represented in the Cyrus Cylinder (line 21), the Bisotun Inscription (DB §2), and Herodotus (7.11).

do not fully appreciate the spread, in various forms, of the Persians' ideological messaging, but both Darius' and Cyrus' original genealogies are incorporated within Herodotus' version. Herodotus, however, was not concerned with reconciling any genealogical discrepancies, even if he was aware of them, or, for that matter, that his rhetorical proclamation from the mouth of Xerxes had too many kings in linear descent.

For much of twentieth-century scholarship, the distinction between the Achaemenid dynastic line of Darius and the Teispid line of Cyrus was assumed to apply to two discrete kingdoms, both to be located in Fars: the "two kingdoms thesis" of early Persian history. In this reconstruction Cyrus the Great's predecessors ruled in the region of Anshan, and Darius' predecessors ruled in the region of Parsa. On that model, the common ancestor in each line, Teispes, divided rule over two discrete regions between his sons Cyrus I and Ariaramnes. Once it was established that the geographic terms Anshan and Parsa (Assyrian *Parsumash*) were essentially synonymous in ancient sources from the early seventh century onward, the two kingdoms thesis became much more problematic to maintain. Arguments have nonetheless persisted in modern scholarship over which of the two lines is to be considered more legitimate. If there were concerns about dynastic preeminence, rivalries among the various Persians clans of the early sixth century—and there most certainly were—they were effectively put to rest when Cyrus became King of the World. Any grander pretensions held by Darius' forbears would have been subsumed to those of Cyrus. In other words, any such issue resolved itself in antiquity when the two lines were unified by Cyrus the Great and then, a generation later, again by Darius I after he took the throne in 522. Most important, as has been discussed already, Darius' marriages to Cyrus' daughters Atossa and Artystone (along with a daughter of Bardiya, Parmys, who was a granddaughter of Cyrus) irrevocably linked the families.[12] Atossa became the mother of Xerxes, and thus Darius ensured that every one of his successors was able to trace a direct bloodline to Cyrus the Great, even though Darius himself could not. As both a preserver and an expander of the realm, Darius I may be considered as important as Cyrus in the Achaemenid Empire's foundation—as what amounts to a second-generation founder. But Cyrus came first, and it is upon his dazzling accomplishments that all else evolved.

Notes

Chapter 1

1. Isaiah 45:1–3.
2. P. Briant, *From Cyrus to Alexander: A History of the Persian Empire*, 2002, 13, translated from the French original, *Histoire de l'empire Perse* (Briant 1996), by Peter T. Daniels.
3. For a recent treatment of the Mongols, with references, see Kradin 2020.
4. See Ristvet 2015: 4–8 for a description of the ceremonies. Wikipedia (accessed September 18, 2020) has a page devoted to it, entitled "2,500-year celebration of the Persian Empire." Note Merhavy 2015 for a contextualized discussion of the phenomenon, also inter alia Aghaie 2000 and McCaskie 2012: 158–63. For more on Cyrus in modern times, see pp. 178–79.
5. Proceedings of these conferences have been published in the Achaemenid History series, which includes many specialized studies as well, published by the Nederlands Instituut voor het Nabije Oosten in Leiden.
6. Recent and soon-to-be published volumes of the *Oxford History of the Ancient Near East*, ed. K. Radner, N. Moeller, and D. T. Potts, provide updated syntheses, with references.
7. This is so despite the incredible distortions the word's meaning underwent in later nationalistic contexts, in the twentieth century the Nazis foremost among them. Some scholars translate the term *Ariya* in the Old Persian inscriptions as "noble" or the like, rather than as an ethnonym. The literature on this phenomenon is extensive; see Wiesehöfer 1996: xi–xii for a useful and succinct overview. Also, on the wider phenomenon, note Yarshater 1983, Gnoli 1989, Good 2010: 23–45, and the contributions to Strootman and Versluys 2017.
8. For an overview of the Elamite language and additional references, see Stolper 2004. Also see Potts 2016 for a thorough survey of Elamite history and culture through and beyond the Achaemenid period.
9. Hdt. 1.125, Xen. *Cyro.* 1.2.5, and Strabo 15.3.1. Historians have yet to reconcile Herodotus' list of tribes with the geopolitical situation that can be gleaned from documentary sources for the sixth century, although some tribal names may be tracked in Elamite administrative documents; note

Kuhrt 2007a: 55–56 for references and Briant 2002: 18–19 and Asheri, Lloyd, Corcella 2007: 163–64 for discussion and references.

10. The Shalmaneser III excerpt is quoted from the text edition of Grayson 1996: 68, inscription A.0.102.14, lines 120–25. Persians and Medes are mentioned in several other inscriptions of Shalmaneser III as well; see Rollinger 1999 and Waters 1999. For the Assyrian toponyms, see Fuchs 2004.

11. For overviews of the Neo-Elamite period, see Stolper 1984: 44–53; Waters 2000 and 2013; Steve, Vallat, and Gasche 2002: 471–78; Henkelman 2008: Chapter 1; Potts 2016: Chapter 8; and Gorris 2020.

12. The Assyrian letter recording this is translated in Fuchs and Parpola 2001: no. 129 and for discussion pp. xxiv–xxxiii and p. liii n. 102.

13. Henkelman 2011: 596–614 for a detailed overview of Persians (usually as groups, not individuals) attested in various documentary sources for this period, including within the so-called Susa Acropole texts, an archive of administrative documents written in Elamite whose historical context is completely uncertain.

14. Anshan also continued to be referenced in administrative documents, but it did not recur in royal inscriptions until the time of Cyrus himself, its last use in royal inscriptions.

15. The quotations are excerpted from various passages from Editions D, F, and A of Ashurbanipal's annals, for which see Novotny and Jeffers 2018. The relief sequence and its epigraphs have been extensively studied; see Russell 1999: Chapter 9 for an accessible version.

16. The free translation here is adapted from Edition A of Ashurbanipal's annals, columns v 126–vi 106; text and translation in Novotny and Jeffers 2018: 248–52. Ashurbanipal's grandfather, the king Sennacherib, used a similarly exaggerated motif when he claimed that he turned Babylon "into a meadow"; Grayson and Novotny 2014: 316–17.

17. For the Arjan tomb and its contents, see the thorough treatment of Álvarez-Mon 2010. For the bowl in particular, see inter alia Majidzadeh 1992 and Stronach 2005.

18. The precise location of many of the toponyms therein is uncertain. The important city of Hidalu was somewhere along the main route between Susa and the later capital of Persepolis; see Map 2 for the route. For the letters, see Parpola 2018: 102–3 and DeVaan 1995: 311–14; note also Waters 2000: 74–75.

19. Copies of these inscriptions were found in Babylon and Nineveh, respectively. Prism H2, column vi, lines 7′–13′ and Ishtar temple inscription,

lines 114–17; Novotny and Jeffers 2018: 270 and 307. Ashurbanipal presumably considered Cyrus' and Pislumê's obeisance as tantamount to declaring themselves Assyrian subjects. However, there is no mention in either short passage of related ritual acts; part of the formal process included a binding oath. That bit of the relevant Assyrian phrasing (and the key Assyrian word, *adê*, used to indicate such binding oaths) is missing in both contexts, whether because it did not happen or because the accounts are simply truncated. For the Assyrian *adê*, see inter alia Fales 2012. Also see Waters 2016 for a parallel situation with Xerxes and the Athenians.

20. Many scholars, though certainly not all, accept this identification of Cyrus of Parsumash with Cyrus I, and it is accepted here. Schmitt 1998: 134–35 etymologizes Arukku as an Iranian name, but this is not a settled issue.

21. The Persepolis Fortification Archive (PFA) is discussed in more detail on pp. 49–50. The asterisk in PFS 93* and other seal labels indicates that the seal impression is inscribed. See Hallock 1969: 24–25 for the type-category. Note Garrison 2011a on the dating of the seal and Garrison 2014 on archaizing imagery; Henkelman 2010 for discussion of these types of disbursements; Waters 2011a: 290–92 and Henkelman 2011: 601–4 for the inscription.

22. Jeremiah 49:35.

23. The word in the Cyrus Cylinder, line 21, that describes Cyrus the Great's relationship to Teispes is written with the cuneiform sign sequence ŠÀ. BAL.BAL, a formulation that represents the Akkadian word *liblibbu*. In royal genealogies, *liblibbu* is applied in a variety of contexts: to refer to "grandfather" (by Ashurbanipal for Sennacherib), "great-grandfather" (by Adad-nirari I for Ashur-uballit), "great-great-grandfather" (by Sin-shar-ishkin for Sargon), and "descendant" (as used by some ninth-century kings). Its application was fluid in genealogical terms. While "descendant" is a safe choice, it is a generic one and *liblibbu* must be therefore translated in context. Cyrus the Great named in order his father (Cambyses I), grandfather (Cyrus I), and then Teispes; the natural inclination is to translate "great-grandfather" for *liblibbu* in that context, though several modern translations favor "descendant." In the only other extant Persian rendering of the genealogy of early kings, Darius I labeled the same Teispes in literal terms as his great-great-grandfather in DB §2. In other words, Darius and his contemporaries represented Teispes as Cyrus the Great's great-grandfather.

24. The Old Persian form of "Vahuka" is disputed, correlative of Akkadian *Umasu* or *Umakush*.

25. Strabo 15.3.6 and Herodotus 1.113–114. Cyrus' upbringing will be further discussed in Chapter 2. The correspondence between Strabo's "Agradates" and Ctesias' "Atradates" (according to Ctesias, Cyrus' father) is close enough to have been conflated in the Greek historiographical tradition. Note Henkelman 2003a: 196 n. 48. Since there were several individuals attested in the historical record who were named Cyrus, the argument has been put forth that there was more than one king among Cyrus' predecessors who had, or took (if a throne-name), the name "Cyrus" before Cyrus the Great, but that they were not all recorded in the Cyrus Cylinder's genealogy.

26. For example, the Assyrian king Esarhaddon (in Assyrian *Aššur-aḫi-iddina*, translated "Ashur has given a brother") took the formal throne-name *Aššur-etel-ilāni-mukin-apli* (translated "Ashur, the prince of the gods, establishes the heir"); Radner 1998: 184. Esarhaddon apparently did not like the ring of the latter, so he continued to use his birth-name even in formal contexts.

27. Note especially for discussion and references Tavernier 2007: 528–30 for Cyrus, including other attestations of the name, and 18–19 for Cambyses (Elamite *Kanbuziya*, Old Persian *Kabūjiya*). Similar arguments surround the etymology of Teispes, Elamite *Zišpiš*, Old Persian *Čišpiš*), for which see Tavernier 2007: 519.

Chapter 2

1. Hdt. 1.95 on awareness of three other versions of Cyrus' life. Pelling 1996 is a seminal treatment for the dream motifs. Assyrian kings not infrequently compared themselves to the destructive power of the great flood, the king "whose passage is the deluge," though in their case it was water, not urine, that inundated the world. There are numerous instances; Esarhaddon offers one example, see Leichty 2011: 184 r. 12. Additional references may be tracked in the Chicago Assyrian Dictionary (vol. A/1) entry for *abūbu* ("devastating flood"), p. 79.

2. Hdt. 1.110. The later writer Justin (1.4.10) conflated Herodotus' version with Cyrus literally suckled by a female dog; inter alia, see Briant 2002: 14–16 for discussion. Parallel stories are found in later Iranian traditions that will be discussed in Chapter 6.

3. Ctesias, Fragments 8d and 9. Hdt. 1.125 listed the Mardians as one of the nomadic Persian tribes. Strabo identified the Mardians as bandits, perhaps applying that characterization from the same tradition as Ctesias.

Mardians have been identified as dwelling in western Fars, but there are a number of theories; cf. the Mardians of northern Iran in Arrian, *Anab.* 3.24.1–3 and 4.6.6.

4. For the Sargon Legend and its analogs, see Lewis 1980; Westenholz 1997: 36–50 for a translation of the related texts. Note Kuhrt 2003: esp. 355–56 for a thorough discussion of the legend's application to Cyrus. This was manifested, among other ways, in Cyrus' restoration work in Akkad (also spelled "Agade"), and Cyrus' continued care for a statue of Sargon found at Sippar.

5. See Zamazalová 2011: esp. 314–16 for discussion of the relevant text of Ashurbanipal describing his education. Xenophon emphasized Persian education on principles of justice (e.g., speaking the truth) as a prerequisite to full participation in Persian society, including holding important offices and other appointments. Hdt. 1.133 on the alternating, drunk-sober approach to decision-making and 1.136 for the emphases on horsemanship, archery, and telling the truth, cf. also Xen. *Cyro.* 1.2.15 and *Anab.* 1.9.3–4. Strabo 15.3.18–19, four centuries after that, provided a more detailed account of Persian youths' education, including what amounts to survival training (for campaign and warfare) for a corps of youths that has suspicious parallels to—meaning it was no doubt influenced by—accounts of the rigorous training of Spartan special forces corps, their so-called secret service. The particulars of Strabo's account are questionable, as is the connection to the Spartan *krupteia*. See Kuhrt 2007a: 629–32 for translation of these passages and additional references.

6. A more detailed overview of the evidence and its problems for the relationships among these early Persian families (esp. those of Cyrus and Darius I) is given in Appendix C. Discussion of the demographics of ancient Iran during this time involves almost complete guesswork. For a grounded treatment, see Wiesehöfer 2009: 76–78.

7. Hdt. 3.2 and also 2.1 for the anecdotes about Cassandane and the Egyptian concubines, 3.3 for the boy Cambyses' vow to invade Egypt. See following discussion and p. 70 for Cyrus' marriage to Astyages' daughter, named Amytis in that tradition, as per Ctesias; Brosius 1996: 41–47 for the phenomenon among the earliest Persian kings. For Philip of Macedon's marriages, see Heckel 2007: 15–16. In the case of Cassandane, her precise relationships to other Persian nobles whom Herodotus identified as Achaemenids is convoluted; see Waters 2004 for discussion.

8. DB §35 for Hystaspes leading military forces. See Sandowicz 2018: 51 for discussion and caveats on identification of Parnaka in the sources.

9. Hdt. 2.1 and Nabonidus Chronicle, column iii, lines 22–24.

10. Ctesias fragments F8d §, F9 §1 and F13 §11–13 for the Cyrus and Amytis sequence. Xen. *Cyro.* 8.5.17–20 and 28 for Cyrus' marriage to a Median princess. The Median Amytis is a bit of a cipher, likely a conflation. A Babylonian priest named Berossus, writing in Greek in the early third century BCE, preserved a tradition of an Amytis, daughter of Cyaxeres, who was married to the Babylonian king Nebuchadnezzar II. That tradition is even more chronologically suspect. For translation of Berossus F8b, see Verbrugghe and Wickersham 1996: 56–57 and note also Brosius 1996: 43–46. In Ctesias, Amytis was described as having a brother, Parmises, who had three sons (F9 §3). Beyond the brief note that they were prisoners of the Scythians, released in a prisoner exchange for the Scythian king Amorges who had been captured by Cyrus, Parmises did not factor into the extant story or the succession. Hdt. 3.88 for Darius I's marriages to Cyrus' daughter and granddaughter and see also p. 205.

11. Tavernier 2007: 212 for the etymology. Other Achaemenid names, such as Darius I's father Hystapes (Old Persian Vishtaspa), the same name as Zoroaster's patron in the Avestan tradition, highlight these links, but their significance is debated. See De Jong 1997: Chapters 1–2 for syntheses and contexts of the related problems; see pp. 151–56 for the religious milieu in Cyrus' time.

12. Hdt. 3.134 for the bedroom scene, a play on a similar motif from the *Iliad* (Book 14, lines 300ff.) when Hera deceives Zeus. Hdt. 7.3 for Atossa's influence in Xerxes' succession.

13. Hellanicus of Lesbos FGH 4 F 178a–b, note Harrison 2011, 141 n. 24. Waters 2017: Chapter 2 for discussion of Semiramis. See also Sancisi-Weerdenburg 1993 and especially Stolper 2018 for attestations of Atossa in the Persepolis Fortification Archive, the latter also for references in the PFA to other of Darius' wives mentioned by Herodotus: Parmys and Phratagoune.

14. Although its stylistic pedigree is somewhat different, PFS 77* is another heirloom seal, perhaps contemporary to PFS 93* and PFS 51 or dating somewhat later; see especially Garrison 2011a: 383–87 for the seal and its context and also for its connections to PFS 93*. Henkelman 2010: 693–701 for the feasts of Irdabama and Irtashduna.

15. On the name *Ṛtastūnā, see Tavernier 2007: 301. Garrison and Root 2001: 83–85 for full treatment of PFS 38 and references. Garrison 2017b: 366–69 for other Assyrianizing seals in the archive.

Chapter 3

1. If there were Median archives, royal inscriptions, or related documents, they are waiting to be discovered. Thus, our presumed knowledge of their language is only through shared roots and presumed cognates traceable in other Iranian languages such as Old Persian. For discussion of the archaeological evidence and further references, see Genito 2005, Stronach 2012, and Gopnik 2017. Dusinberre 2002 provides an overview of so-called Median artifacts and the interminable problem of identifying forgeries. Note Radner 2013: 449 for discussion of Median and other Iranian guests (hostages) at the Assyrian royal court, a parallel for the case of Arukku discussed in Chapter 1. The study of Median language remains in the rarefied realm of historical linguistics; see Rossi 2010 for context and cf. remarks of Briant 2002: 24–25.

2. Hdt 1.96–106. For the definitive deconstruction of the Median Empire, see the contributions in Lanfranchi, Roaf, and Rollinger 2003, with Waters 2005 for a review thereof.

3. The Iranian Zagros of the mid-first century millennium contained many discrete groups of Iranian-speakers and other ethnicities. Some dwelt in urban or semi-urban environments, while others were pastoralists; note Reade 2003: 149–50 for interesting, modern parallels.

4. Modern scholars have attempted to identify some Medes named in Assyrian sources with those of early Median kings mentioned in the Greek tradition. Assyrians encountered a certain Daiukku (late eighth century) and Kashtaritu (early seventh century), regional rulers in the Zagros Mountains, who have been equated with Herodotus' Median kings Deioces and Phraortes, respectively. Beyond the linguistic contortions involved in the identification, it is difficult to make a good historical fit with either one; see Fuchs 1999a, 1999b, and 2000.

5. Three Median city-lords rebelled against Ashurbanipal, were defeated, and were brought to Nineveh for punishment. Text and translation in Novotny and Jeffers 2018: 65: iii 92–iv 5.

6. The lines from the Book of Nahum are from a much longer passage (1:15–3:19) reveling in the destruction of Nineveh, translation from May and Metzger 1973: 1133–35.

7. Hdt. 1.134 and Jeremiah 25.25 (the omen of the cup of wrath), 51.11, and 51.27–28 (omens against Babylon).

8. Column i, lines 24–28, Whether or not this Median threat was real or manufactured is a matter of debate; note discussion in Rollinger 2003: 291–305.

The Sippar Cylinder's content deals mainly with temple restorations; note also Beaulieu 1989: 34, Inscription 15 and pp. 106–10.

9. See the *Chicago Assyrian Dictionary*, vol. 16 (Ṣ): 179–85 *ṣiḫru* for various examples of each of the meanings. For the translation "young" see, e.g., Briant 2002: 31; and Kuhrt 2007a: 56. For "insignificant" (or similar) see, e.g., Rollinger 1999: 129; Beaulieu 2000: 311, and n. 7; and Schaudig 2001: 437.

10. Column ii, lines 1–4, translation after Kuhrt 2007a: 50; Akkadian text in Grayson 1975a: 106.

11. Hdt. 1.108–130.

12. Fragment 8d for the version as preserved by Nicolas of Damascus. Ctesias' *Persica* was widely read in antiquity, and influential. Despite its manifold problems, it is possible to identify several Near Eastern motifs as inputs; for the Cyrus saga in particular see Waters 2017: Chapter 4.

13. Ctesias F8d §12–13. Xen. *Cyro.* 8.2.7–8 for similar gifts; see discussion in Briant 2002, 304–7 for numerous other examples. The link between horses and Persian identity has long been noted as a feature of Achaemenid royal inscriptions (e.g., DPd § 2 describing Persia as a land of good horses and good men); see, e.g., Root 2010: 199 for discussion. Herodotus relayed two, slightly different versions (3.85–87) of a story how a groomsman named Oibaras enabled Darius' accession through a trick. The character also appears (as Soebaris) in Justin 1.6–7, which echoed Ctesias' version but has the added detail of Soebaris marrying Cyrus' otherwise-unattested sister(!). All this testifies to an independent tradition of this character that preceded both Herodotus and Ctesias, and one is hard-pressed to conceive the character as entirely a product of Greek imagination. See for further discussion and references Waters 2011b and Rollinger 2018.

14. In Mesopotamian omen literature, the appearance of a lion in the protasis seems to attract a reference to a rival in the apodosis; see A. L. Oppenheim's observation 1956: 278 n. 75 with references. This may find an echo in Ctesias' narrative. Note also a related variant from the fourth-century BCE Ionian Greek historian Deinon, preserved among the second-century CE writer Athenaeus' collection of anecdotes, wherein Cyrus is compared to a powerful wild boar; Athenaeus 14.633d–e, translation in Kuhrt 2007a: 632.

15. The insult appears often in this sequence. The Persians were also called terebinth-eaters, the full significance of which continues to be debated. The terebinth has been associated with various plants, used as a food and for its oil in antiquity, linked by Strabo (15.3.18) and other writers with

the earliest days of the Persians under Cyrus, perhaps already by Ctesias' time steeped in nostalgia. According to Plutarch (*Art.* 3.2, F17), chewing terebinth was part of the coronation ritual for a new king; see especially Sancisi-Weerdenburg 1995: 286–92.

16. Ctesias, *Indica*, F45 §9. Polyaenus, a writer of the second century CE, recorded in his work entitled *Stratagems* (7.11.12) that during Darius I's Scythian expedition in the 510s a treacherous Scythian guide led the king and his army into a region with no water. In dire straits, Darius performed an elaborate ritual with his royal implements (scepter, robe, etc.), and through divine intercession was able to make it rain. In Polyaenus' Greek text, the god was named Apollo, but the story may have had Persian origins. See Briant 2002: 239–40 for discussion. On the king's connection to the divine, Waters 2021 with references.

17. A later Median general named Datis was one of the leaders of the Persian expedition sent by Darius I against Greek Eretria and Athens that culminated in the Battle of Marathon in 490. When Darius I seized power in 522, beyond the six noble Persians honored explicitly by name (DB §68), several other individuals who fought for Darius are also mentioned. These include some individuals explicitly identified as Medes, such as a general named Taxmaspada (DB §33). Darius also included the Medes in the rhetorical pronouncement that "neither Persian nor Mede nor anyone of our family" dared to act against Gaumata, until he did (DB §12–13). These inclusions are suggestive of the prominent role the Medes held in the Empire before and during Darius' reign. For that matter, memory of an independent Media remained prominent as well. Two of the challengers Darius I defeated in 522–521, Fravartish and Ciçantakhma, explicitly claimed to have been of the family of Cyaxares, the Mede who overthrew Assyria (DB §24–34). Regardless of Astyages' place in the Median tradition, it is not surprising that a later Median rebel avoided identification with the Median king defeated by Cyrus.

18. The end of Urartu—however that is to be defined—is usually dated earlier than the mid-sixth century on the basis of archaeological evidence; see Khatchadourian 2016: 88 and 222 with references. Dusinberre 2013: 15–26 for an overview of Anatolian geography and kingdoms during this period.

19. See Cahill 2019 for a recent treatment.

20. Hdt. 1.7–14 for the story of Gyges. The report of Gugu of Luddi is relayed in Ashurbanipal's annals, Edition A ii 95–125, Novotny and Jeffers 2018: 237–38.

21. Hdt. 1.73–74.
22. Nabonidus Chronicle, column ii, lines 15–16. Cyrus' march through what is assumed Babylonian territory will be revisited in Chapter 4.
23. Rollinger and Kellner 2019 provide a thorough review of the evidence and context for this passage, with references to previous literature; cf. Van der Spek 2021.
24. For Croesus' testing of the Greek oracles and the Delphic oracle's response, see Hdt. 1.46–49, 1.53–54, and 1.90–91.
25. Hdt. 1.53, 1.56, and 1.152–153 on Croesus, the Spartans, and Cyrus.
26. On Cyrus as his own messenger, Hdt. 1.79. For the archaeological evidence, see inter alia Greenwalt 1992 and Cahill 2010 for discussion and additional bibliography. Babylonian administrative documents from the later fifth century refer to a community of Lydians ("Sardians") living in Nippur, who were perhaps descendants of initial deportees; see Van der Spek 2014: 256 n. 185 and 258, with references. A reference from the late first century BCE (Tacitus, *Annals*, 3.62) refers to Cyrus consecrating a temple to "Persian Artemis" in Hierocaesaria in eastern Anatolia.
27. Hdt. 1.141 for the anecdote of the flute-player.
28. Hdt. 1.87 on Apollo's intervention. A translation of Bacchylides' poem may be found in Kuhrt 2007a: 65–66.
29. Ctesias F9 §3–5.

Chapter 4

1. Pirngruber 2017 provides a useful summary, with references. Records kept in these sanctuaries, from Babylon itself and other major cities, show a level of continuity in the administration and functioning of these organizations into the early Achaemenid period and beyond. See among others Waerzeggers 2010a and 2014 and also Jursa 2015.
2. The generally dim view of the last Babylonian king has been tempered only in recent scholarship. An assessment of the advantages gained from Babylonian control of trade routes running through the northern Arabian peninsula has encouraged modern scholars to re-evaluate Nabonidus' strategy and the virtues of his efforts there to increase Babylon's wealth by opening new doors to the oasis routes of the Arabian peninsula. Nonetheless, the representation of an aloof, indifferent, or slightly off-balance king has been difficult to shake in modern scholarship. It is difficult to understand Nabonidus' extended absence from his capital for many

reasons, but especially in consideration of Cyrus' rise and military activities during the 540s.

3. Nabonidus Chronicle, column ii, lines 13–18, for Cyrus' crossing the Tigris. See Beaulieu 1989: 197–202 for an intriguing reconstruction of this period.

4. Later traditions are severely conflated, e.g., Justin 1.7 places the conquest of Babylonian before that of Lydia and has Croesus providing the Babylonians assistance.

5. Hdt. 1.178–191.

6. Hdt. 1.189. The import and value of the horses to the Persians has been much remarked, and this passage is often cited. Horses were considered sacred both to Auramazda and to Mithra, so these instances give grist to the mill in speculations about Cyrus' religious beliefs, discussed in Chapter 5. Kuhrt 2007a: 562–66 contains a selection of excerpts from Greek and Roman writers on which these associations are based.

7. Hdt. 1.191

8. Nabonidus chronicle, column iii, lines 8–28. The verb (Akkadian *dakû*) has a range of meanings—to kill, to fight, to defeat, etc.—and modern translations thus differ. Similarly, for line 14, the term for "army" (from the cuneiform sign ERÍN, a logogram for Akkadian *ummānu*) can also be translated as "people" or "populace." Cf. translations of Grayson 1975a: 109–11; Glassner 2004: 236–39; Kuhrt 2007a: 50–51; and Lambert 2007. The translation here is adapted from Kuhrt's.

9. Xen. *Cyro.* 4.6.1–11, 5.2.1–22, and 7.5.26–30 on Gobryas; see Hyland 2018 for discussion.

10. Cyrus Cylinder, line 17 for the delivery of Nabonidus to Cyrus. For the Dynastic Prophecy, column ii, lines 20–21; Grayson 1975b: 32–33 and note also van der Spek 2014: 251 for comparison of this account and that of Berossus, Fragment 10a.

11. Note Stolper 2013: 41–42 and especially 47–49; Schaudig 2019a: 17 and 2019b: 69.

12. Finkel 2013: 29 for the fragments from another copy. The Nabonidus Chronicle (column iii, lines 18–20) referred to a proclamation of Cyrus that was read to all the people of Babylon.

13. Cyrus Cylinder, line 36.

14. Cyrus Cylinder, line 17 and column iv, line 126 of the Babylonian creation epic, called "When on High" as titled from its Akkadian incipit: *Enūma eliš*. For discussion of this and several other examples, see Schaudig 2019b.

15. The Akkadian in transliteration reads: *šar kiššati šarru rabû šarru dannu šar Bābili šar Šumeri ù Akkadi šar kibrāti erbetti*. Notably, Cyrus shifted

the order of these standard titles, so that King of the World (*šar kiššati*) came first in his list. For Nabonidus, see, e.g., the Eḫulḫul Cylinder, lines 1–2, Schaudig 2001: 415. Assyrian examples, of which there are scores, include a stamped brick from the Esagila processional, lines 1–2 (Esarhaddon, Frame 1995: 167, etc.); a barrel cylinder dealing with restoration of Nēmet-Enlil, Babylon, line 3 (Ashurbanipal, Frame 1995: 197, etc.). Note Beaulieu 1989: 137–43 on Nabonidus' attitude toward Assyrian kings.

16. Jursa 2014: 132–33 for description of family connections; also Frahm 2017: 194–95.

17. Cyrus Cylinder, line 43; for Ashurbanipal's dedication, Frame 1995: 196–98 (inscription B.6.33.1)

18. See Kuhrt 2003: 354–55 on Nabonidus' and Cyrus' interests in the kings of Akkad.

19. The names and common titles were perhaps identifiable to many citizens, even if they were otherwise illiterate in cuneiform. For the question of literacy among the ancient Babylonians, see Veldhuis 2011.

20. This was the main temple complex in Uruk during the Neo-Babylonian into the early Achaemenid periods, but its history is much older. Many of the surviving administrative texts that reference Gobryas, Cyrus' governor of Babylon and Across-the-River discussed previously, come from this complex. See Stolper 2003: 266 for some examples; Kozuh 2014 provides a thorough overview of the Eanna complex in this period.

21. Museum numbers: BM 90731 from the British Museum; W 1141, W 1142, and W 1814 from the Vorderasiatisches Museum. Dr. J. Marzahn kindly confirmed that the whereabouts of the copies in Vorderasiatisches Museum are unknown, cf. also Schaduig 2001: 548, and see discussion in Waters 2019.

22. For example, Esarhaddon "ruled all the lands" (Frame 1995: 178; Esar. B.6.31.12, and similar phrasing occurs in several other Assyrian royal inscriptions). See Seux 1967: 292–320 for combinations in title with *šarru* ("king").

23. Perhaps Cyrus' slight change in the formula in the Ur brick may be considered as anticipatory to Darius' use of Old Persian *bumi* as an expression of dominion over one world (see Chapter 5). Note Herrenschmidt 1976 (English translation, 2014) with Lincoln 2012: 124–25 and 146 for fuller discussion and references. Compare Briant 2002: 909–10 and Waters 2016.

24. George 1993: 114, no. 653 has a list of kings who left inscriptions at the Temple of Nanna-Suen, with references, likewise for the Eanna temple complex at Uruk, pp. 67–68.
25. Column vi, lines 18–22 for erasing of Nabonidus' monuments. What remains of the Verse Account is often disjointed because of the damaged tablet. See Kuhrt 2007a: 75–80 for a translation of the extant text, and note discussion of Waerzeggers 2012b. In column vi, lines 9–12, there is an invocation of Nebuchadnezzar II (r. 605–562); the text is too broken to determine the context of that passage, but it would not be surprising for Cyrus to link his reign not only to Ashurbanipal (see above) but also to the most successful king of the immediately preceding Babylonian dynasty.
26. Excerpts quoted from Verse Account, column i, lines 3–4 and 19–20. There is a litany of offenses and outrages that spans dozens of lines, much of which echoed and expanded on those relayed in the Cyrus Cylinder. Another example referred to Nabonidus' plans to make counterfeit temples and to cease the New Year celebration; compare Verse Account col. ii, lines 2–17 and Cyrus Cylinder, lines 4–8. Daniel 4:28–33 for the madman Nebuchadnezzar.
27. Nebuchadnezzar had attempted to control Judea with his own appointed governors to no avail, an involved sequence relayed in his own inscriptions and in 2 Kings: 24–25; Kuhrt 1995: 590–93 for a succinct overview.
28. It is also a curiosity how the return of deported subject peoples played among the contemporary Babylonians, their former masters. With Cyrus as a new master over all of them, one neither Babylonian nor Assyrian, it may be safe to assume that the Babylonians were far more concerned about their own fates: in other words, how (or rather "if") the new king would adhere to long-standing traditions. Babylon had long possessed what was called in Akkadian *kidinnutu*, a somewhat nebulous status that freed its citizens from corvée and other obligations, along with which went a great amount of prestige; see Kuhrt 2014b for discussion. Cyrus' royal proclamations and care for the reinstitution, or continuation, of important cultic rites were no doubt reassuring.
29. Cyrus Cylinder, lines 30–32. Note the important commentary on this passage at Schaudig 2019a: 19 n. 5. As a potential analog, one Babylonian text dating from the fourth year of Cyrus' reign refers to attempts to reorganize cultic practices in Eshnunna and Akkad, for which see Jursa 2007: 77–78, also Beaulieu 1989b.
30. Isaiah 44:28.

31. While a fascinating subplot, that tension is beside the point here; see Schniedewind 2019: 111–13 and Sweeney 2019.

32. Book of Ezra 1:2–4 and 6:2–5, excerpt quoted from the Aramaic version of 6:3–4, translation slightly adapted from Kuhrt 2007a: 84–85. The first version of the decree is in Hebrew, the second in Aramaic; the Aramaic version is held to be the more reliable. Doubts of the decree's authenticity persist nonetheless, and the bibliography is enormous. Among others see Bedford 2001; Fried 2017: 52–68; Silverman 2020: 121–25. Note also the provision in Ezra 6:10 to pray for the king and his family, an echo of the sentiment expressed in Hdt. 1.131; see Kuhrt 2007b, 136–37. Add to that Cyrus Cylinder, line 36, which includes the phrase "All the people of Babylon pray for my kingship." Though some translations render "pray" as "bless" (the Akkadian verb *karābu* contains both nuances), the same sentiment may be invoked here. A fuller account of the refoundation of the temple was given in Josephus' *Jewish Antiquities* (11.3–21), written in the later first century CE.

Chapter 5

1. DB §6. Some elements of Darius' list remain opaque, for example, to whom specifically the phrase "those of the sea" referred. Some peoples whom we would expect to see on the list, such as the Judeans, were subsumed under larger administrative units, in their case Babylonia.

2. Hdt. 1.134.

3. The terminology of these various levels of officialdom is not always consistent over time and place, however, which can complicate our understanding.

4. Hdt. 1.153–154; this episode is discussed on p. 78.

5. For the Elamite-Iranian ethnogenesis and the Persepolis Fortification archive, see pp. 12 and 49–50, respectively. Stolper 1992: 267–69 gives examples and a brief overview of the Neo-Elamite archives. The diversity in workers' ethnicities was not unique to Persepolis; it was no doubt similar among the workers at Pasargadae, though we have not yet found surviving documentation there. Many aspects of the *kurtash* are yet unclear. The people mentioned in these tablets may have been brought to Persepolis and elsewhere, whether by virtue of a specific call (e.g., obligation to provide service to the crown) or by force, and required to work on select projects. That Persians also could be labeled *kurtash* in these texts gives pause to any assumption that the word indicates deportees.

6. A translation of Darius' foundation charter (DSf) and related texts may be found in Kuhrt 2007a: 492–97.

7. Hdt. 8.98. Xenophon attributed this courier system to Cyrus, *Cyro.* 8.6.17–18. For remains of one of these staging-posts, see Mousavi 1989.

8. Hdt. 5.52–53 for a description of the road from Sardis to Susa. Maritime trade networks were already extensive from the Mediterranean to the Indian Ocean; Hdt. 4.42–46 described various Persian (and earlier) kings' efforts to track routes. Hallock 1969: 688 for *halmi* and 744 for *pirradaziš*. Dandamaev 1992: 78–80 for references to Gubaru.

9. See Chapter 4, n. 8.

10. Stolper 1985 for the seminal treatment of the Murashu archive, pp. 70–103 on the *haṭru*-system.

11. The asterisk indicates that the Old Persian word is reconstructed, not extant in a surviving text. Cf. the overviews in Wiesehöfer 2001: 89–93; Briant 2002: 783–800; and Kuhrt 2007a: 713–17. On the chiliarch, see Briant 2002: 258–59; Henkelman 2002; Keaveney 2010.

12. Hdt. 7.61–100

13. Cyrus Cylinder, lines 20–22, see also Chapter 4, n. 15. King of the Four Quarters is one of the oldest titles in the Mesopotamian corpus. See Seux 1967: 292–320 for epithets with *šar* (for *šarru*, i.e., "king"). For Neo-Assyrian conceptions of empire and kingship, see inter alia the seminal treatment of Tadmor 1999 and for Achaemenid conceptualizations Kuhrt 2010.

14. Old Persian *aivam parūvnām xšāyaθiyam, aivam parūvnām framātāram.* The sense of empire as one land, rule over one earth, rested in part on the interpretation of the Old Persian word *bumi*. When considered within a Zoroastrian, or Mazdaean, context, tying it to elements of the creation myths, its interpretation is an involved topic. See in particular Herrenschmidt 1976/2014 and Lincoln 2012: 124–25 and 146 for fuller discussion and references, Briant 2002: 909–10, and Waters 2016. Achaemenid *bumi* was usually translated by Akkadian *qaqqaru* in those trilingual formulae where a similar sense of totality was at issue; for *qaqqaru*, note the *Assyrian Dictionary* vol. 13 (Q): 123 (mng. 8c2′). Hallock 1969: 734 and Hinz and Koch 1987: 954–55 for the corresponding Elamite word *murun*. For additional references and variants of Elamite *likume rišakka* see Hinz and Koch 1987: 827. For Assyrian expression, the literature is vast; see Liverani 2017 for a recent treatment.

15. See discussion and references collected in Llewellyn-Jones 2013.

16. On Cyrus' splendor, compare, e.g., Xen., *Cyro.* 8.3.14 and Cyrus Cylinder, line 18. Aster 2012 on Akkadian *melammu*. Henkelman 2008: 364–68 and Garrison 2017a: 155–56 on Elamite *kitin*. Note also Lincoln 2012, Chapter 24, and Waters 2021. Canepa 2020: 317 on *xvarnah* (the normalized English rendering of the word varies).

17. See Chapter 4 for Cyrus and Cambyses at the New Year Festival. Xen., *Cyro.* 1.2.1 for one example of Cyrus' attractiveness (and see pp. 119–20). Quintus Curtius Rufus 3.3.17–19 for the Persian king's formal attire. Greek and Roman literary portrayals may be balanced by assessment of the sculptures from palatial Persepolis, but how well those monumental edifices matched Cyrus' initial representations at Pasargadae, or elsewhere, must remain uncertain. For the Achaemenid court, note especially Kuhrt 2007a: Chapter 12, the contributions to Jacobs and Rollinger 2010, and Llewellyn-Jones 2013.

18. Hdt 1.98.

19. See pp. 21–22 in Chapter 1 for Ashurbanipal's sack of Susa. Hdt. 1.188 on water from the Choaspes; on the modern identification of the river, see Potts 2005b. Kuhrt 2007a: 585 n. 3 cites an interesting modern parallel from *The Independent* newspaper, London, February 23, 1991: "In 1902 the Maharajah of Jaipur visited London. He brought with him two silver jars weighing 345 kg apiece, which he had had made especially for the visit. They were each to carry 9,000 litres of pure and holy Ganges water, since he could drink no other."

20. DSf §12 for the quoted excerpt.

21. The curious phenomenon on the disconnect between the Achaemenids and later periods in Iran will be discussed in Chapter 6. Stronach 1978 is the main excavation report, the introduction to which includes discussion and references to previous, important work there by Ernst Herzfeld and Ali Sami, among others; see pp. 107–12 for the so-called royal garden and its layout. Many of the illustrations herein are courtesy of David Stronach, from his 1978 publication or subsequent works. See Boucharlat 2009, 2011, 2014a, and 2019; Gondet et al. 2016 and 2018 for updates on recent work and interpretations. Note also Callieri 2017: 394–97 for discussion of a monumental gate from the site of Tol-e Ajori, slightly more than two miles west of the Persepolis Terrace, its Babylonian analogs (especially the Ishtar Gate) suggesting an origin with Cyrus or Cambyses. This find gives a glimpse into how much remains to be discovered about Cyrus and his successors.

22. Plut., *Life of Artaxerxes* 3.1–2.

23. Strabo. 15.3.8. Hdt. 1.125 on the Persian tribes, and see pp. 62–70 for Ctesias' version of the war against Astyages.

24. See Gondet, Mohammadkhandi, and Gopnik 2021 for recent survey work in this area and for evidence of fortifications elsewhere on the site.

25. Quotation from Stronach 1978: 26, on which this description is based. The reasons for the tomb's association with the mother of Solomon are not known, likewise the reasons for its popularity among women. The latter phenomenon brings to mind a story from Ctesias' *Persica* that when the Persians led by Cyrus were reeling from the Medes' attack at the site that would become Pasargadae, the women rallied the men to victory. Castigating the retreating men, the women displayed their private parts and asked if the men wished to return from whence they came. Whether this anecdote was a Greek trope meant to serve as comic relief is unclear, as it is related in several later authors' excerpts stemming from Ctesias, e.g., Justin 1.6.13–15 (F8e*, see Stronk 2010: 310–11). On the name of, and traditions surrounding, the Madar-i Suliman (Tomb of Cyrus) and several other monuments from Pasargadae and Persepolis through time, note Coloru 2017, esp. 99–103.

26. Arrian, *Anab.* excerpted from 6.29.4–10, translation adapted from Wiesehöfer 2016: 55–56. Other ancient references are conveniently collected in Stronach 1978: 24.

27. Note Henkelman 2003b for thorough discussion and references. In Elamite, the word is *shumar*, the precise meaning of which is still disputed. Cyrus' fondness for horses has been discussed elsewhere herein.

28. For the suggestion of the figure as a "mythologized Cyrus," see the seminal discussion at Root 1979: 300–3. If Darius I even briefly experimented with a blurring of the line dividing king and god in his imagery, he could have done worse than lionizing his famed predecessor, with whom he claimed familial kinship. This interpretation is admittedly speculative, though it is notable that the Pasargadae figure uses a similar hand gesture as does Darius in his physical address to Auramazda (and vice versa) at Bisotun and Naqsh-i-Rustam. Note inter alia Root 2013, Garrison 2017a, and Waters 2021 for further discussion. For a similar image on an Achaemenid cylinder seal (BM 108963), see Garrison, Jones, and Stolper 2018.

29. Note Stronach 1978: 61–62 for the capital figures. Kawami 1972 and Stronach 2019: 53–63 for the reliefs. Several Assyrian parallels may be noted, for example, a relief panel from the North Palace of Nineveh (reign of Ashurbanipal, c. 650 BCE) displaying a *lahmu, ugallu,* and smiting god (BM 118918).

30. No clear evidence for the Hanging Gardens in Babylon has been found, or at least agreed upon—some scholars locate them in Nineveh, a controversy that still spins in academic circles; compare, e.g., Rollinger 2013 and Dalley 2013.

31. A²Sd. Translation after Kuhrt 2007a: 403–5. Several Greek authors commented on these parks, and they are mentioned also in Elamite and other texts, see idem, p. 1000 for references. Strabo (15.3.7) indicated that Cyrus' tomb was also situated in such a setting. See Boucharlat 2019 for a recent overview of the Pasargadae gardens and associated waterworks.

32. Xen., *Oikonomikos* 4.20.

33. See pp. 128–31 on the Tomb of Cyrus and especially Coloru 2017. Callieri 2017: 392–93 for discussion of these two towers' significance, with references. Parallels for the Zendan and Ka'bah-i Zadrusht remain elusive, but note the tower from Samadlo, Georgia; see Knauss 2006: 87f and Fig. 9. On the Tall-i Takht see Stronach 1978: 11–23 and 146–55.

34. Xen., *Cyro.* 8.3.12, inter alia. Daryaee 2013b for a succinct and useful overview of the problem. Cyrus' affinity for his horses recurs in the sources, and horses in turn were associated with the sun and sun god.

35. Note the thorough and seminal work of Henkelman 2008; see also the contributions to Henkelman and Redard (eds.) 2017 for these wider questions and also Garrison 2017b.

36. DB §62, Elamite version, for "god of the Iranians." The reference to an Assara-Mazaš, which looks to be an Akkadian rendering of Auramazda, in an Assyrian gods list from the time of Ashurbanipal must be noted here, though its significance remains unclear; see Gaspa 2017: 145–46 for discussion and references.

Chapter 6

1. Hdt 1.177 and 1.153 on Cyrus' return to "upper Asia." On Cyropolis, note Arrian 4.2.2 and 3.14 and Strabo 11.11.4; see Briant 2021: 55–56 for discussion.

2. Hdt. 1.214 and cf. 1.95.

3. Several modern treatments deal with this phenomenon; note the discussion of Darbo-Peschanski 2013: 99–100 as one example. See pp. 86–87 on Cyrus' diverting two rivers during his Babylonian campaign.

4. Hdt. 1.207 on Croesus' advice to attack.

5. Hdt. 1.209–10 for the dispatch homeward of Cambyses and Croesus and for Cyrus' dream. The winged disk and its association with Auramazda

(and the king) is a broad-ranging subject; see Garrison 2017b for overviews with references and Ornan 2005 for the iconographic figure's history.

6. Ctesias, F9 §7. The account of the campaign suggests a close parallel, in structure and theme, to another that Ctesias related in the *Persica*, that of Semiramis against one Strabrobates (F1b). Semiramis' and Cyrus' eastern campaigns were linked in later tradition, e.g., Arrian, *Anab.*, 6.24.1–3, probably an extension of Ctesias' presentation. Berossos, via Eusebius, also referred to Cyrus' death on campaign in the northeast (F11); see Verbrugghe and Wickersham 1996: 61 for translation.

7. In historical terms, the succession would have been arranged much earlier; compare the explicit mentions and presentations of Cambyses in the Cyrus Cylinder, lines 27 and 35, and in the celebration of the Babylonian New Year as relayed by the Nabonidus Chronicle, discussed pp. 90–91.

8. See pp. 46–47 and 70 for Cyrus' marriage to Amytis. Xen, *Cyro.* 8.7 for Cyrus' lengthy final speech and arrangements.

9. Plato *Laws* 694a–b. Part of this portrayal remains embedded in the centrality of a Western education grounded in Greek and Roman texts, still evident today but not nearly as prevalent as even a few decades, let alone centuries, ago. See Ricks 2020 for a recent treatment of the phenomenon as it was manifested among the United States' founding fathers.

10. Xen., *Cyro.* 8.5.17–20.

11. Excerpted from Xen., *Anab.* 1.9, translation from Kuhrt 2007a: 506–7.

12. Excerpted from DNb §2, also copied by Xerxes at Persepolis (XP1); translation after Kuhrt 2007a: 504–5; see her notes for comments on factors impacting the translation, with references.

13. Hdt. 9.122.

14. For example, Xen. *Cyro.* 8.1.1 and 8.1.44; Hdt. 3.89 for the comparison of Cyrus, Cambyses, and Darius.

15. Nelsestuen 2017 for a fuller analysis of these passages in their Greek context.

16. Isaiah 45:1–3 and cf. Cyrus Cylinder, line 15.

17. Isaiah 42: 1–6 and chapters 44–45. See Silverman 2020, especially 41–44, 61–71, and 112–17, for discussion and references of these passages, and also for parallels between Yahweh and Auramazda as creator gods.

18. See for a balanced treatment of this issue, Kuhrt 2007b, 117–42; note also Van der Spek 2014.

19. Pp. 130–31 for the Arrian passage on Alexander and Cyrus' tomb. For Alexander's disbursements of Persian clothing and gifts, note Diodorus Siculus 17.7.5; for Persian women honored, see e.g., Ctesias F8d §43–44

inter alia and cf. Xen., *Cyro.* 8.5.21. Plut., *Alex.* §69.1–2 on Alexander's continuation of the custom. On Cyrus' generosity, prominent examples include Xen. *Cyro.* 8.3.1–8 and 8.3.23. Briant 2002: 304–7 for other examples, and Olbrycht 2014 for Alexander's adaptation of Persian garments, accoutrements, and customs.

20. Arrian 3.16.3–5 and Quintus Curtius Rufus 5.1.17–23 for Alexander's entry into Babylon. Cyrus Cylinder, lines 17–19, for Cyrus' entry into Babylon. For a more detailed discussion, see Kuhrt 1990. For Alexander's place in the *longue durée* of Achaemenid and Hellenistic history, cf. Briant 2002: 875–76 and Fox 2007.

21. Sachs and Hunger 1988, text no. 330.

22. Justin 41.5–6 on Mithridates' genealogical connections. Note the complex and varying perspectives on the Achaemenid legacy even within Iran itself during the subsequent Seleucid and Parthian periods; see especially Strootman 2017 and Canepa 2017.

23. That perspective of course precludes the Parthian view of the dynamic, one that is much more difficult to delineate. See below and note for detailed discussion Shayegan 2011: Chapter 3 and Shayegan 2017.

24. Conversely, the Greeks of the Greek mainland were not under direct Achaemenid rule. They may have been formally claimed as such by Darius I and Xerxes, but many Greeks would have viewed it differently; see Waters 2016.

25. Horace *Odes* 2.2.17–21 for Phraates IV. Tacitus, *Annals* 6.31.1, and Herodian 6.2.1–2 on Parthian territorial claims. Justin 41.5.5–6 on the comparison of Arsaces with his famous predecessors.

26. Ammianus Marcellinus 23.6.7–8 on Cyrus and Darius; Valerius Maximus, *Facta et Dicta Memorabilia* 1.7.5 on Astyages' dream; Suetonius, *Div. Jul.* §87 on Caesar's wish. Cicero, *Letters to Quintus* 1.1.23 on Cyrus and characteristics of a just empire, *Letters to Families* 9.25.1 on his readiness for the Parthians; see Schulde 2019: 182–84 for additional references.

27. A number of studies may be consulted on this phenomenon. Note inter alia Yarshater 1983; Gnoli 1989; Dulęba 1995; Bivar 2000; Shayegan 2011 and 2017; the contributions to Strootman and Versluys 2017; and Canepa 2018: 251–90. Mari 2016 for the curious and conflated remnants about Cyrus preserved in Armenian tradition.

28. The anglicization of titles of these various Iranian works varies significantly. Kai Khosrow's rise to the throne has also been compared to the circumstances of Xerxes' accession. Davis 2006: 275–78 for the story of Kai Khosrow. Davidson 2019: 237–40 for Kai Khosrow and Cyrus, with suggested parallels to the Cyrus Cylinder; Jamzadeh 2004 for a Xerxes connection.

29. See especially Daryaee 2019 for Sasanians' orientation to the ancient Iranian tradition preserved in the *Avesta*, and see Wiesehöfer 2017: esp. 385–87, for discussion and references on the Sasanian idea of *Ērānshahr*.

30. Lerner 2017 for a discussion of this phenomenon with several examples, note also Daryaee 2021.

31. Quoted from Garthwaite 2005: 251, which see for further context on this controversial celebration.

32. UN Photo #144182, https://www.unmultimedia.org/s/photo/detail/144/0144182.html. A copy of the press release on the gift of the Cyrus Cylinder replica to the United Nations may be viewed via the online archives of the Dag Hammarskjöld Library of the United Nations, https://ask.un.org/faq/194027 (accessed December 22, 2020). The Cyrus Cylinder, after its return from a loan to Iran in 2010, embarked on a US exhibition tour through museums in five cities (see in particular Curtis 2013: esp. 6–17) that sparked several presentations, lectures, and colloquia; see as an example the proceedings of an international conference hosted by UCLA, published in Shayegan (ed.) 2019.

33. See especially Van der Spek 2014: 233–34 n. 1 for a lengthy and detailed list of recent discussions of the uses (and abuses) of the Cyrus Cylinder in context of modern notions of human rights.

34. Cyrus Cylinder, lines 30–34, and see pp. 105–6 for discussion.

35. The phrasing "rule-bound environment" is after Tuplin 2015, which see for copious references and discussion. A Neo-Babylonian example, a text entitled "King of Justice" (translation in Foster 2005: 870–74), demonstrates that the idea that the king was responsible to maintain justice still held currency, unsurprisingly, into Cyrus' times.

36. Hdt. 3.31.

37. Note Sandowicz 2018: 36–27 and 2019: ix–xiii for an overview of what we know, and do not know, of the Neo-Babylonian justice and court system.

38. For an excerpt from Darius' tomb inscription, see p. 167. The Old Persian terms *arika* ("disloyal") and *drauga* ("Lie") are both replete with symbolic significance.

Appendix A

1. For overviews, see Haubold et al. 2019 (astronomical diaries); Waerzegers 2018 and 2021 for the chronicles; Jursa 2010 for economic and administrative texts; Kuhrt 2014a for correspondence.

2. Wiesehöfer 1996: 223–42, for a succinct and compelling overview.

3. See Eckhardt 2017; Razmjou 2020; and Silverman 2020 for recent discussions of this material, with references to a wide field of scholarship.

Appendix C

1. Cyrus Cylinder line 20 for the Assyrian and Babylonian titles co-opted by Cyrus, lines 12 and 21 for application of the title "King of Anshan"; the same title was used in Cyrus' Ur brick inscriptions, lines 1 and 3, and likewise in Nabonidus' Sippar Cylinder, column i, line 27.

2. For earlier references and discussion, see Waters 2004: 94, Potts 2005a: 14–15, and note also Briant 2002: 16–18 and 23. For different perspectives on Cyrus' choice of title, compare Waters 2011a; Henkelman 2011; Stronach 2013; and Zournatzi 2018. Potts 2016: esp. 97 and 128–29 for charts of titles used in earlier periods, also Malbran-Labat 1995: 176–79.

3. The so-called Dynastic Prophecy (ii 17) refers to a "king of Elam" who, from context of the broken section, must be Cyrus the Great. The text survives from a Seleucid era copy, though the original composition date is uncertain; see Grayson 1975b: 32–33 and Kuhrt 2007a: 80–81.

4. Translations of these texts are available in Foster 2005: 369–91.

5. The Nabonidus Chronicle referred to Cyrus the Great both as "king of Anshan" (ii 1) and "king of Parsu" (ii 15), a scribal conflation of the synonymous toponyms. The extant copy of the chronicle dates from the Seleucid period; the date of the original is uncertain.

6. Kuhrt 2007a: 141–57 for a full translation of the Old Persian version with notes.

7. The translation "line" follows primarily the Akkadian version's NUMUN (*zēru*: "seed" or "line"); the logogram NUMUN is also used in the Elamite version. The Old Persian version contains the word *taumā-*, which is often translated "family" but also has a wider sense of "lineage" or "clan"; see Brandenstein and Mayrhofer 1964: 145 and note Rollinger 1998: 183–86.

8. DB §10.

9. See also pp. 135–36 and also Figure 5.4c. The two inscriptions are labeled CMa and CMc, based on the standard abbreviations used to refer to Achaemenid-era inscriptions, labeled based on their initial attribution to Cyrus: uppercase letters for king (C̲yrus) and for provenience (M̲urghab, the modern name for Pasargadae), and a lowercase letter to distinguish discrete inscriptions from the same location. Though doubts about their attribution rose immediately, the original labels are still used to avoid confusion in tracking discussions through the scholarly literature. For

summaries and discussions of the problem, see inter alia Stronach 1990 and 1997; Waters 1996; Huyse 1999; and Briant 2002: 16 and 877. Another inscription, labeled CMb in the scholarly literature, consists of roughly thirty fragments that are not able to be confidently reassembled and are likely from more than one inscription.

10. DB §70.

11. Hdt. 1.125 for the Persian tribes, and see pp. 12–13. Hdt. 7.11 for Xerxes' rehearsal of his lineage; for a detailed treatment of the full passage, Hdt. 7.11, note especially Harrison 2015.

12. Hdt. 3.88 and see above, pp. 47–48.

Bibliography

Aghaie, K. 2000. "Islam and Nationalist Historiography: Competing Historical Narratives of the Iranian Nation in the Pahlavi Period." *Studies in Contemporary Islam* 2: 21–47.

Álvarez-Mon, J. 2010. *The Arjān Tomb: At the Crossroads of the Elamite and the Persian Empires.* Leuven: Peeters.

Álvarez-Mon, J., G. Basello, and Y. Wicks (eds.). 2018. *The Elamite World.* London: Routledge.

Amiet, P. 1973. "La glyptique de la fin de l'Élam." *Arts Asiatique* 28: 3–32.

Asheri, D., A. Lloyd, and A. Corcella. 2007. *A Commentary on Herodotus Books I–IV.* Oxford: Oxford University Press.

Aster, S. 2012. *The Unbeatable Light:* Melammu *and Its Biblical Parallels.* Münster: Ugarit-Verlag.

Bae, C. 2001. "Comparative Studies of King Darius's Bisitun Inscription." PhD diss., Harvard University.

Barajomovic, G. 2011. "Pride, Pomp and Circumstance: Palace, Court, and Household in Assyria, 879–612 BCE." In *Royal Courts in Dynastic States and Empires: A Global Perspective*, ed. J. Duindam, T. Artan, and M. Kunt. Leiden: Brill, 27–61.

Barnett, R. D. 1976. *Sculptures from the North Palace of Assurbanipal at Nineveh (668–627 BC).* London: British Museum.

Barnett, R. D., E. Bliebtreu, and G. Turner. 1998. *Sculptures from the Southwest Palace of Sennacherib at Nineveh.* London: British Museum Press.

Beaulieu, P.-A. 1989. *The Reign of Nabonidus, King of Babylon 556–539 BC.* New Haven, CT: Yale University Press.

Beaulieu, P.-A. 2000. "The Sippar Cylinder of Nabonidus." In *The Context of Scripture*, Vol. II, ed. W. Hallo and K. L. Younger. Leiden: Brill, 310–13.

Beaulieu, P.-A. 2003. "Nabopolassar and the Antiquity of Babylon." *Eretz Israel* 27: 1–9.

Beaulieu, P.-A. 2007. "Nabonidus the Mad King: A Reconsideration of His Steles from Harran and Babylon." In *Representations of Political Power: Case Histories from Times of Change and Dissolving Order in the Ancient Near East*, ed. M. Heinz and M. Feldman. Winona Lake, IN: Eisenbrauns, 137–66.

Beaulieu, P.-A. 2017. "Assyria in Late Babylonian Sources." In *A Companion to Assyria*, ed. E. Frahm. Malden, MA: Wiley-Blackwell, 549–55.

Bedford, P. 2001. *Temple Restoration in Early Achaemenid Judah.* Leiden: Brill.

Bivar, A. 2000. "The Role of Allegory in the Persian Epic." *Bulletin of the Asia Institute*, n.s. 14: 19–26.

Boucharlat, R. 2009. "The 'Paradise' of Cyrus at Pasargadae, the Core of the Royal Ostentation." In *Bau- und Gartenkultur zwischen "Orient" und "Okzident": Fragen zu Herkunft, Identität und Legitimation*, ed. J. Ganzert and J. Wolschke-Bulmahn. Munich: Martin Meidenbauer Verlag, 47–64.

Boucharlat, R. 2011. "Gardens and Parks at Pasargadae: Two 'Paradises'?" In *Herodot und das persisiche Weltreich*, ed. R. Rollinger, B. Truschnegg, and J. Wiesehöfer. Wiesbaden: Harrassowitz Verlag, 557–74.

Boucharlat, R. 2013. "Southwestern Iran in the Achaemenid Period." In *The Oxford Handbook of Ancient Iran*, ed. D. T. Potts. Oxford: Oxford University Press, 503–27.

Boucharlat, R. 2014a. "Archaeological Approaches and Their Future Directions in Pasargadae." In *World Heritage in Iran: Perspectives on Pasargadae*, ed. A. Mozaffari. Surrey: Ashgate, 29–60.

Boucharlat, R. 2014b. "Fire Altars and Fire Temples in the First Millennia BC/AD in the Iranian World: Some Remarks." In *Proceedings of the 8th International Congress on the Archaeology of the Ancient Near East*, Vol. 1, ed. P. Bieliński et al. Wiesbaden: Harrassowitz Verlag, 7–25.

Boucharlat, R. 2016. "À propos de *paradayadām* et paradis perse: perpléxité de l'archéologue et perspectives." In *Des contrées avestiques à Mahabad, via Bisoton: études offertes en hommage à Pierre Lecoq*, ed. Celine Redard. Paris: Recherches et Publications, 61–80.

Boucharlat, R. 2019. "Cyrus and Pasargadae: Forging an Empire—Fashioning 'Paradise.'" In *Cyrus the Great: Life and Lore*, ed. M. R. Shayegan. Boston: Ilex Foundation and Harvard University Press, 131–49.

Brandenstein, W., and M. Mayrhofer. 1964. *Handbuch des Altpersischen*. Wiesbaden: Harrassowitz Verlag.

Brereton, G. (ed.). 2018. *I Am Ashurbanipal, King of the World, King of Assyria*. London: Trustees of the British Museum.

Briant, P. 1996. *Histoire de l'empire Perse: De Cyrus à Perse*. Paris: Fayard.

Briant, P. 2002. *From Cyrus to Alexander: A History of the Persian Empire*, trans. P. Daniels. Winona Lake, IN: Eisenbrauns.

Briant, P. 2021. "From the Mediterranean to the Indus Valley: Modalities and Limitations of the Achaemenid Imperial Space." In *The Limits of Universal Rule: Eurasian Empires Compared*, ed. Y. Pines, M. Biran, and J. Rüpke. Cambridge: Cambridge University Press, 49–78.

Brosius, M. 1996. *Women in Ancient Persia (559–331 BC)*. Oxford: Oxford University Press.

Cahill, N. 2010. "The Persian Destruction of Sardis / Sardeis'teki Pers Tahribi." In *Lidyalılar ve dünyaları / The Lydians and Their World*, ed. N. Cahill. Istanbul: Yapı Kredi Yayınları, 339–61.

Cahill, N. 2019. "Inside Out: Sardis in the Achaemenid and Lysimachean Periods." In *Spear-won Land: Sardis from the King's Peace to the Peace of Apamea*, ed. A. Berlin and P. Kosmin. Madison: University of Wisconsin Press, 11–36.

Callieri, P. 2017. "Achaemenid 'Ritual Architecture' vs. 'Religious Architecture': Reflections on the Elusive Archaeological Evidence of the Religion of the Achaemenids." In *Persian Religion in the Achaemenid Period*, ed. W. Henkelman and C. Redard. Wiesbaden: Harrassowitz Verlag, 385–400.

Canepa, M. 2017. "Rival Images of Iranian Kingship and Persian Identity in Post-Achaemenid Western Asia." In *Persianism in Antiquity*, ed. R. Strootman and M. Versluys. Stuttgart: Franz Steiner Verlag, 201–22.

Canepa, M. 2018. *The Iranian Expanse: Transforming Royal Identity through Architecture, Landscape, and the Built Environment, 550 BCE–642 CE*. Berkeley: University of California Press.

Canepa, M. 2020. "The Parthian and Sasanian Empires." In *The Oxford World History of Empires*, Vol. 2, ed. P. Bang, C. Bayly, and W. Scheidel. Oxford: Oxford University Press, 290–324.

Coloru, O. 2017. "Once Were Persians: The Perception of Pre-Islamic Monuments in Iran from the 16th to the 19th Century." In *Persianism in Antiquity*, ed. R. Strootman and M. Versluys. Stuttgart: Franz Steiner Verlag, 87–106.

Curtis, J. 2013. *The Cyrus Cylinder and Ancient Persia: A New Beginning for the Middle East*. London: The British Museum.

Curtis, J., and St. John Simpson (eds.). 2010. *The World of Achaemenid Persia*. London: I. B. Tauris.

Dalley, S. 2013. *The Mystery of the Hanging Garden of Babylon: An Elusive World Wonder Traced*. Oxford: Oxford University Press.

Dandamaev, M. 1989. *A Political History of the Achaemenid Empire*, trans. W. J. Vogelsang. Leiden: Brill.

Dandamaev, M. 1992. *Iranians in Achaemenid Babylonia*. Costa Mesa, CA: Mazda Publishers.

Darbo-Peschanski, C. 2013. "Herodotus and *historia*." In *Herodotus*, Vol. 2: *Herodotus and the World*, ed. Rosario Vignolo Munson. Oxford: Oxford University Press, 78–105.

Da Riva, R. 2008. *The Neo-Babylonian Royal Inscriptions: An Introduction*. Münster: Ugarit-Verlag.

Da Riva, R. 2013. *The Inscriptions of Nabopolassar, Amel-Marduk, and Neriglissar*. Berlin: de Gruyter.

Daryaee, T. (ed.). 2013a. *Cyrus the Great: An Ancient Iranian King*. Santa Monica, CA: Afshar Publishing.

Daryaee, T. 2013b. "Religion of Cyrus the Great." In *Cyrus the Great: An Ancient Iranian King*, ed. T. Daryaee. Santa Monica, CA: Afshar Publishing, 16–27.

Daryaee, T. 2019. "On Forgetting Cyrus and Remembering the Achaemenids in Late Antique Iran." In *Cyrus the Great: Life and Lore*, ed. M. R. Shayegan. Boston: Ilex Foundation and Harvard University Press, 221–31.

Daryaee, T. 2021. "Balkanization of Antiquity in Contemporary Iranian Memory." In *Iran and Its Histories. From the Beginning through the Achaemenid Empire*, ed. T. Daryaee and R. Rollinger. Wiesbaden: Harrassowitz Verlag, 31–44.

Davidson, O. 2019. "Traces of Poetic Traditions about Cyrus the Great and His Dynasty in the Šāhnāme of Ferdowsi and the Cyrus Cylinder." In *Cyrus the Great: Life and Lore*, ed. M. R. Shayegan. Boston: Ilex Foundation and Harvard University Press, 232–41.

Davis, D. (trans.). 2006. *Shahnameh: The Persian Book of Kings*. New York: Viking.

De Jong, A. 1997. *Traditions of Magi: Zoroastrianism in Greek and Latin Literature*. Leiden: Brill.

De Vaan, J. M. C. T. 1995. *"Ich bin eine Schwertklinge des Königs": Die Sprache des Bēl-ibni*. Neukirchen: Ugarit-Verlag.

Dulęba, W. 1995. *The Cyrus Legend in the Šāhnāme*. Krakow: The Enigma Press.

Dusinberre, E. 2002. "An Excavated Ivory from Kerkenes Dağ, Turkey: Transcultural Fluidities, Significations of Collective Identity, and the Problem of Median Art." In *Medes and Persians. Fresh Assessments of the Arts and Archaeologies of Empire*, ed. M. C. Root. *Ars Orientalis* 32: 17–54.

Dusinberre, E. 2003. *Aspects of Empire in Achaemenid Sardis*. Cambridge: Cambridge University Press.

Dusinberre, E. 2013. *Empire, Authority, and Autonomy in Achaemenid Anatolia*. Cambridge: Cambridge University Press.

Eckhardt, B. 2017. "Memories of Persian Rule: Constructing History and Ideology in Hasmonean Judea." In *Persianism in Antiquity*, ed. R. Strootman and M Versluys. Stuttgart: Franz Steiner Verlag, 249–66.

Fales, F. M. 2012. "After Taʿyinat: The New Status of Esarhaddon's *adê* for Assyrian Political History." *Revue d'Assyriologie* 106: 133–58.

Farrokh, K. 2007. *Shadows in the Desert: Ancient Persia at War*. Oxford: Osprey Publishers.

Feldman, M. 2007. "Darius I and the Heroes of Akkad: Affect and Agency in the Bisitun Relief." In *Ancient Near Eastern Art in Context: Studies in Honor of Irene Winter by Her Students*, ed. J. Cheng and M. Feldman. Leiden: Brill, 265–93.

Finkel, I. (ed.). 2013. *The Cyrus Cylinder: The King of Persia's Ancient Proclamation from Babylon*. London: I. B. Tauris.

Foster, B. 2005. *Before the Muses: An Anthology of Akkadian Literature*. 3rd ed. Bethesda, MD: CDL Press.

Fox, R. L. 2007. "Alexander the Great: 'Last of the Achaemenids'?" In *Persian Responses: Political and Culture Interactions with(in) the Achaemenid Empire*, ed. C. Tuplin. Swansea: The Classical Press of Wales, 267–312.

Frahm, E. 2013. "Rising Suns and Falling Stars: Assyrian Kings and the Cosmos." In *Experiencing Power, Generating Authority: Cosmos, Politics, and the Ideology of Kingship in Ancient Egypt and Mesopotamia*, ed. J. Hill, P. Jones, and A. Morales. Philadelphia: University of Pennsylvania Museum, 97–120.

Frahm, E. 2017. "The Neo-Assyrian Period (c. 1000–609 BCE)." In *A Companion to Assyria*, ed. E. Frahm. Malden, MA: Wiley-Blackwell, 161–208.

Frame, G. 1992. *Babylonia 689–627 BC: A Political History*. Leiden: Nederlands Instituut voor het Nabije Oosten.

Frame, G. 1995. *Rulers of Babylonia: From the Second Dynasty of Isin to the End of Assyrian Domination (1157–612 BC)*. RIM Babylonian Periods 2. Toronto: University of Toronto Press.

Fried, L. 2004. *The Priest and the Great King: Temple-Palace Relations in the Persian Empire*. Winona Lake, IN: Eisenbrauns.

Fried, L. 2017. *Ezra: A Commentary*. Sheffield: Sheffield Phoenix Press.

Fuchs, A. 1999a. "Daiukku." In *The Prosopography of the Neo Assyrian Empire*, Vol. I, Part 2, ed. K. Radner. Helsinki: The Neo-Assyrian Text Corpus Project, 369.

Fuchs, A. 1999b. "Daīku." In *The Prosopography of the Neo Assyrian Empire*, Vol. I, Part 2, ed. K. Radner. Helsinki: The Neo-Assyrian Text Corpus Project, 370.

Fuchs, A. 2000. "Kashtaritu." In *The Prosopography of the Neo Assyrian Empire*, Vol. II, Part 1, ed. H. Baker. Helsinki: The Neo-Assyrian Text Corpus Project, 608.

Fuchs, A. 2004. "Parsua(š)." *Reallexikon der Assyriologie und Vorderasiatischen Archäologie* 10 (5/6): 341–42.

Fuchs, A., and S. Parpola. *The Correspondence of Sargon II, Part III: Letters from Babylonia and the Eastern Provinces*, SAA XV. Helsinki, 2001.

Gadd, C. J. 1928. *Ur Excavation Texts I. Royal Inscriptions*. Text. London: Trustees of the British Museum and the Museum of the University of Pennsylvania.

Garrison, M. B. 1991. "Seals and the Elite at Persepolis: Some Observations on Early Achaemenid Persian Art." *Ars Orientalis* 21: 1–29.

Garrison, M. B. 2011a. "The Seal of 'Kuraš the Anshanite, son of Šešpeš' (Teispes), PFS 93*." In *Elam and Persia*, ed. J. Álvarez-Mon and M. Garrison. Winona Lake, IN: Eisenbrauns, 375–405.

Garrison, M. B. 2011b. "By the Favor of Auramazda: Kingship and the Divine in the Early Achaemenid Period." In *More Than Men, Less Than Gods: Studies on Royal Cult and Imperial Worship*, ed. P. Iossif, A. Chankowski, and C. Lorber. Leuven: Peeters, 15–104.

Garrison, M. B. 2014. "Glyptic Studies as Art History." In *Critical Approaches to Ancient Near Eastern Art*, ed. B. Brown and M. Feldman. Berlin: Walter de Gruyter, 481–513.

Garrison, M. B. 2017a. "Beyond Auramazdā and the Winged Symbol: Imagery of the Divine and Numinous at Persepolis." In *Persian Religion in the Achaemenid Period*, ed. W. Henkelman and C. Redard. Wiesbaden: Harrassowitz Verlag, 185–246.

Garrison, M. B. 2017b. *The Ritual Landscape at Persepolis: Glyptic Imagery from Persepolis Fortification and Treasury Archives*. Chicago: University of Chicago Press.

Garrison, M. B. and W. Henkelman. 2020. "The Seal of Prince Aršāma: From Persepolis to Oxford." In *Aršāma and His World: The Bodleian Letters in Context*, Vol. 2: *Bullae and Seals*, ed. M. Garrison, W. Henkelman, and D. Kaptan. Oxford: Oxford University Press, 46–166.

Garrison, M. B., C. Jones, and M. W. Stolper. 2018. "Achaemenid Elamite Administrative Tablets, 4: BM 108963." *Journal of Near Eastern Studies* 77: 1–14.

Garrison, M. B., and M. C. Root. 2001. *Seals on the Persepolis Fortification Tablets*, Vol. 1: *Images of Heroic Encounter*. Chicago: Oriental Institute of the University of Chicago Press.

Garthwaite, G. 2005. *The Persians*. Malden, MA: Blackwell Publishing.

Gaspa, S. 2017. "State Theology and Royal Ideology of the Neo-Assyrian Empire as a Structuring Model for the Achaemenid Imperial Religion." In *Persian Religion in the Achaemenid Period*, ed. W. Henkelman and C. Redard. Wiesbaden: Harrassowitz Verlag, 125–84.

Genito, B. 2005. "The Archaeology of the Median Period: An Outline and a Research Perspective." *Iranica Antiqua* 40: 315–40.

George, A. R. 1993. *House Most High: The Temples of Ancient Mesopotamia*, Winona Lake, IN: Eisenbrauns.

George, A. R. 1996. "Studies in Cultic Topography and Ideology." *Bibliotheca Orientalis* 53: 379–84.

Glassner, J.-J. 2004. *Mesopotamian Chronicles*. Atlanta: Society of Biblical Literature.

Gnoli, G. 1989. *The Idea of Iran: An Essay on Its Origin*. Rome: Is.M.E.O.

Gondet, S., et al. 2016. "Field Report on the 2015 Current Archaeological Works of the Joint Iran-French Project on Pasargadae and Its Territory." *International Journal of Iranian Heritage* 1 (1): 60–87.

Gondet, S., et al. 2018. "Field Report on the 2016 Archaeological Project of the Joint Iran-France Project on Pasargadae and Its Surrounding Territory." *International Journal of Iranian Heritage Studies* 1 (2): 1–28.

Gondet, S., K. Mohammadkhandi, and H. Gopnik. 2021. "The 2015–2016 Survey Campaigns at Pasargadae: Results and Observations on the Cyrus' Capital Layout and Its Latter Evolutions." In *Achaemenid Studies Today*, ed. G. Basello, P. Callieri, and A. V. Rossi. Napoli: Università degli Studi di Napoli "L'Orientale."

Good, I. 2010. "When East Met West: Interpretative Problems in Assessing Eurasian Contact and Exchange in Antiquity." *Archäologische Mitteilungen aus Iran und Turan* 42: 23–45.

Gopnik, H. 2017. "The Median Confederacy." In *King of the Seven Climes: A History of the Ancient Iranian World (3000 BCE–651 CE)*, ed. T. Daryaee. Irvine, CA: UCI Jordan Center of Persian Studies, 39–62.

Gorris, E. 2020. *Power and Politics in the Neo-Elamite Kingdom*. Leuven: Peeters.

Grayson, A. K. 1975a. *Assyrian and Babylonian Chronicles*. Locust Valley, NY: J. J. Augustin.

Grayson, A. K. 1975b. *Babylonian Historical-Literary Texts*. Toronto: University of Toronto Press.

Grayson, A. K. 1991. *Assyrian Rulers of the Early First Millennium BC I*. RIMA 2. Toronto: University of Toronto Press.

Grayson, A. K. 1996. *Assyrian Rulers of the Early First Millennium BC II (858–745 BC)*. RIMA 3. Toronto: University of Toronto Press.

Grayson, A. K., and J. Novotny. 2014. *The Royal Inscriptions of Sennacherib, King of Assyria (704–681 BC), Part 2*. RINAP 3/2. Winona Lake, IN: Eisenbrauns.

Greenewalt, C. 1992. "When a Mighty Empire Was Destroyed: The Common Man at the Fall of Sardis, ca. 546 BC." *Proceedings of the American Philosophical Society* 136: 247–71.

Hall, E. 1989. *Inventing the Barbarian: Greek Self-Definition through Tragedy*. Oxford: Oxford University Press.

Hallock, R. T. 1969. *Persepolis Fortification Tablets*. OIP 92. Chicago: University of Chicago Press.

Harrison, T. 2011. *Writing Ancient Persia*. London: Bristol Classical Press.

Harrison, T. 2015. "Herodotus on the Character of Persian Imperialism (7.5–11)." In *Assessing Biblical and Classical Sources for the Reconstruction of Persian Influence, History and Culture*, ed. A. Fitzpatrick-McKinley. Wiesbaden: Harrassowitz Verlag, 9–48.

Haubold, J., J. Steele, and K. Stevens (eds.). 2019. *Keeping Watch in Babylon: The Astronomical Diaries in Context*. Leiden: Brill.

Heckel, W. 2007. *The Conquests of Alexander the Great*. Cambridge: Cambridge University Press.

Helm, P. 1981. "Herodotus' *Mêdikos Logos* and Median History." *Iran* 19: 85–90.

Henkelman, W. 2002. "Exit der Posaunenbläser: On Lance-Guards and Lance-Bearers in the Persepolis Fortification Archive." *ARTA: Achaemenid Research on Texts and Archaeology* 2002 (7).

Henkelman, W. 2003a. "Persians, Medes, and Elamites: Acculturation in the Neo-Elamite Period." In *Continuity of Empire(?): Assyria, Media, Persia*, ed. G. Lanfranchi, M. Roaf, and R. Rollinger. Padua: S.a.r.go.n. Editrice de Libreria, 181–232.

Henkelman, W. 2003b. "An Elamite Memorial: The *šumar* of Cambyses and Hystaspes." In *A Persian Perspective: Essays in Memory of Heleen Sancisi-Weerdenburg*, ed. W. Henkelman and A. Kuhrt. Achaemenid History 13. Leiden: Nederlands Instituut voor het Nabije Oosten, 101–72.

Henkelman, W. 2008. *The Other Gods Who Are: Studies in Elamite-Iranian Acculturation Based on the Persepolis Fortification Texts*. Leiden: Nederlands Instituut voor het Nabije Oosten.

Henkelman, W. 2010. "'Consumed before the King': The Table of Darius, That of Irdabama and Irtaštuna, and That of His Satrap, Karkiš." In *Der Achämenidenhof/The Achaemenid Court*, ed. B. Jacobs und R. Rollinger. Wiesbaden: Harrassowitz Verlag, 667–775.

Henkelman, W. 2011. "Cyrus the Persian and Darius the Elamite: A Case of Mistaken Identity." In *Herodot und das persische Weltreich/Herodotus and the Persian Empire*, ed. R. Rollinger, B. Truschnegg, and J. Wiesehöfer. Wiesbaden: Harrassowitz Verlag, 577–634.

Henkelman, W., and C. Redard (eds.). 2017. *Persian Religion in the Achaemenid Period*. Wiesbaden: Harrassowitz Verlag.

Herrenschmidt, C. 1976/2014. "Désignations de l'empire et concepts politiques de Darius Ier d'après ses inscriptions en vieux-perse." *Studia Iranica* 5 (1976), translated into English in *Excavating an Empire: Achaemenid Persia in Longue Durée*, ed. T. Daryaee, A. Mousavi, and K. Rezakhani. Costa Mesa, CA: Mazda Publishers, 12–36.

Hinz, W., and H. Koch. 1987. *Elamisches Wörterbuch*, 2 vols. Berlin: Dietrich Reimer.

Holtz, S. 2009. *Neo-Babylonian Court Procedure*. Leiden: Brill.

Huyse, P. 1999. "Some Further Thoughts on the Bisitun Monument and the Genesis of the Old Persian Script." *Bulletin of the Asia Institute* 13: 45–66.

Hyland, J. 2018. "Hystaspes, Gobryas, and Elite Marriage Politics in Teispid Persia." *The Digital Archive of Brief Notes and Iran Review* (DABIR) 5: 30–35.

Hyland, J. 2019. "The Achaemenid Messenger Service and the Ionian Revolt." *Historia* 68 (2): 150–69.

Jacobs, B. 2011. "Achaemenid Satrapies." In *Encyclopædia Iranica*, online edition, available at http://www.iranicaonline.org/articles/achaemenid-satrap ies, accessed October 13, 2020.

Jacobs, B., and R. Rollinger (eds.). 2010. *Der Achämenidenhof/The Achaemenid Court*. Wiesbaden: Harrassowitz Verlag.

Jamzadeh, P. 2004. "A Shahnama Passage in an Achaemenid Context." *Iran* 39: 383–88.

Jursa, M. 2007. "The Transition of Babylonia from the Neo-Babylonian Empire to Achaemenid Rule." In *Regime Change in the Ancient Near East and Egypt: From Sargon of Agade to Saddam Hussein*, ed. H. Crawford. Oxford: Oxford University Press, 73–94.

Jursa, M. 2010. *Aspects of the Economic History of Babylonia in the First Millennium BC*. Münster: Ugarit-Verlag.

Jursa, M. 2014. "The Neo-Babylonian Empire." In *Imperien und Reiche in der Weltgeschichte: Epochenübergreifende und globalhistorische Vergleiche*, ed. Sabine Fick. Wiesbaden: Harrassowitz Verlag, 121–48.

Jursa, M. 2015. "Families, Officialdom, and Families of Royal Officials in Chaldean and Achaemenid Babylonia." In *Tradition and Innovation in the Ancient Near East*, ed. A. Archi. Winona Lake, IN: Eisenbrauns, 597–606.

Kaptan, D. 2002. *The Daskyleion Bullae: Seal Images from the Western Achaemenid Empire*. Leiden: Nederlands Instituut voor het Nabije Oosten.

Kawami, T. 1972. "A Possible Source for the Sculptures of the Audience Hall, Pasargadae." *Iran* 10: 146–48.

Kent, R. G. 1953. *Old Persian: Grammar, Texts, Lexicon*. 2nd ed. New Haven, CT: Yale University Press.

Khatchadourian, L. 2016. *Imperial Matter: Ancient Persia and the Archaeology of Empires*. Oakland: University of California Press.

King, L. W., and R. C. Thompson. 1907. *Sculptures and Inscription of Darius the Great, on the Rock of Behistûn in Persia*. London: The British Museum.

Kleber, K., with J. Hackl. 2010. "*Dātu ša šarri*: Gesetzgebung in Babylonien unter den Achämeniden." *Journal for Ancient Near Eastern and Biblical Law* 16: 49–75.

Knauss. F. 2006. "Ancient Persia and the Caucasus." *Iranica Antiqua* 41: 79–118.

Kozuh, M. 2014. *The Sacrificial Economy: Assessors, Contractors, and Thieves in the Management of Sacrificial Sheep at the Eanna Temple of Uruk (ca. 625–520 BC)*. Winona Lake, IN: Eisenbrauns.

Kradin, N. 2020. "The Mongol Empire and the Unification of Eurasia." In *The Oxford World History of Empire*, Vol. 2, ed. P. Bang, C. Bayly, and W. Scheidel. Oxford: Oxford University Press, 507–32.

Kuhrt, A. 1990. "Alexander and Babylon." In *The Roots of the European Tradition*, ed. H. Sancisi-Weerdenburg and H. Drijvers. Leiden: Nederlands Instituut voor het Nabije Oosten, 121–30.

Kuhrt, A. 1995. *The Ancient Near East, c. 3000–330 BC*, 2 vols. London: Routledge.

Kuhrt, A. 2003. "Making History: Sargon of Agade and Cyrus the Great of Persia." In *A Persian Perspective: Essays in Memory of Heleen Sancisi-Weerdenburg*, ed. W. Henkelman and A. Kuhrt. Leiden: Nederlands Instituut voor het Nabije Oosten, 347–61.

Kuhrt, A. 2007a. *The Persian Empire: A Corpus of Sources from the Achaemenid Period*. London: Routledge.

Kuhrt, A. 2007b "The Problem of Achaemenid 'Religious Policy.'" In *Die Welt der Götterbilder*, ed. B. Groneburg and H. Spieckermann. Berlin: Walter de Gruyter, 117–42.

Kuhrt, A. 2010. "Achaemenid Images of Royalty and Empire." In *Concepts of Kingship in Antiquity*, ed. G. Lanfranchi and R. Rollinger. Padua: S.a.r.g.o.n. Editrice de Libreria, 87–105.

Kuhrt, A. 2014a. "State Communications in the Persian Empire." In *State Correspondence in the Ancient World*, ed. K. Radner. Oxford: Oxford University Press, 112–40.

Kuhrt, A. 2014b. "Even a Dog in Babylon Is Free." In *Legacy of Momigliano*, ed. T. Cornell and O. Murray. London: The Warburg Institute, 77–88.

Lambert. W. G. 2007. "Cyrus' Defeat of Nabonidus." *Nouvelles Assyriologiques Brèves et Utilitaires* 2007 no. 14.

Lanfranchi, G., M. Roaf, and R. Rollinger (eds.). 2003. *Continuity of Empire(?): Assyria, Media, Persia*. Padua: S.a.r.go.n. Editrice de Libreria.

Leichty, E. 2011. *The Royal Inscriptions of Esarhaddon, King of Assyria (680–669 BC)*. RINAP 4. Winona Lake, IN: Eisenbrauns.

Lecoq, P. 1997. *Les inscriptions de la Perse achéménide*. Paris: Gallimard.

Lerner, J. 2017. "Ancient Persianisms in Nineteenth-Century Iran: The Revival of Persepolitan Imagery under the Qajars." In *Persianism in Antiquity*, ed. R. Strootman and M. Versluys. Stuttgart: Franz Steiner Verlag, 107–20.

Lewis, B. 1980. *The Sargon Legend: A Study of the Akkadian Text and the Hero Who Was Exposed at Birth*. Cambridge, MA: American Schools of Oriental Research.

Lincoln, B. 2012. *"Happiness for Mankind": Achaemenian Religion and the Imperial Project*. Leuven: Peeters.

Liverani, M. 2017. *Assyria: The Imperial Mission*. Winona Lake, IN: Eisenbrauns.

Llewellyn-Jones, L. 2013. *King and Court in Ancient Persia 559 to 331 BCE*. Edinburgh: Edinburgh University Press.

Llewellyn-Jones, L., and J. Robson. 2010. *Ctesias' History of Persia: Tales of the Orient*. London: Routledge.

Luukko, M., and G. Van Buylaere. 2002. *The Political Correspondence of Esarhaddon*. SAA 16. Helsinki: Helsinki University Press.

Machinist, P. 2006. "Kingship and Divinity in Imperial Assyria." In *Text, Artifact, and Image: Revealing Ancient Israelite Religion*, ed. G. Beckman and T. Lewis. Providence, RI: Brown University, 151–88.

Majidzadeh, Y. 1992. "The Arjan Bowl." *Iran* 30: 131–44.

Malbran-Labat, F. 1995. *Les inscriptions royales de Suse: Briques de l'époque paleo-élamite à l'Empire néo-élamite*. Paris: Réunion des musées nationaux.

Mari, F. 2016. "Cyrus the Great in Movsēs Xorenac'i, *Patmut'iwn Hayoc'*: Telescoping the King." In *Greek Texts and Armenian Traditions: An Interdisciplinary Approach*, ed. F. Gazzano, L. Pagani, and G. Traina. Berlin: Walter de Gruyter, 115–42.

Masroori, C. 1999. "Cyrus II and the Political Utility of Religious Toleration." In *Religious Toleration: "The Variety of Rites" from Cyrus to Defoe*, ed. J. C. Laursen. New York: St. Martin's Press, 13–36.

May, H., and B. Metzger. 1973. *The New Oxford Annotated Bible with the Apocrypha*, revised edition. Oxford: Oxford University Press.

McCaskie, T. 2012. "'As on a Darkling Plain': Practitioners, Publics, Propagandists, and Ancient Historiography." *Comparative Studies in Society and History* 54 (1): 145–73.

Miroschedji, P. de. 1985. "La fin du royaume d'Anšan et de Suse et la naissance de l'Empire perse." *Zeitschrift für Assyriologie und Vorderasiatische Archäologie* 75: 265–306.

Miroschedji, P. de. 1990. "La fin de l'Élam: Essai d'analyse et d'interpretation." *Iranica Antiqua* 25: 48–95.

Moeller, N., D. T. Potts, and K. Radner. *The Oxford History of the Ancient Near East*, Vol. 4. Oxford: Oxford University Press.

Moeller, N., Potts, D. T., and Radner, K. 2022. *The Oxford History of the Ancient Near East*, Vol. 5. Oxford: Oxford University Press.

Mousavi, A. 1989. "The Discovery of an Achaemenid Station at Deh-Bozan in the Asadabad Valley." *Archäologische Mitteilungen aus Iran* 22: 135–38.

Mozaffari. A. (ed.). 2014. *World Heritage in Iran: Perspectives on Pasargadae*. Surrey: Ashgate.

Naveh, J., and Shaked, S. 2012. *Ancient Aramaic Documents from Bactria (fourth century BCE) from the Khalili Collection*. London: Khalili Family Trust.

Nelsestuen, G. 2017. "*Oikonomia* as a Theory of Empire in the Political Thought of Xenophon and Aristotle." *Greek, Roman, and Byzantine Studies* 57: 74–104.

Novotny, J., and J. Jeffers. 2018. *The Royal Inscriptions of Ashurbanipal (668–631 BC), Aššur-etal-ilāni (630–627 BC), and Sîn-šarra-iškun (626–612 BC), Kings of Assyria*. RINAP 5/1. University Park, PA: Eisenbrauns.

Nylander, C. 1967. "Who Wrote the Inscriptions at Pasargadae?" *Orientalia Suecana* 16: 135–80.

Olbrycht, M. 2014. "'An Admirer of Persian Ways': Alexander the Great's Reforms in Parthia-Hyrcania and the Iranian Heritage." In *Excavating an Empire: Achaemenid Persia in Longue Durée*, ed. T. Daryaee, A. Mousavi, and K. Rezakhani. Costa Mesa, CA: Mazda Publishers, 37–62.

Olbrycht, M. 2019. "The Shaping of Political Memory: Cyrus and the Achaemenids in the Royal Ideologies of the Seleucid and Parthian Periods." In *Cyrus the Great: Life and Lore*, ed. M. R. Shayegan. Boston: Ilex Foundation and Harvard University Press, 198–220.

Olmstead, A. T. 1948. *History of the Persian Empire*. Chicago: University of Chicago Press.

Oppenheim, A. L. 1956. *The Interpretation of Dreams in the Ancient Near East: With a Translation of an Assyrian Dream-book*. Transactions of the American Philosophical Society, n.s. 46. Philadelphia: American Philosophical Society, 179–373.

Ornan, T. 2005. "A Complex System of Religious Symbols: The Case of the Winged Disc in Near Eastern Imagery in the First Millennium

BCE." In *Crafts and Images in Contact*, ed. C. Suter and C. Uehlinger. Göttingen: Academic Press Fribourg, 207–41.

Parpola, S. 2018. *The Correspondence of Assurbanipal, Part I: Letters from Assyria, Babylonia, and Vassal States*. SAA XXI. Helsinki: The Neo-Assyrian Text Corpus Project.

Pelling, C. 1996. "The Urine and the Vine: Astyages' Dreams at Herodotus 1.107–8." *Classical Quarterly* 46: 68–77.

Perrot, J. (ed.). 2010. *The Palace of Darius at Susa: The Great Royal Residence of Achaemenid Persia*. Translated by G. Collon. London: Iran Heritage Foundation.

Pirngruber, R. 2017. *The Economy of Late Achaemenid and Seleucid Babylonia*. Cambridge: Cambridge University Press.

Pongratz-Leisten, B. 2002. "'Lying King' and 'False Prophet': The Intercultural Transfer of a Rhetorical Device within Ancient Near Eastern Ideologies." In *Ideologies as Intercultural Phenomena: Proceedings of the Third Annual Symposium of the Assyrian and Babylonian Intellectual Heritage Project*, ed. A. Panaino and G. Pettinato. Milan: Università di Bologna, 215–43.

Pongratz-Leisten, B. 2015. *Religion and Ideology in Assyria*. Berlin: Walter de Gruyter.

Pongratz-Leisten, B. 2019. "'Ich bin ein Babylonier': The Political-Religious Message of the Cyrus Cylinder." In *Cyrus the Great: Life* and Lore, ed. M. R. Shayegan. Boston: Ilex Foundation and Harvard University Press, 92–105.

Porter, B., and K. Radner. 1998. "*Aššur-aḫi-iddina*." In *The Prosopography of the Neo-Assyrian Empire* 1/I, A, ed. K. Radner. Helsinki: The Neo-Assyrian Text Corpus Project, 145–52.

Potts, D. T. 1999. "Elamite Ūlā, Akkadian Ulaya, and Greek Choaspes: A Solution to the Eulaios Problem." *Bulletin of the Asia Institute* 13: 27–44.

Potts, D. T. 2005a. "Cyrus the Great and the Kingdom of Anshan." In *Birth of the Persian Empire*, ed. V. Curtis and S. Stewart. London: I. B. Tauris, 7–28.

Potts, D. T. 2005b. "Neo-Elamite Problems." *Iranica Antiqua* 40: 165–70.

Potts, D. T. 2016. *The Archaeology of Elam: Formation and Transformation of an Ancient Iranian State*. 2nd ed. Cambridge: Cambridge University Press.

Radner, K. 1998. "*Aššūr-etel-ilāni-mukīn-apli*." In *The Prosopography of the Neo-Assyrian Empire* 1/I, A, ed. K. Radner. Helsinki: The Neo-Assyrian Text Corpus Project.

Radner, K. 2013. "Assyria and the Medes." In *The Oxford Handbook of Ancient Iran*, ed. D. T. Potts. Oxford: Oxford University Press, 442–56.

Razmjou, S. 2013. "The Cyrus Cylinder: A Persian Perspective." In *The Cyrus Cylinder: The King of Persia's Ancient Proclamation from Babylon*, ed. I. Finkel. London: I. B. Tauris, 104–26.

Razmjou, S. 2020. "The Textual Connections between the Cyrus Cylinder and the Bible, with Particular Reference to Isaiah." In *Studies in Ancient Persia and the Achaemenid Period*, ed. John Curtis. London: James Clarke & Co. Ltd, 158–74.

Reade, J. 2003. "Why Did the Medes Invade Assyria?" In *Continuity of Empire(?): Assyria, Media, Persia*, ed. G. Lanfranchi, M. Roaf, and R. Rollinger. Padua: S.a.r.g.o.n. Editrice e Libreria, 149–56.

Ricks, T. 2020. *First Principles: What America's Founders Learned from the Greeks and Romans and How That Shaped Our Country*. New York: Harper.

Ristvet, L. 2015. *Ritual, Performance, and Politics in the Ancient Near East*. Cambridge: Cambridge University Press.

Roaf, M. 2003. "The Median Dark Age." In *Continuity of Empire(?): Assyria, Media, Persia*, ed. G. Lanfranchi, M. Roaf, and R. Rollinger. Padua: S.a.r.g.o.n. Editrice e Libreria, 13–22.

Rollinger, R. 1998. "Der Stammbaum des achaimenidischen Königshauses oder die Frage des Legitimität der Herrschaft de Dareios." *Archäologische Mitteilungen aus Iran und Turan* 30: 155–209.

Rollinger, R. 1999. "Zur Lokalisation von Parsu(m)a(š) in der Fārs und zu einigen Fragen der frühen persischen Geschichte." *Zeitschrift für Assyriologie und Vorderasiatische Archäologie* 89: 115–39.

Rollinger, R. 2003. "The Western Expansion of the Median 'Empire': A Re-examination." In *Continuity of Empire(?): Assyria, Media, Persia*, ed. G. Lanfranchi, M. Roaf, and R. Rollinger. Padua: S.a.r.g.o.n. Editrice e Libreria, 289–320.

Rollinger, R. 2013. "Berossos and the Monuments: City Walls, Sanctuaries, Palaces and the Hanging Garden." In *The World of Berossos*, ed. Johannes Haubold, Giovanni B. Lanfranchi, Robert Rollinger, and John Steele. Wiesbaden: Harrassowitz Verlag, 137–62.

Rollinger, R. 2018. "Herodotus and the Transformation of Ancient Near Eastern Motifs: Darius I, Oebares, the Neighing Horse." In *Interpreting Herodotus*, ed. T Harrison and E. Irwin. Oxford: Oxford University Press, 203–36.

Rollinger, R. 2020. "The Medes of the 7th and 6th c. BCE: A Short-Term Empire or Rather a Short-Term Confederacy?" In *Short-term Empires in World History*, ed. R. Rollinger, J. Degen, and M. Gehler. Wiesbaden: Springer, 187–213.

Rollinger, R., and A. Kellner. 2019. "Once More the Nabonidus Chronicle (BM 35382) and Cyrus' Campaigns in 547 BC." *Ancient West and East* 18: 153–76.

Root, M. C. 1979. *The King and Kingship in Achaemenid Art: Essays on the Creation of an Iconography of Empire*. Leiden: Brill.

Root, M. C. 2010. "Palace to Temple-King to Cosmos: Achaemenid Foundation Texts in Iran." In *From the Foundations to the Crenellations: Essays on Temple Building in the Ancient Near East and Hebrew Bible*, ed. M. Boda and J. Novotny. Münster: Ugarit-Verlag, 165–210.

Root, M. C. 2013. "Defining the Divine in Achaemenid Persian Kingship: The View from Bisitun." In *Every Inch a King: Comparative Studies on Kings and Kingship in the Ancient and Medieval Worlds*, ed. L. Mitchell and C. Melville. Leiden: Brill, 23–65.

Rosavich, V. 1984. "The Romans' View of the Persians." *The Classical World* 78 (1): 1–8.

Rossi, A. 2010. "Elusive Identities in Pre-Achaemenid Iran: The Medes and the Median Language." In *Iranian Identity in the Course of History*, ed. C. Cereti. Roma: Istituto Italiano per l'Africa e l'Oriente, 289–330.

Rung, E. 2015. "The End of the Lydian Kingdom and the Lydians after Croesus." In *Political Memory in and after the Persian Empire*, ed. J. Silverman and C. Waerzeggers. Atlanta: SBL Press, 7–26.

Russell, J. 1991. *Sennacherib's Palace without Rival at Nineveh*. Chicago: University of Chicago Press.

Russell, J. 1999. *The Writing on the Wall: Studies in the Architectural Context of Late Assyrian Palace Inscriptions*. Winona Lake, IN: Eisenbrauns.

Sachs, A., and H. Hunger, 1988. *Astronomical Diaries and Related Texts from Babylonia I: Diaries from 652 BC to 262 BC*. Vienna: Verlag der Österreichischen Akademie der Wissenschaften.

Sami, A. 1956. *Pasargadae: The Oldest Imperial Capital of Iran*, trans. R. Sharp. Shiraz: Musavi Print.

Sancisi-Weerdenburg, H. 1988. "Was There Ever a Median Empire?" In *Method and Theory: Proceedings of the London 1985 Achaemenid History Workshop. Achaemenid History III*, ed. H. Sancisi-Weerdenburg and A. Kuhrt. Leiden: Nederlands Instituut voor het Nabije Oosten, 197–212.

Sancisi-Weerdenburg, H. 1993. "Exit Atossa: Images of Women in Greek Historiography on Persia." In *Images of Women in Antiquity*, ed. A. Cameron and A. Kuhrt. Detroit: Wayne State University Press, 20–33.

Sancisi-Weerdenburg, H. 1994. "The Orality of Herodotus' Medikos Logos or: the Median Empire Revisited." In *Continuity and Change. Achaemenid History VIII*, ed. H. Sancisi-Weerdenburg, A. Kuhrt, and M. C. Root. Leiden: Nederlands Instituut voor het Nabije Oosten, 39–55.

Sancisi-Weerdenburg, H. 1995. "Persian Food: Stereotypes and Political Identity." In *Food in Antiquity*, ed. J. Wilkins, D. Harvey, and M. Dobson. Exeter: University of Exeter Press, 286–302.

Sandowicz, M. 2018. "Before Xerxes: The Role of the Governor of Babylonia in the Administration of Justice under the First Achaemenids." In *Xerxes and Babylonia: The Cuneiform Evidence*, ed. C. Waerzeggers and M. Seire. Leuven: Peeters, 35–62.

Sandowicz, M. 2019. *Neo-Babylonian Dispute Documents in the British Museum*. Münster: Zaphon.

Schaudig, H. 2001. *Die Inschriften Nabonids von Babylon und Kyros' de Großen*. AOAT 256. Münster: Ugarit-Verlag.

Schaudig, H. 2019a. "The Text of the Cyrus Cylinder." In *Cyrus the Great: Life and Lore*, ed. M. R. Shayegan. Boston: Ilex Foundation and Harvard University Press, 16–25.

Schaudig, H. 2019b. "The Magnanimous Heart of Cyrus: The Cyrus Cylinder and Its Literary Models." In *Cyrus the Great: Life and Lore*, ed. M. R. Shayegan. Boston: Ilex Foundation and Harvard University Press, 67–91.

Schlude, J. 2019. "Cyrus the Great and Roman Views of Ancient Iran." In *Cyrus the Great: Life and Lore*, ed. M. R. Shayegan. Boston: Ilex Foundation and Harvard University Press, 183–97.

Schmitt, E. 1970. *Persepolis III: The Royal Tombs*. Chicago: University of Chicago Press.

Schmitt, R. 1982. "Achaemenid Throne-names." *Annali dell'Istituto Orientale di Napoli* 42: 83–95.

Schmitt, R. 1993. "Cyrus." In *Encyclopædia Iranica*, ed. E. Yarshater. Vol. VI, Fasc. 5. New York: Columbia University Center for Iranian Studies, 515–16.

Schmitt, R. 1998. "Arukku." In *The Prosopography of the Neo-Assyrian Empire* 1/ I, A, ed. K. Radner. Helsinki: The Neo-Assyrian Text Corpus Project, 134–35.

Schmitt, R. 2000a. "Kuraš." In *The Prosopography of the Neo Assyrian Empire*, 2/I, H, ed. H. Baker. Helsinki: The Neo-Assyrian Text Corpus Project, 639.

Schmitt, R. 2000b. *Naqsh-i Rustam and Persepolis*. London: Corpus Inscriptionum Iranicarum.

Schmitt, R. 2014. *Wörterbuch der altpersischen Königsinschriften*. Wiesbaden: Reichert.

Schniedewind, W. 2019. "Cyrus and Post-Collapse Yehud." In *Cyrus the Great: Life and Lore*, ed. M. R. Shayegan. Boston: Ilex Foundation and Harvard University Press, 106–16.

Seux, M. J. 1967. *Épithètes royales Akkadiennes et Sumériennes*. Paris: Letouzey et Ané.

Shayegan, M. R. 2011. *Arsacids and Sasanians: Political Ideology in Post-Hellenistic and Late Antique Persia*. Cambridge: Cambridge University Press.

Shayegan, M. R. 2017. "Persianism: Or Achaemenid Reminiscences in the Iranian and Iranicate World(s) of Antiquity." In *Persianism in Antiquity*, ed. R. Strootman and M. Versluys. Stuttgart: Franz Steiner Verlag, 401–55.

Shayegan, M. R. (ed.). 2019. *Cyrus the Great: Life and Lore*. Boston: Ilex Foundation and Harvard University Press.

Silverman, J. 2020. *Persian Royal-Judaean Elite Engagements in the Early Teispid and Achaemenid Empire*. London: T&T Clark.

Silverman, J., and C. Waerzeggers. (eds.). 2015. *Political Memory in and after the Persian Empire*. Atlanta: SBL Press.

Sonik, K. 2015. "Divine (Re-)Presentation: Authoritative Images and a Pictorial Stream of Tradition in Mesopotamia." In *The Materiality of Divine Agency*, ed. B. Pongratz-Leisten and K. Sonik. Berlin: Walter de Gruyter, 142–93.

Starr, I. M. 1990. *Queries to the Sungod: Divination and Politics in Sargonid Assyria.* SAA IV. Helsinki: The Neo-Assyrian Text Corpus Project.

Steve, M-J., F. Vallat, and H. Gasche. 2002. "Suse." In *Supplément au Dictionnaire de la Bible*, fascicle 73–74, ed. J. Briend and M. Quesnel. Paris: Létouzey et Ané, 359–529.

Stolper, M. W. 1984. "Political History." In *Elam: Surveys of Political History and Archaeology*, ed. E. Carter and M. W. Stolper. Berkeley: University of California Press, 3–102.

Stolper, M. W. 1985. *Entrepreneurs and Empire.* Leiden: Nederlands Instituut voor het Nabije Oosten.

Stolper, M. W. 1992. "'Neo Elamite Legal Tablet with Seal Impression' and 'Neo-Elamite Administrative Tablet with Seal Impression.'" In *The Royal City of Susa: Ancient Near Eastern Treasures in the Louvre*, ed. P. Harper, J. Aruz, and P. Tallon. New York: The Metropolitan Museum of Art, 267–69.

Stolper, M. W. 2003. "'No One Has Exact Information Except for You': Communication between Babylon and Uruk in the First Achaemenid Reigns." In *A Persian Perspective: Essays in Memory of Heleen Sancisi-Weerdenburg*, ed. W. Henkelman and A. Kuhrt. Achaemenid History 13. Leiden: Nederlands Instituut voor het Nabije Oosten, 265–87.

Stolper, M. W. 2004. "Elamite." In *The Cambridge Encyclopedia of the World's Ancient Languages*, ed. R. Woodard. Cambridge: Cambridge University Press, 59–94.

Stolper, M. W. 2013. "The Form, Language, and Contents of the Cyrus Cylinder." In *Cyrus the Great: An Ancient Iranian King*, ed. T. Daryaee. Santa Monica, CA: Afshar, 40–52.

Stolper, M. W. 2018. "Atossa Re-Enters: Cyrus' Other Daughter in Persepolis Fortification Texts." In *L'Orient est son jardin: hommage à Rémy Boucharlat*, ed. S. Gondet and E. Haerinck. Leuven: Peeters, 449–66.

Stronach, D. 1978. *Pasargadae: A Report on the Excavations Conducted by the British Institute of Persian Studies from 1961 to 1963.* Oxford: Oxford University Press.

Stronach, D. 1990. "On the Genesis of the Old Persian Cuneiform Script." In *Contribution à l'histoire de l'Iran: mélanges offerts à Jean Perrot*, ed. F. Vallat. Paris: ERC, 195–203.

Stronach, D. 1997. "Darius at Pasargadae: A Neglected Source for the History of Early Persia." *Topoi Orient-Occident* Suppl. 1: 351–63.

Stronach, D. 2003. "Early Achaemenid Iran: New Considerations." In *Symbiosis, Symbolism, and the Power of the Past*, ed. W. Dever and S. Gitin. Winona Lake, IN: Eisenbrauns, 133–44.

Stronach, D. 2005. "The Arjan Tomb: Innovation and Acculturation in the Last Days of Elam." *Iranica Antiqua* 40: 179–96.

Stronach, D. 2012. "The Territorial Limits of Ancient Media: An Architectural Perspective." In *Stories of Long Ago: Festschrift für Michael D. Roaf*, ed. H. Baker, K. Kaniuth, and A. Otto. Münster: Ugarit Verlag, 667–84.

Stronach, D. 2013. "Cyrus and the Kingship of Anshan: Further Perspectives." *Iran* 51: 55–69.

Stronach, D. 2019. "Cyrus, Anshan, and Assyria." In *Cyrus the Great: Life and Lore*, ed. M. R. Shayegan. Boston: Ilex Foundation and Harvard University Press, 46–66.

Stronk, J. 2010. *Ctesias' Persian History, Part 1: Introduction, Text, and Translation*. Düsseldorf: Wellem Verlag.

Strootman, R. 2017. "Imperial Persianism: Seleukids, Arsakids, and *Fratarakā*." In *Persianism in Antiquity*, ed. R. Strootman and M. J. Versluys. Stuttgart: Franz Steiner Verlag, 177–200.

Strootman, R., and Versluys, M. (eds.). 2017. *Persianism in Antiquity*. Stuttgart: Franz Steiner Verlag.

Sweeney, M. 2019. "Contrasting Portrayals of the Achaemenid Monarchy in Isaiah and Zecharia." In *Cyrus the Great: Life* and Lore, ed. M. R. Shayegan. Boston: Ilex Foundation and Harvard University Press, 117–30.

Tadmor, H. 1998. "Nabopalassar and Sin-shum-lishir in a Literary Perspective." In *Festschrift für Rykle Borger zu seinem 65. Geburtstag am 24. Mai 1994*, ed. S. Maul. Groningen: Styx, 353–57.

Tadmor, H. 1999. "World Dominion: The Expanding Horizon of the Assyrian Empire." In *Landscapes: Territories, Frontiers, Horizons in the Ancient Near East*, ed. L. Milano et al. Padua: S.a.r.g.o.n. Editrice de Libreria, 55–62.

Tavernier, J. 2007. *Iranica in the Achaemenid Period (ca. 550–330 BC): Lexicon of Old Iranian Proper Names and Loanwords Attested in Non-Iranian Texts*. Leuven: Peeters.

Tolini, G. 2005. "Quelques éléments concernant la prise de Babylone par Cyrus (octobre 539 av. J.-C.)." *ARTA: Achaemenid Research on Texts and Archaeology* 2005 (3).

Trumpelman, L. 1967. "Zur Entstehungsgeschichte des Monumentes Dareios' I. von Bisutun und zur Datierung der Einführung der altpersischen Schrift." *Archäologischer Anzeiger* 82: 281–98.

Tuplin, C. 2015. "The Justice of Darius: Reflections on the Achaemenid Empire as a Rule-bound Environment." In *Assessing Biblical and Classical Sources for the Reconstruction of Persian Influence, History and Culture*, ed. A. Fitzpatrick-McKinley. Wiesbaden: Harrassowitz Verlag, 73–126.

Vallat, F. 1997. "Cyrus l'usurpateur." *Topoi: Orient-Occident* 1997, Suppl. 1: 423–34.

Vallat, F. 2011. "Darius l'hériter légitime, et les premiers Achéménides." In *Elam and Persia*, ed. J. Álvarez-Mon and M. Garrison. Winona Lake, IN: Eisenbrauns, 263–84.

Van der Spek, R. 2014. "Cyrus the Great, Exiles, and Foreign Gods: A Comparison of Assyrian and Persian Policies on Subject Nations." In *Extraction and Control: Studies in Honor of Matthew W. Stolper*, ed. M. Kozuh et al. Chicago: The Oriental Institute, 233–64.

Van der Spek, R. 2021. "The Nabonidus Chronicle on the Ninth Year of Nabonidus (547–6 BC): Babylonia and Lydia in Context." In *Achemenet. Vingt ans après*, ed. D. Agut-Labordère et al. Leuven: Peeters, 414–28.

Veldhuis, N. 2011. "Levels of Literacy." In *The Oxford Handbook of Cuneiform Culture*, ed. K. Radner and E. Robson. Oxford: Oxford University Press, 68–89.

Verbrugghe, G., and J. Wickersham. 1996. *Berossos and Manetho: Introduced and Translated*. Ann Arbor: University of Michigan Press.

Vogelsang, W. 1986. "Four Short Notes on the Bisitun Text and Monument." *Iranica Antiqua* 20: 121–40.

Vogelsang, W. 1992. *The Rise and Organisation of the Achaemenid Empire: The Eastern Iranian Evidence*. Leiden: Brill.

Waerzeggers, C. 2003. "The Babylonian Revolts against Xerxes and the End of Archives." *Archiv für Orientforschung* 50: 150–73.

Waerzeggers, C. 2010a. *The Ezida Temple of Borsippa: Priesthood, Cult, Archives*. Achaemenid History 15. Leiden: Nederlands Instituut voor het Nabije Oosten.

Waerzeggers, C. 2010b. "Babylonians in Susa. The Travels of Babylonian Businessmen to Susa Reconsidered." In *Der Achämenidenhof/The Achaemenid Court*, ed. B. Jacobs and R. Rollinger. Wiesbaden: Harrassowitz Verlag, 777–813.

Waerzeggers, C. 2011. "The Babylonian Priesthood in the Long Sixth Century BC." *Bulletin of the Institute of Classical Studies* 54: 59–70.

Waerzeggers, C. 2012a. "The Babylonian Chronicle: Classification and Provenance." *Journal of Near Eastern Studies* 71: 285–98.

Waerzeggers, C. 2012b. "Very Cordially Hated in Babylonia? Zeria and Remfit in the Verse Account." *Altorientalische Forschungen* 39: 316–20.

Waerzeggers, C. 2014. *Marduk-rēmanni: Local Networks and Imperial Politics in Achaemenid Babylonia*. Leuven: Peeters.

Waerzeggers, C. 2018. "Manuscript and Archive: Who Wrote and Read Babylonian Chronicles?" In *Conceptualizing Past, Present and Future*, ed. S. Fink and R. Rollinger. Münster: Ugarit Verlag, 335–46.

Waerzeggers, C. 2021. "Writing History under Empire: The *Babylonian Chronicle* Reconsidered." *Journal of Ancient Near Eastern History* 8: 279–317.

Waterfield, R. (trans.). 1998. *Herodotus: The Histories*. Oxford: Oxford University Press.

Waters, M. 1996. "Darius and the Achaemenid Line." *Ancient History Bulletin* 10: 11–18.

Waters, M. 1999. "The Earliest Persians in Southwestern Iran: The Textual Evidence." *Iranian Studies* 32: 99–107.

Waters, M. 2000. *A Survey of Neo-Elamite History.* SAAS 12. Helsinki: State Archives of Assyria.

Waters, M. 2004. "Cyrus and the Achaemenids." *Iran* 42: 91–102.

Waters, M. 2005. "Media and Its Discontents." *Journal of the American Oriental Society* 125: 517–33.

Waters, M. 2008. "Cyrus and Susa." *Revue d'Assyriologie* 102: 115–18.

Waters, M. 2010. "Cyrus and the Medes." In *The World of Achaemenid Persia*, ed. J. Curtis and St. John Simpson. London: British Museum and I. B. Tauris, 63–71.

Waters, M. 2011a. "Parsumaš, Anšan, and Cyrus." In *Elam and Persia*, ed. J. Álvarez-Mon and M. Garrison. Winona Lake, IN: Eisenbrauns, 285–96.

Waters, M. 2011b. "The Oibaras Saga in Ctesias." In *Ktesias's Welt/Ctesias' World*, ed. J. Wiesehöfer, R. Rollinger, and G. Lanfranchi. Wiesbaden: Harrassowitz Verlag, 489–98.

Waters, M. 2013. "Elam, Assyria, and Babylonia in the Early First Millennium BC." In *The Oxford Handbook of Ancient Iran*, ed. D. T. Potts. Oxford: Oxford University Press, 478–92.

Waters, M. 2014a. *Ancient Persia: A Concise History of the Achaemenid Empire, 550–330 BCE.* Cambridge: Cambridge University Press.

Waters, M. 2014b. "Darius the First, the Ninth King." In *Excavating an Empire: Achaemenid Persia in Longue Durée*, ed. T. Daryaee, A. Mousavi, and K. Rezakhani. Costa Mesa, CA: Mazda Publishers, 63–70.

Waters, M. 2016. "Xerxes and the Oathbreakers: Empire and Rebellion on the Northwestern Front." In *Revolt and Resistance in the Ancient Classical World and the Near East: In the Crucible of Empire*, ed. J. Collins and J. G. Manning. Leiden: Brill, 93–102.

Waters, M. 2017. *Ctesias' Persica and Its Near Eastern Context.* Madison: University of Wisconsin Press.

Waters, M. 2019. "Cyrus Rising: Reflections on Word Choice, Ancient and Modern." In *Cyrus the Great: Life and Lore*, ed. M. R. Shayegan. Boston: Ilex Foundation and Harvard University Press, 26–45.

Waters, M. 2021. "To Be or Not to Be (Divine): The Achaemenid King and Essential Ambiguity in Image, Text, and Historical Context." In *Art/ifacts and ArtWorks in the Ancient World*, ed. K. Sonik. Philadelphia: University of Pennsylvania Museum of Archaeology and Anthropology, 159–82.

Waters, M. forthcoming. "By All Means, Auramazda: Help, Support, and Protect the King." In *Contextualizing Iranian Religions in the Ancient World*, proceedings of the 2020 UCLA Melammu Symposium. Verlag der Österreichischen Akademie der Wissenschaften.

Weidner, E. 1931–1932. "Die älteste Nachricht über das persische Königshaus. Kyros I. ein Zeitgenosse Aššurbânaplis." *Archiv für Orientforschung* 7: 1–7.

Westenholz, J. 1997. *Legends of the Kings of Akkade*. Winona Lake, IN: Eisenbrauns.

Wiesehöfer, J. 1996. *Ancient Persia*, trans. A. Azodi. London: I. B. Tauris.

Wiesehöfer, J. 2009. "The Achaemenid Empire." In *The Dynamics of Ancient Empires: State Power from Assyria to Byzantium*, ed. I. Morris and W. Scheidel. Oxford: Oxford University Press, 66–98.

Wiesehöfer, J. 2016. "Cyrus the Great and the Sacrifices for a Dead King." In *Ancient Historiography on War and Empire*, ed. T. Howe et al. Oxford: Oxbow Books, 55–61.

Wiesehöfer, J. 2017. "Ērān ud Anērān: Sasanian Patterns of Worldview." In *Persianism in Antiquity*, ed. R. Strootman and M. Versluys. Stuttgart: Franz Steiner Verlag, 381–92.

Winter, I. 2008. "Touched by the Gods: Visual Evidence for the Divine Status of Rulers in the Ancient Near East." In *Religion and Power: Divine Kingship in the Ancient World and Beyond*, ed. N. Brisch. Chicago: University of Chicago, 75–102.

Winter, I. 2010. *On Art in the Ancient Near East*, Vol. 1: *Of the First Millennium* BCE. Leiden: Brill.

Yarshater, E. 1983. "Iranian National History." In *The Cambridge History of Iran*, Vol. 3: *The Seleucid, Parthian and Sasanid Periods*, ed. E. Yarshater. Cambridge: Cambridge University Press, 359–477.

Zamazalová, S. 2011. "The Education of Neo-Assyrian Princes." In *The Oxford Handbook of Cuneiform Culture*, ed. K. Radner and E. Robson. Oxford: Oxford University Press, 313–30.

Zarghamee, R. 2013. *Discovering Cyrus: The Persian Conqueror Astride the Ancient World*. Washington, DC: Mage Publishers.

Zawadzki, S. 2010. "The Portrait of Nabonidus and Cyrus in Their(?) Chronicle: When and Why the Present Version Was Composed." In *Who Was King? Who Was Not King? The Rulers and the Ruled in the Ancient Near East*, ed. P. Charvat and P. Marikova. Prague: Institute of Archaeology of the Academy of Sciences of the Czech Republic, 142–54.

Zawadzki, S. 2012. "The End of the Neo-Babylonian Empire: New Data Concerning Nabonidus's Order to Send the Statues of Gods to Babylon." *Journal of Near Eastern Studies* 71: 47–52.

Zournatzi, A. 2018. "Cyrus the Great as a 'King of the City of Anshan.'" *Tekmeria* 14: 149–80.

Index